Social Work and Sociology

Discussing the relationship between social work and sociology, this book explores how the two have become more and more divided, moving from one single discipline, to two separate, but related, fields.

Both sociology and social work focus on social problems, social structure, social integration and how individuals respond to and live within cultural and structural constraints. Today, both disciplines face the possibility of losing some of their most important characteristics to individualising trends, the disappearance of the importance of 'the social' and pressure towards solely evidence-based knowledge.

In addition to casting light on areas that have been in the shadows of the mainstream narrative, the contributions to this book will raise new questions, contributing to continuing discussions between and within each discipline.

This book was originally published as a special issue of *Nordic Social Work Research*.

Irene Levin is a Professor in the Department of Social Work, Child Welfare and Social Policy at Oslo University College, Norway.

Marit Haldar is Professor in the Department of Social Work, Child Welfare and Social Policy at Oslo University College, Norway.

Aurélie Picot is a Fellow in the Department of Social Work, Child Welfare and Social Policy at Oslo University College, Norway.

Social Work and Sociology

Historical and contemporary perspectives

Edited by
Irene Levin, Marit Haldar and Aurélie Picot

LONDON AND NEW YORK

First published 2016
by Routledge
2 Park Square, Milton Park, Abingdon, Oxon, OX14 4RN, UK

and by Routledge
711 Third Avenue, New York, NY 10017, USA

Routledge is an imprint of the Taylor & Francis Group, an informa business

© 2016 Taylor & Francis

All rights reserved. No part of this book may be reprinted or reproduced or utilised in any form or by any electronic, mechanical, or other means, now known or hereafter invented, including photocopying and recording, or in any information storage or retrieval system, without permission in writing from the publishers.

Trademark notice: Product or corporate names may be trademarks or registered trademarks, and are used only for identification and explanation without intent to infringe.

British Library Cataloguing in Publication Data
A catalogue record for this book is available from the British Library

ISBN 13: 978-1-138-67361-8

Typeset in Times New Roman
by RefineCatch Limited, Bungay, Suffolk

Publisher's Note
The publisher accepts responsibility for any inconsistencies that may have arisen during the conversion of this book from journal articles to book chapters, namely the possible inclusion of journal terminology.

Disclaimer
Every effort has been made to contact copyright holders for their permission to reprint material in this book. The publishers would be grateful to hear from any copyright holder who is not here acknowledged and will undertake to rectify any errors or omissions in future editions of this book.

Contents

Citation Information   vii
Notes on Contributors   ix

Introduction – Social work and sociology: historical separation and current challenges   1
Irene Levin, Marit Haldar and Aurélie Picot

1. Sociological social workers: a history of the present?   7
   Ian Shaw

2. The other Chicago school – a sociological tradition expropriated and erased   25
   Michael Seltzer and Marit Haldar

3. The theoretical foundation of social case work   42
   Siri Fjeldheim, Irene Levin and Eivind Engebretsen

4. Evidence and research designs in applied sociology and social work research   56
   Kjeld Høgsbro

5. The help system and its reflection theory: a sociological observation of social work   71
   Werner Schirmer and Dimitris Michailakis

6. Why social work and sociology need psychosocial theory   85
   Elizabeth Frost

7. Complex issues, complex solutions: applying complexity theory in social work practice   98
   Sheila Fish and Mark Hardy

8. What happens to the social in social work?   115
   Jorid Krane Hanssen, Gunn Strand Hutchinson, Rolv Lyngstad and Johans Tveit Sandvin

Index   127

Citation Information

The chapters in this book were originally published in *Nordic Social Work Research*, volume 5, supplement 1 (September 2015). When citing this material, please use the original page numbering for each article, as follows:

Introduction
Social work and sociology: historical separation and current challenges
Irene Levin, Marit Haldar and Aurélie Picot
Nordic Social Work Research, volume 5, supplement 1 (September 2015) pp. S1–S6

Chapter 1
Sociological social workers: a history of the present?
Ian Shaw
Nordic Social Work Research, volume 5, supplement 1 (September 2015) pp. S7–S24

Chapter 2
The other Chicago school – a sociological tradition expropriated and erased
Michael Seltzer and Marit Haldar
Nordic Social Work Research, volume 5, supplement 1 (September 2015) pp. S25–S41

Chapter 3
The theoretical foundation of social case work
Siri Fjeldheim, Irene Levin and Eivind Engebretsen
Nordic Social Work Research, volume 5, supplement 1 (September 2015) pp. S42–S55

Chapter 4
Evidence and research designs in applied sociology and social work research
Kjeld Høgsbro
Nordic Social Work Research, volume 5, supplement 1 (September 2015) pp. S56–S70

Chapter 5
The help system and its reflection theory: a sociological observation of social work
Werner Schirmer and Dimitris Michailakis
Nordic Social Work Research, volume 5, supplement 1 (September 2015) pp. S71–S84

CITATION INFORMATION

Chapter 6
Why social work and sociology need psychosocial theory
Elizabeth Frost
Nordic Social Work Research, volume 5, supplement 1 (September 2015) pp. S85–S97

Chapter 7
Complex issues, complex solutions: applying complexity theory in social work practice
Sheila Fish and Mark Hardy
Nordic Social Work Research, volume 5, supplement 1 (September 2015) pp. S98–S114

Chapter 8
What happens to the social in social work?
Jorid Krane Hanssen, Gunn Strand Hutchinson, Rolv Lyngstad and Johans Tveit Sandvin
Nordic Social Work Research, volume 5, supplement 1 (September 2015) pp. S115–S126

For any permission-related enquiries please visit:
http://www.tandfonline.com/page/help/permissions

Notes on Contributors

Eivind Engebretsen is Professor in the Department of Social Work, Child Welfare and Social Policy, Oslo and Akershus University College of Applied Sciences, Oslo, Norway.

Sheila Fish is Research Analyst at the Social Care Institute for Excellence, London, UK.

Siri Fjeldheim is a Fellow in the Department of Social Work, Child Welfare and Social Policy, Oslo and Akershus University College of Applied Sciences, Oslo, Norway.

Elizabeth Frost is Associate Professor in the Department of Health and Applied Sciences, University of the West of England, Bristol, UK.

Marit Haldar is Professor in the Department of Social Work, Child Welfare and Social Policy at Oslo University College, Norway.

Jorid Krane Hanssen is Associate Professor in the Faculty of Social Sciences, University of Nordland, Bodø, Norway.

Mark Hardy is Lecturer in the Department of Social Policy and Social Work, University of York, York, UK.

Kjeld Høgsbro is Professor in the Department of Sociology and Social Work, Aalborg University, Aalborg, Denmark.

Gunn Strand Hutchinson is Associate Professor in the Faculty of Social Sciences, University of Nordland, Bodø, Norway.

Irene Levin is Professor in the Department of Social Work, Child Welfare and Social Policy at Oslo University College, Norway.

Rolv Lyngstad is Professor in the Faculty of Social Sciences, University of Nordland, Bodø, Norway.

Dimitris Michailakis is Professor at the TEFSA Platform for Theory-Driven Research, Department of Social and Welfare Studies, University of Linköping, Norrköping, Sweden.

Aurélie Picot is a Fellow in the Department of Social Work, Child Welfare and Social Policy at Oslo University College, Norway.

Johans Tveit Sandvin is Professor in the Faculty of Social Sciences, University of Nordland, Bodø, Norway.

NOTES ON CONTRIBUTORS

Werner Schirmer is Associate Professor at the TEFSA Platform for Theory-Driven Research, Department of Social and Welfare Studies, University of Linköping, Norrköping, Sweden.

Michael Seltzer is Professor in the Faculty of Social Sciences, Oslo and Akershus University College of Applied Sciences, Oslo, Norway.

Ian Shaw is Emeritus Professor in the Department of Social Policy and Social Work, University of York, York, UK and Professor in the Department of Sociology and Social Work, University of Aalborg, Aalborg, Denmark.

INTRODUCTION

Social work and sociology: historical separation and current challenges

This special issue represents a continuation of work done in recent years in exploring the relationships between social work and sociology. Part of this work has been done at conferences around the world where historical as well as contemporary issues were discussed and where theoretical as well as practical areas became the focus of attention. During the World Congress of Sociology in Gothenburg in 2010, a group of persons interested in the relationships between social work and sociology gathered to discuss common areas of interest. Those participating in this gathering and others showing interest in its discussions shared educational backgrounds in either sociology or social work. The participants at this initial get-together included sociologists teaching in social work programmes and social workers teaching in sociology programmes and most of them published in journals known to 'belong' to the other disciplines. Common to all participants at this meeting was the feeling that their professional belonging was not solely related to one or the other of the disciplines.

With this special issue, we wish to continue the discussion of how this relationship between these two disciplines can be looked upon today without deleting the historical experiences. Once upon a time, social work and sociology were one discipline and in this issue, we ask the question: What has happened with the division into two? Both disciplines focus on social problems, social structure, social integration and how individuals respond to and live within cultural and structural constraints. Today, both disciplines face a possibility of losing some of their most important characteristics to individualising trends, the disappearance of the importance of 'the social' and pressure towards solely evidence-based knowledge. Our aim here is not only to attend to disciplinary similarities and differences, but also to cast light on areas that have been in the shadows of the mainstream narrative. In addition, we hope that the articles in this special issue will raise new questions and will contribute to continuing discussions between and within each discipline.

By defining one discipline as theoretical and the other as practical, shared achievements together with instances of interdisciplinary knowledge production become easily hidden or invisible. We hope that the articles will shed light on these, answer questions about interdisciplinary relationships and challenge predefined assumptions. First, let us look in the rear-view mirror and see what history can tell about this relationship.

Historical separation

Today, social work and sociology are two separate disciplines, while this was not the case in earlier times. When reading the history, we realise that the division between the two goes along lines involving conceptualisations of theory and practice as well as the politics of gender. The opening of University of Chicago in 1892 was also a beginning of an academic career in sociology for the women being accepted as students at the Department of Sociology. The new study was like a magnet on the women wishing to understand more of the rapidly changing American society being more and more industrialised. In some respects, the department became for the women a 'heaven in a heartless world' as Deegan (1990) put it. On the other hand, the department failed to satisfy a number of specific interests of the women. Even though the sociology department gave them new opportunities, their interests were more concerned with how things worked in a fast changing world. Using contemporary terminology, one could say that their interests were not focused on theory alone but also on practical work. For the women, the results were nothing in itself, but the most important was the consequences the result had for those involved.

At the university, the men were looked upon as abstract thinkers and the women became practical data collectors. The analyses these women produced were often seen as merely mirroring their knowledge as mothers and having no relationship to theory (Deegan 1990). However, accomplishments and successes in the world of the university were not a must for these women. Their main interest and primary goal was to work for a changing society. Many left the university and turned to Hull House, the first settlement in the USA – also located in Chicago.

In 1920, the University of Chicago opened its first programme in social work education. In connection with this, all the women studying at the sociology department left their studies there to begin at the social work department. To move the women was not something done against the will of the women themselves. On the contrary, it was, for many, a relief because the new department offered them new possibilities including escape from feelings of being treated by men of the sociology department as second-class sociologists because of their concern with how things worked in society as well as interest in the individual. In the practical world, they could study the themes and use the methods they felt were crucial for answering the big questions of the day and contribute to a new and better society.

The establishment of a separate institute for social work led to the segregation between women and men: after the social work institute was established, the sociology department at the University of Chicago became a near-total male bastion, while the department of social work had nearly no men among its students and faculty. Applied sociology was defined as belonging outside of the boundaries of the university and became what today could be defined as social work. Consequently, both disciplines suffered major losses in the wake of this change – sociology lost the creativity of the women and social work lost the legitimacy of the men (Deegan 1990).

Current challenges

Within current social work, there is a strong tendency to make use of individually oriented methods, such as motivational interviewing, coaching and techniques drawn from cognitive behavioural therapy. In current sociology, agency and individual freedom, for instance, have become much used concepts in explaining societal change and development. In the past two decades, we have witnessed transformations in ideology that have made it difficult to see anything but individuals in society, and structures have become more invisible. Consequently, what once were understood as societal problems are increasingly perceived as an aggregate of individual conditions.

We see a similar tendency in the downgrading of social-oriented schemes in the welfare apparatuses figuring centrally in the Scandinavian welfare model (Esping-Andersen 1990). We are currently witnessing the large-scale privatisation of social welfare systems and the opening of long-standing publicly owned infrastructural arrangements to competitive bidding on a near-daily basis.

How may these and related changes be explained? Politically, part of the explanation may be traced back to a large and relatively prosperous middle class whose economic success has been produced in great part by the workings of the Scandinavian welfare model. Paradoxically, the political rationale underpinning the many transformations of the welfare state leading to greater inequality in society gains much of its support among those whose prosperity has been made possible by the very same welfare state in the form, for example, of tuition-free higher education, child care systems and child benefits making possible dual-income families, low-cost medical care and other services.

A process paralleling the same development appears to be taking place in theoretical accounts of the workings of society, where structural theories have become unfashionable. Structuralism conceptualises human existence as basically communal. This implies that every human being presupposes that other humans live in the same world, that the world is not one's own, but rather shared with all others, even if it is perceived differently (Østerberg 1982, 144). There is an inner relation between society and its individual members. Society is not simply an accumulation of single individuals connected by outer relations. Durkheim, the father of structuralism, argued that when the collective consciousness and social practices of a society lose their religious character, the individual then becomes the object of religious reverence. A cult worshiping the dignity of the individual person then arises (Durkheim [1964] 1893, 407). This was something new, as the collective consciousness previously had been directed towards society. In its new form, the collective consciousness of the individuals becomes directed towards the individuals themselves. Durkheim feared that increasing egoistic individualism would lead to the 'ensuing dissolution of society' ([1964] 1893, 172). He later emphasised that 'communal life is impossible without the existence of interests superior to those of the individual' ([1973] 1898, 44).

In the realm of contemporary social theory, the growing emphasis on the individual and individualisation makes it easier to overlook the communal and the social than at earlier times. The social structural dimensions of society are taken for granted and social processes are often silenced. These developments raise the question of whether both social work and sociology are in danger of losing some of their specific features, as 'the social' becomes less important. If sociologists and social workers increase their cooperative efforts, they will be better equipped and more able to meet these challenges. For this reason, one central aim of this special issue is to stimulate debates and discussions about the theoretical ideas and concepts connecting as well as separating the two disciplines.

Theoretical intersections

Even though we have made a clear distinction in this special issue between social work and sociology, we would like to emphasise that the boundaries between the two disciplines are not that clear cut. It is usual to give a kind of ownership of a certain theory to a specific discipline. We are accustomed to hearing and reading: 'sociological theories' or 'the philosopher said'. For certain purposes, this is valid and of importance.

But this naming also constitutes a framing. And in an issue where questions of theories and belongings are discussed, it is important also to focus on immanent power within concepts and hierarchies.

A question to be asked is to whom belongs a theory? Do, for instance, Michel Foucault's ideas belong to philosophy? History? Sociology? Or Social Work? What about Erving Goffman? Is he within social psychology, sociology or social work or social anthropology? Mary Richmond? Is she only within social work? And can her theories be used or connect with or have similarities to theories in psychology, sociology and anthropology – just to take some examples. That question can be asked about almost all social theorists. This is of special importance when we discuss what we call *sociological* theories in *practical* social work. What is explicitly expressed and what is implicitly taken for granted?

Whatever the answers to the questions posed, the way we express ourselves also includes power and hierarchy. And our way of expressing ourselves through our use of language is also a way of reproducing power and hierarchy. According to Dorothy Smith, this reproduction of power through language is immanent and ideological – almost like a genetic code (Smith 1993). However, as several of the articles in this special issue demonstrate, theoretical innovation evolves from intersections with as well as interaction between disciplines. And in so doing, these help us to interrogate our immanent and near-automatic ways of expressing ourselves.

The composition of this special issue reflects the diversity of perspectives in contemporary social work research. As readers will discover, the authors of the articles included here build on a wide range of theoretical perspectives such as applied sociology, complexity theory, theories of social systems, actor network theory and psychosocial studies. Individually and collectively, the articles aim to destabilise traditional disciplinary boundaries and the division between theoretical research and practice to enrich our knowledge of social work and sociology's identity and knowledge bases.

Before we present a brief overview of the articles, we would like to thank all the contributing authors as well as reviewers for their patient cooperation. A special thanks goes to the co-editor of the journal, Monica Kjørstad, for her help and support during the whole process. Without her contribution, we would not have reached the result as smoothly as we have done. Because of all that help, we present the current volume in the hope that it will be used in discussing the relationship between social work and sociology from the past, present and future perspectives.

Structure of the special issue

The special issue comprises two parts. The first part includes four articles reassessing the historical foundations of social work and sociology. The four articles included in the second part focus upon the contribution of recent theoretical developments within both social work and sociology to the conceptualisation and practice of social work and sociology.

Ian Shaw, in 'Sociological social workers: a history of the present?', introduces us to neglected figures of a field he describes as 'sociological social work'. In so doing, he raises questions about the nature and boundaries of social work as a discipline and a profession. The article explores the thinking of sociological social workers about the environment, the case and social work intervention. It focuses, as well as, their ties to early constructionism.

In 'The other Chicago school – a sociological tradition expropriated and erased', Michael Seltzer and Marit Haldar bring a fresh look into the historical relationship of social work and sociology. The authors ask how male sociologists from the Chicago school and the women from Hull House understand the relationship between structure and agency, uncovering striking contrasts between them.

The contribution by Siri Fjeldheim, Eivind Engebretsen and Irene Levin, 'The theoretical foundation of social case work' explores the theoretical foundations of social work. The authors return to social work's early history and examine Mary Richmond's book 'What is social case work' from 1922. They highlight three main aspects in Richmond's writings: (1) the basic categories of processes and human interdependence, (2) the concept of 'personality' and (3) the concept of 'man in environment'.

Kjeld Høgsbro's article, 'Evidence and research designs in applied sociology and social work research' also stresses the importance of a historical awareness for understanding the present. The author asks how the relationships between applied sociology and policy-making have evolved across time. The author reviews methodological discussions within applied sociology and draws lessons for apprehending current challenges.

The special issue's final section suggests how current theoretical developments within both sociology and social work can enhance our understanding of social work as a discipline, a profession and a practice, and constitute a resource for sociologists and social workers in responding to the challenges they are currently facing.

In 'The help system and its reflection theory: a sociological observation of social work', Werner Schirmer and Dimitris Michailakis ask how the relationship between social work and sociology can be understood. To develop a theoretical understanding of social work, the authors draw on Niklas Luhmann's theory of social systems. Moreover, they stress the implications of this renewed understanding for social work research – notably the inescapability of normativity.

Liz Frost's article 'Why social work and sociology need psychosocial theory', examines a recent theoretical development at the boundaries between sociology and social work. The author asks how psychosocial studies can help in bridging the gap between social work and sociology. The author attributes the difficult dialogue between social work and sociology to the sociological theories that have been used, notably the influence of post-structuralism. Then, she puts forward psychosocial theory as a valuable alternative.

In 'Complex issues, complex solutions: applying complexity theory in social work practice', Sheila Fish and Mark Hardy ask how social work can respond to current requirements for accountable decision-making. To answer this question, the authors turn towards complexity theory. They report about their own unsuccessful attempt to apply complexity theory to social work practice. They then explain how this experience led them to reconsider the usefulness of complexity theories.

The concern with how to strengthen social work's knowledge base in order to respond to current pressures on social work is also at the core of the article 'What happens to the social in social work?'. In this article, Jorid Krane Hanssen, Gunn Strand Hutchinson, Rolv Lyngstad and Johans Tveit Sandvin question scholarly interpretations framing individualisation, standardisation and pressures for evidence-based practice as a decline of the social.

References

Deegan, Mary-Jo. 1990. *Jane Addams and the Men of the Chicago School, 1892–1918*. New Brunswick: Transaction Books.

Durkheim, Emile. ([1964] 1893). *De la division du travail social* [The Division of Labor in Society]. Translated by George Simpson. New York: The Free Press.

Durkheim, Emile. ([1973] 1898). "Individualism and the Intellectuals." Translated by Mark Traugott. In *Emile Durkheim on Morality and Society*, edited by Robert Bellah, 43–57. Chicago: University of Chicago Press.

Esping-Andersen, Gøsta. 1990. *The Three Worlds of Welfare Capitalism*. Princeton: Princeton University Press.

Østerberg, Dag. 1982. *Sosialfilosofi* [Social Philosophy]. Oslo: Gyldendal.

Smith, Dorothy. 1993. "The Standard North American Family: SNAF as an Ideological Code." *Journal of Family Issues* 14 (1): 50–65.

Irene Levin, Marit Haldar and Aurélie Picot
Guest Editors
Oslo and Akershus University College, Norway

Sociological social workers: a history of the present?

Ian Shaw[a,b]

[a]*Sociology and Social Work, University of Aalborg, Aalborg, Denmark;* [b]*Department of Social Policy and Social Work, University of York, York, UK*

> I argue that there is a submerged cluster of people who, at one or other stage of their careers, took positions in relation to social problems, social work practice, modes of understanding, and research practice that reflected and anticipated – knowingly or not – something we might call a Chicago-enriched sociological social work. They are Harriett Bartlett, Stuart Queen, Ada Sheffield, Erle Fisk Young and Pauline Young. Several of the themes that emerge from a review of their work are today, as then, as much sociology as social work. In closing, I consider three questions. How can we generally explain the presence of this distinctive strand of thinking and practice? Why did it drift into subterranean obscurity? Why should it matter to us? I communicate my sense that the work of these people was premised on a fruitful but never fully realised relationship between 'sociology' and 'social work'. Conjunctions between the largely forgotten heritage of Chicago social work and sociology would allow a less 'pre-tuned' discussion of how the respective fields are constituted, and how practitioners of either might pursue their profession.

This study forms part of a larger project about the identity and purpose of social work, the terms of which proceed from the general premise that social work as commonly apprehended in western countries emerged out of the late nineteenth century as part of extensive social, economic, religious, industrial, educational, political and philosophical shifts. These movements were manifested in what from the 1860s were referred to in newly minted and fluid language as the social sciences. In late nineteenth century, Europe and North America, the emerging outlines of what would become social work shared particularly with sociology that, as a distinct way of practice and thought, it 'came into being in the face of momentous historical changes and from the first was shaped by the experience of those changes' (Abrams 1982, 3). In that swirl of developments, led perhaps by the process of western industrialisation, 'Again and again we find the concern for facts and for rationalisation mixed up with a counteracting moral sensibility' (Abrams 1968, 31). The social conditions and intellectual history of the period are deeply intertwined.

The larger project consists of four questions. *First*, how should we approach the history of social work? Is social work in its form of the moment a story of enlightenment, a rising from the pit of metaphysics, tradition and authority-led presuppositions – or one of a fall from grace? Or is history not linear at all but perhaps cyclical, or even fragmentary and without any meaning – with 'hope but no guarantees'

(Denzin 1997, 10)? Or alternatively is the history of social work to be understood through a genealogy of how orders of knowledge come to hold sway, such that history is the story told by the winners?

Second, within this broad concern with a kind of historical strategy, when thinking about social work how should we understand the nature and boundaries of what we think of as professions and disciplines? In what sense if at all is social work distinctive? Chambon has thought about social work in this general way (Chambon 2012) as more generally has Abbott in relation to social work in the USA (Abbott 1995; cf. also Shaw 2007, 2009, 2011a; Höjer and Dellgran 2014).

Third, how has research as a form of practice developed as part of the core and periphery of what in different ways has been regarded as social work? I have begun to explore the virtually uncultivated field of the history of social work research methods and practices (e.g. Shaw 2015). *Finally*, questions of the identity of social work considered in these ways properly raise 'so what?' questions – in what ways might such an exploration be of relevance and value to current social work and sociology?

This article contributes especially to the second and, by implication, the fourth of these questions. In addition, although I do not deal here with the first question (cf. Shaw 2015), the analysis gives little support to an enlightenment history of social work.

An objection

It may help to anticipate a response heard from time to time, especially to the east of the Atlantic. Why should time be devoted to something that by and large is just yet another American tale? For those (and they should not be ignored) who think that USA academic social work is entirely 'other', I would respond that the social work flow of ideas, people and practices back and forth between Europe and North America has been influential, but not well understood. To treat it defensively serves social work badly (cf. Shaw 2014, 2015).

But those who are familiar with early USA social work and its relation to sociology may puzzle over the absence of figures such as Mary Richmond, Jane Addams and Edith Abbott from the following pages. Each has significance for understanding the identity and course of social work and, to some extent, sociology. Indeed, in the case in particular of Richmond and Abbott this has probably been underestimated.[1] The historiography in relation to Jane Addams is neither clear-cut nor uncomplicated. Her significance in relation to both social work and sociology may have been over-interpreted by those within critical social work practice and feminist sociology. Addams is without doubt important as a cultural (and countercultural) figure, and impossible to ignore if we are to understand, for example, the roots of community organisation, but she may figure less often and less influentially in social work's history than some may wish, partly, it would seem, by her own choice.[2] To my knowledge, none of the people who figure in this article stood in intellectual or practical proximity to these founding social work notables.

With regard to the general stance taken here towards Chicago sociology and social work, Platt observed that there has been a secondary industry around the Chicago School of debunking myths. She observes of her own work in terms that also apply to the work analysed here, that while her article fell into the myth-debunking category, 'it argues that different accounts may be appropriate to their own terms of reference' (Platt 1994, 57).

Encountering a puzzle

I have become unsettled regarding conventional accounts of both social work and sociology in the USA and the UK (cf. Shaw 2009, 2014). But rather than pursue that line, I want to focus on the significance of a cluster of people who appeared to reflect a quite different sense of identity. The first hints I heard of their existence were from appreciative remarks made by Ernest Burgess about Ada Sheffield, and from passing references to Pauline Young in the work of Ray Lee (e.g. Lee 2004). My general argument is that there is a submerged cluster of people who, at least at one or other stage of their careers, took positions in relation to social problems, social work practice, modes of understanding, and research practice that reflected and even anticipated – knowingly or not – something we might call a Chicago-enriched sociological social work. The people I have in mind are Harriett Bartlett, Stuart Queen, Ada Sheffield, Erle Fisk Young and Pauline Young. The list is not complete – I could have added Faye and Maurice Karpf. The Chicago sociologists I have in mind, in addition to Burgess and Shaw, are Frederick Thrasher and Walter Reckless.[3]

One or two reservations are necessary. I am not sure how far they saw their standpoints as presenting consciously taken counter-positions to what was developing around them. Nor do I think they were particularly aware that they occupied common ground with one another. Finally, they did little to sustain or develop their position, and by the time of the USA's entry into the Second World War little was left to be seen. But the encounter with these people may prove somewhat as follows. We may have been to a wedding – or perhaps more likely a funeral – to discover family relatives of whom we have never or only very vaguely heard. How should one greet them? There is a British TV series, 'Who Do You Think You Are?', in which some well-known figure traces their family tree to discover unexpected and sometimes discomforting ancestors, in the light of whom their sense of who *they* are is unsettled. Discovering that our family is larger than and somewhat different from what we knew, what if anything ought we to do about it?

I will give brief biographical information about each one. The subsequent majority of the article is given over to suggesting the shared and overlapping themes of their work, asking in doing so if they can be seen as holding coherent frames of reference. 'Coherent' in the sense that Foucault speaks of a discourse – as groups of verbal performances that are not linked to one another grammatically (as sentences) or at a logical level (as formally coherent) or even psychologically (for example, as a conscious project) but at the statement level, as a way of speaking (Foucault 2002). In conclusion, I will briefly consider three questions. How can we generally explain the presence of this distinctive strand of thinking and practice? Why did it drift into relative obscurity? I close by hinting at possible ways this history may matter for social work and sociology today.

Biographical sketches

Ada Sheffield, 1869–1943

Ada Sheffield was Boston-based. She worked in the Boston charities field and was Director of a new Mother's Aid Programme. Her tenure was short-lived; when, in 1914, the city's first Catholic mayor did not reappoint her. She was Director of the Research Bureau on Social Case Work. She authored two significant books – *The Social Case History: Its Construction and Content* (1920) and *Case Study Possibilities: A Forecast*

(1922). The latter is a brief but remarkable text that drew appreciative comments from Ernest Burgess. She later (1937) wrote *Social Insight in Case Situations*. A careful appreciative account of aspects of her contribution to social work theory is given in Kemp, Whittaker, and Tracy (1997). She was sister of the poet T.S. Eliot – Ada Eliot Sheffield was her name. Her brother regarded her as 'a very exceptional woman' (*Letters* Vol. 4). She died in 1943.

Erle Fisk Young, 1888–1953

Erle Young[4] was a graduate student in the Chicago Sociology Department in the second and third decades of the last century, and a lecturer in the Graduate School of Social Service Administration coordinating a course in Advanced Social Case Work. He undertook research studies in Sociology of which Robert Park said 'seem destined to me to change fundamentally our whole conception of case histories' (Park 1924, 263). He moved to the University of Southern California where he appears to have spent the whole of his life thereafter. He wrote almost entirely in the field of social work, including several editions of *The Social Workers' Dictionary*, on family case work, race, and more broadly on social welfare. He was married to Pauline Young, with whom he completed some coauthoring.

Stuart Queen, 1890–1987

Stuart Queen was born in Fredonia, Kansas. He entered Pomona College in 1906, majoring in Greek. In 1908, Queen transferred to University of Nebraska at Lincoln, where he developed his lifelong interest in sociology. Queen received a PhD in Sociology from the University of Chicago in 1919.

Queen was professor of Social Economy and Director of the School of Social Work at Simmons College (1920–1922), professor of Sociology at University of Kansas (1922–1930), and professor of Sociology at Washington University, St. Louis (1932–1958). Queen's published works include the following: *The Passing of the County Gaol* (1920), and *Social Work in the Light of History* (1922), and a number of papers on social work's relation to sociology. His unpublished – and apparently unread – autobiography is in the Special Collections at Chicago.

Pauline Young, b. 30 May 1896

Pauline Young[5] (nee Vislick) was born in 'Russian Poland'. I know nothing of her early life, but she migrated to USA in 1913, and married in 1918. She had three children. She entered Chicago for her degree in 1915 and credits the influence of Small, Park and W.I. Thomas. She worked as a family case worker in 1917 through to 1918 and graduated in 1919. She worked as a researcher between 1918 and 1925 in both Chicago and Los Angeles, where she gained her MA in 1925. Bogardus seems to have been the key influence here – 'Dr Bogardus started me on independent field research in immigrant communities and taught me the application of objective, scientific methods in the treatment of the field data' – and she had a research fellowship with him in 1925. Burgess was also a key figure. In 1928, she wrote an article asking 'Should case records be written in the first person?' in the same year that Burgess was writing on that theme (Burgess 1928). She dedicated her 'Interviewing' book to him – as 'Teacher and Friend'.

Her main books were (1932) *The Pilgrims of Russian Town* (Young 1932), *Interviewing in Social Work: a Sociological Analysis* (Young 1935), and *Scientific Social Surveys and Research* (Young 1942). She occasionally wrote jointly with Erle Young.

Harriett Bartlett, 1897–1987

Harriett M. Bartlett was a moving force in the continued development of the fields of medical social work and social work education. Born on 18 July 1897, in Lowell, Massachusetts, she graduated from Vassar in 1918. In 1920, she earned a Social Service Certificate from the London School of Economics and Political Science. She was awarded an MA in Sociology from the University of Chicago in 1927 and in 1969 received an honorary Doctorate from Boston University.

Between the years of 1921 and 1945, Bartlett was employed in various capacities by the Social Service Department of Massachusetts General Hospital in Boston. For the academic year 1940–1941, she was an associate professor for the Graduate School of Social Work at the University of Southern California. From 1947 to 1957, Bartlett was a professor and director of Medical Social Work at Simmons College School of Social Work in Boston.

A major study on social work practice, conducted during the 1960s, resulted in the publication of perhaps her best known book, *The Common Base of Social Work Practice*. Describing herself as 'I'm a keeper … I have kept everything', her extensive papers are archived in the University of Minnesota Libraries. Social Welfare History Archives.[6]

Social work ideas and practice

I will illustrative the dominant *motifs* in the writing and work of these five figures. In various respects, their work can be seen as giving a sociological 'shape' to social work practice. This is so in three central ways:

- Through their understanding of social environments.
- In the meaning they gave to the 'case'.
- In the direct practice of social work intervention.

Running through much of this work can be detected a proto-social constructionism, that in some cases anticipates the subsequent work in Chicago sociology. In each case, this brought a conscious deliberating sense of the relationship between social work and sociology. I will deal with each of these points in the following pages.

The environment

Kemp, Whittaker, and Tracy (1997) plausibly suggest that Ada Sheffield foreshadowed later standpoints regarding social work as focusing on the person in the environment. While her practice prescriptions tend to the general, her perspective is unequivocal. She places centre stage 'personality and situation' – 'the individual's biographical endowment, and the relationships which show the interplay between this native endowment and his social milieu' (Sheffield 1922, 10). Case workers should think of the relation between individual and milieu and when dictating to their stenographer bear these relations in mind. This 'holds promise … of a gain in power to give practical help to clients ...' (14). Clients are likely to have 'limited group connections' (9), and hence, different methods are needed to study group connections. One cannot individualise unless cases are understood in social contexts.

Pauline Young shared with Sheffield – though without any apparent direct influence – the approach to the person within the situation. In a letter of February 1928 to the sociologist L.L. Bernard she concludes as follows:

> While in the field as social worker, social investigator, or research worker I was strongly impressed with the complexity of the social forces underlying social situations, with the necessity for studying these situations objectively rather than evaluatively,[7] and in their entire social setting rather than as isolated problems. The importance of understanding the mores and the folkways[8] of a group in relation to personal and group behavior has been repeatedly brought home to me.

Harriet Bartlett, looking back on her decision to register in the Sociology Department at Chicago, identifies herself similarly when she recalls

> We were social workers who came out of case work but ourselves through our interest had an urge ... to see things more broadly, to see people not just (as) personalities but people who were working and living and growing up in a social environment. (Department of Sociology. Interviews with Graduate Students. Special Collections)

How far such understandings of social work became part of social work programmes at that period may be doubted. Stuart Queen was on the move from Boston to Kansas having directed the social work programme at Boston, when he wrote in a slightly jaundiced way about the failings of social work training, indicating the need for a more community-based conceptualisation of the social work task. He concludes 'Perhaps the most important reason why social work has not yet become a profession is the persistence of the apprenticeship system' which produces social workers 'ignorant of the relation of social work in general to the community life as a whole' (Queen 1922, 25).

The case

The centrality of the sociological ideas of social forces and seeing problems within 'entire social settings' deeply influenced how early social workers of sociological inclination understood the idea of a case. Indeed, it is plausible to argue that 'case work' was the origin of sociologists' development of the method of case studies. The almost taken-for-granted assumption about the intertwining of sociology and case work, sociologists and case workers, follows, in Sheffield's view, as of necessity. Thus, from 'the influence of schools of social work and of sociologists' (Sheffield 1922, 38), 'case-work agencies ... will gradually become what may be described as social laboratories' where 'study of ... cases would go on simultaneously with treatment'. The question of how to regard the 'case' was wholly germane to her view of social work. Sheffield realises that when sociologists use words like 'personality' they are not thinking of free agents but 'established modes of activity – within which personality and circumstance are inseparable terms'. Personality is 'a web-like creation of self, interacting with other selves in a succession of situations' (10). Yet 'no one yet has subjected to methodological analysis and interpretation the data amassed in social histories' (12).

It is intriguing to note that the ever-aware Ernest Burgess was familiar with her work and extolled at some length her social work writing in her book on *Case Study Possibilities* for presenting a social view of the individual over against the 'atomic view of the individual' adopted by 'most medical men' (Burgess 1928, 526), and affirms 'with her theoretic statement I find myself in complete agreement' (525). Burgess asks 'how does the life-history method of the sociologist differ from the case-study method in abnormal psychology and psychiatry?' (1930, 317). He gives a Meadian answer when he says 'The sociological life history is secured, not for the purpose of discovering *mental* experiences of the person as he reflects over them and continually recognises them in the perspective of the present' (317). He anticipates later narrative methods when he concludes

> It follows from this that the best life history documents are not secured in response to a series of questions. In fact, the aim is to obtain a life history that is spontaneous and original. The ideal is the unguided rather than the guided interview as a stimulus. (318)

We get a sense by clear inference as to what Burgess saw as good interviewing – and he had tasked his students to undertake such interviews over a long period so was not talking simply hypothetically. He says:

> The chief criterion of a good case document is that it be revealing, that it penetrate beneath the conventional mask each human being wears, and that it freely admits one into the inner recesses of the memories and wishes, fears and hopes, of the other person. (371–372)

He immediately goes on to refer to what he sees as needed, as a consequence, in the researcher – 'a sense for the dramatic in all human life' (372), defending it by saying it 'seems to show that the inhibitions to personal revelations are not generally so much in the subject as in the attitude of the inquirer' (372).

The processes by which these ideas worked their way from one to another are perhaps illustrated when Pauline Young says in a letter to Bernard in 1928 'Dr. E.F. Young taught me the case method as applied to social research'. As with almost all the key figures of the time Harriet Bartlett valued the sociological stance on the idea of the case.

> I'm glad I came at the time that the case study was regarded as a professional and possibly scientific instrument. There were ways of evaluating this material; it could be other than just used for helping people, trying to understand. (Department of Sociology, Interviews with Graduate Students, Special Collections.)

Queen continued to work on the application of case study methods in sociology (Queen 1928).

Social work intervention

It was Pauline Young more than others who elaborated the direct intervention consequences of their thinking. It is worth emphasising how Pauline Young and Ada Sheffield expounded the conjunction between sociology and social work. Whereas the dominant convention, to this day, is for social workers to set out the value of research findings as a practice *resource*, Young and Sheffield talk primarily in terms of the value for practice of sociological *method*. Bill Reid set the distinction in clear terms in 1998, while stating his prioritising of research as a *resource*.

> Historically, the influence of science on direct social work practice has taken two forms. One is the use of the scientific method to shape practice activities, for example, gathering evidence and forming hypotheses about a client's problem. The other form is the provision of scientific knowledge about human beings, their problems and ways of resolving them. (Reid 1998, 3)

Young made her contribution especially in the field of reflections on interviewing. As early as 1928, social workers were producing work that the sociologist Ray Lee describes as 'the early development of a – to modern eyes – quite sophisticated understanding of interview practice by social workers in the United States' (Lee 2004, 291). Pauline Young's book on social work interviewing – significantly subtitled 'a sociological analysis' and dedicated, as we have seen, to Ernest Burgess 'Teacher and Friend' – is unambiguously a practice text. Yet she speaks in a voice strange to social work, now as much as at any time. It is her constant easy movement between what today would be seen as different even dissonant literatures that is so striking. Interviewing, she insists, 'is itself a phenomenon in the general field of social interaction, and the problems which it faces have to do for the most part with social situations' (Young 1935, x). There is a Foreword by Joanne Colcord of Russell Sage Foundation's Charity Organisation Department, who remarks of Young's bibliography that 'a large proportion of the material listed comes out of other disciplines than that of social work' (xvi).

Young observes at one point that

> The research interview is more concerned with the analysis of the fundamental processes involved in social situations, social problems and human behaviour than with their diagnosis. The research interview, as such, has little or no immediate interest in practical problems and does not undertake to find solutions for them. (36)

This at first glance seems to make a traditional dichotomy between social work interviews and research interviews, but the subsequent context makes this difficult to sustain. She is not talking about interviews that researchers do, but more about an orientation towards interviewing, and notes that it is not the case that any interview is just one or the other. Most important, she is working through the different kinds of *social work* interview. She discusses kinds of knowledge – for her they are 'spatial or material' and 'social and personal' and has eight tests of a successful interview that entail assumptions far distant from the psychiatric hegemony of some of the social work schools:

> Have I rendered the interviewee articulate? ...
>
> Have I seen and understood the interviewee's problems and position from his point of view?
>
> Have I succeeded in learning his attitudes? ...
>
> Did I enter his life?
>
> Have I enlarged his social world? ...
>
> Have I invaded the personality of the interviewee or secured his story against his will or his knowledge?
>
> Did I secure important data ...?
>
> Did I learn the cause of his behavior?
>
> Did I impose my views or plans ...? (Young 1935, 85–86)

Her sociologically driven social work practice is worked out in an earlier article with Erle Young, titled 'Getting at the boy himself: through the personal interview' (Young and Young 1928). In terms that recall Sheffield, they say of boys that

> Scores of correlated and uncorrelated facts are known about them. The thing, however, about which we know least is the boy *himself* ... In short, we know the boy's external

characteristics but not his personal and intimate life. To learn that we must gain access into the world in which he lives and in which he has his being … He cannot be studied or understood apart from this world. (Young and Young 1928, 409)[9]

As she remarks elsewhere, 'common language must be rooted in common experiences; "facts are *facts* only in a world of discourse"' (Young [1928] 1929, 499). Young and Young talk in cultural terms of 'boy life', and through two life history case studies conclude that the boy and the city 'are two aspects of a single process. They represent an intimate relationship of two interacting forces' (412).

They make an interesting connection between interviewing and intervention when they say that 'Just as the formal methods of interviewing ordinarily employed in social case work fail to get to the inner story of the boy, so formal methods of discipline fail to reform him since they are not based on sympathetic insight' (414). They say that 'The informal interview method may be used as a therapeutic device and may be made the starting point for social reconstruction' (Young and Young 1928, 414). They argue the implications for how service interventions are structured in concluding that the agencies of society do not respond to boys as a whole. 'The social problems presented by the boy are not due to the fact that the city lacks mechanisms for the social control of boys but rather that there is such a multiplicity of social controls' (413).

I have suggested in passing reference to Burgess that the sociological social work outlined in the previous paragraphs has very close and self-aware affinities to work undertaken by those who were more wholly sociologists in identity. In addition to Burgess, the work of Clifford Shaw falls into that category (Shaw 1966; cf. Shaw 2009),[10] as does some of the oeuvre of Frederick Thrasher and Walter Reckless (e.g. Reckless 1928, 1929; Thrasher 1927, 1928a, 1928b, 1928c; cf. Shaw 2011a, 2015). The strand of thinking and service development usually called clinical sociology is deceptive in its relevance. It has its roots in Shaw's Chicago community intervention programmes, was formalised by Louis Wirth (e.g. Wirth 1931), and has continued to attract some interest (e.g. Deegan 1986). But clinical sociology remained a low key movement within sociology and does not appear to have directly influenced or perhaps even interested the cluster of people who figure in this article.

Proto-social constructionism, representation and language

We have heard Young remark that 'facts are facts only in a world of discourse' (Young [1928] 1929, 499). Several years earlier Ada Sheffield was fashioning a conception of sociological social work that strikingly foreshadowed later constructionist and symbolic interactionist formulations. As with many of her contemporaries, Sheffield had much to say about recording social work, including sensitivity to shifts in technology. In her book on the social case history (Sheffield 1920), she devotes a chapter to writing the 'narrative' – the client story. Despite her general sense of social progress and commitment to 'science', she does not take a naïve position. For example, she sees one consequence of typewriter as being that 'dictation to a stenographer lapses into the prolix and redundant style of ordinary talk' (81). Issues of fact selection would not have arisen in same way in pen and ink days.

I do not know if she was familiar with Mead's thinking[11] but she anticipates a constructionist stance when she says of the case worker that 'selection of facts amounts to an implicit interpretation of them' (Sheffield 1922, 48) and quotes herself as saying that the traditions and training of the observer more or less condition the *nature* of the fact-items that make their appearance ... In this sense the subject-matter of much social study is unstable. Not only do two students perceive different facts, they actually in a measure make different facts to be perceived. (49)

Thus, 'For a long time to come these interpretations of conduct and social situation must be thought of as tentative'. She offers a further safeguard that has an enduring ring when she says 'the social student ... should exercise caution in condensing the original record of these items in the case histories' – 'compression is in itself a process of interpretation', and by doing so 'a student is imposing his own diagnosis upon them in a way that is not open to review by other students' (49).

Throughout she reflects on the difficulties of language. '[A]ny advance in the scientific standing of case work is conditioned ... upon a refining of our descriptive vocabulary' (1922, 19). She has a short section on 'The need of a social terminology' where she uses phrases like 'socially irrelevant anger', 'affectionate parental monopoly' and 'self-sufficient family life', observing that 'they supply a worker with a set of expectations as to the possibilities within a case. And she will work with the inspiring conviction that she is testing her observations by ideas destined to count in a science of society' (19).

She returns to language and how 'Speech-habits seem but symbols of one's habitual nearness to or remoteness from book-culture' (24), and the interpretation of client speech. Social workers use 'blanket terms' without addressing the variation within. 'This poverty and vagueness of nomenclature both spring from and occasion a vagueness of thought' (43). She is not unwilling to argue the implications for the then almost universal reliance on questionnaires in community surveys. Questionnaires are 'not adapted to the study of material in which the import of the fact-items is not yet identified' (62). Respectful towards the social world, she says that 'Whether systematic interpretation and the building up of diagnostic terms can be brought to a uniformity and exactness that these terms may be used for statistics one would not venture to predict' (63f).

Sociology and social work

Given the sociological thrust of the social work sketched above, how conscious were this constellation of people of the implications of their work for how the identity of 'sociology' and 'social work' as they were then understood, and for the relationship between them? Pauline Young's exposition of social work practice suggests that for her the interweaving was of the essence of the order of knowledge. Bartlett suggests something similar. She had worked for some years as a social worker in London and Massachusetts before taking her sociology masters at Chicago in 1926–1927. Asked in 1972 why she opted to take that path rather than register in the Graduate School of Social Service Administration she said she had thought she

> might want to go into something broader ... I preferred to go into the social science approach rather than the school of social work, which was very early then. They were pretty well involved with social welfare programmes and things like that, and not themselves working out the concepts and principles as much as I wanted. It was more directly service and operational.[12]

Sociologists were 'seeking to come closer to real social experience... Talking in terms of moving towards a more scientific approach' but 'it was at a stage where it hadn't moved to become extremely scientific in another way'.[13] In this connection, and speaking of social work education, she says:

> we were required at that time to have a thesis and it developed as a rather narrow and technical approach to the process of writing a thesis, with the research viewed as that – how do you get the data and how do you analyze them and how you work it out and write it. Some of us feel that since then social work has still not learned enough.

By way of contrast 'It was good for me to try to understand without trying immediately to change or influence the situation'.

Stuart Queen seems to have moved to a more conventional position on the relation between the disciplines, even if one that made him stand out from the mainstream of interwar sociology. Recalling in his unpublished autobiography his experience of the classroom at Chicago, Queen illustrates how George Herbert Mead shaped those who heard him on issues relevant to social work. His lectures

> constantly raised questions in my mind, for example: How does all this help to understand the problem of crime? If the offender does not freely choose to break the law, on what basis can he be punished? If his behaviour is not the direct product of his heredity or of his environment, what is there that can be changed in order to reform the delinquent or protect society, or both?

'I began to understand what Mead meant by "symbolic interaction" between an active individual and his environment, especially other people' (Stuart Alfred Queen Papers. Special Collections Research Centre, University of Chicago Library). Queen's *Social Work in the Light of History* (Queen 1922) was a conscious attempt to 'make a sociological interpretation' by following Mead's ideas of primary and secondary relations and by his analysis of movements of thought in the nineteenth century. He expressed his settled position in a letter in 1951 to fellow sociologist Howard Odom where he spoke of

> ... my concern about the relationship between sociology and social work. First of all I have insisted upon their differentiation as two distinct fields of interest and activity. Second, I have pointed out that they have, actually and potentially, numerous points of contact and possible collaboration. I look upon sociology as one of the foundation stones for the profession of social work, not forgetting that this is only one of many functions which may be performed.

His gaze was from sociology towards social work – albeit an unflagging and persistently interested gaze. Towards the end of his life, he looked back on the shifts in the relationships between sociology and social work, such that 'these two fields early appeared to be indistinguishable, sometimes separate but friendly, later openly hostile, and lately mutually helpful; but usually without formal planning' (Queen 1981, 35). He concludes 'I doubt if the relations between the two professions ever have been adequately thought through or wisely planned.' While 'on the whole ... (relations) have been more helpful than harmful' this appeared to him to have been 'fortuitous' (37).

The one who perhaps did more than others, at least in his early career, to think through and work for a mutually valuable interrelation was Erle Fisk Young. Walter Reckless was asked in 1972 what he thought were the reasons for poor relations between the School of Social Service Administration and Sociology. He replied:

> ... the sociology students all felt this was crazy stuff, do you see what I mean? It had no university standing. This you could understand; this was one of the earliest schools of social work ... in the country, and the opinion among the sociology students was that

social work was just sort of a fantasy and was not a university subject. Unfortunately, don't you see?

> They tried to cement it – Erle Fiske Young tried to cement it. He was in both, he took work both in sociology and he went out to the University of Southern California and his wife also, Pauline Young, she was primarily studying the methodology in sociology and she wrote books on it and so on. She was the (wife)[14] of Erle Fiske Young and he did much to cement the two departments, but in those days there was considerable estrangement. And the social work people did not like the sociologists and the sociologists didn't like the social worker.[15]

He provided possibly one of the few avenues of communication between faculty in the two departments. Norman Haynor – a graduate student in Sociology at the time – talked of the extent to which they were encouraged to do courses in other departments. 'I had a course with Erle Young ... not living anymore now of course. He taught a course in advanced case work. Burgess encouraged me to take that course. It turned out to be particularly helpful'.[16]

It seems that he was at the heart of much of the day to day work on drawing up the maps of Chicago that became a central part of the Chicago School's output. Fay Karpf recalled in the 1972 interview referred to in an earlier endnote 'Erle Young and I made the first four ecological maps and we really did ourselves proud ... I mean they were beautiful' (cf. Young 1925). Young's report to the of his study on 'Natural Areas and Community Organisation' shows how he and his mentors were already thinking in terms that came out in later papers by Burgess and Park when he says,

> Practically it raises the question: How far can the present use of arbitrarily chosen units of study (such as census districts, wards, and so on) be replaced in both theoretical and practical investigation by the natural area as a unit? Social service agencies, in particular, will profit by the adoption of such a unit. (Office of the President. Box 77, Folder 22)

But it is his demonstration of the possibility of collaborative or at least conjunctive work that most distinguishes his significance.

Questions

In conclusion, three questions raise their heads. How do we explain this strand of sociological social work? Why did it become forgotten in both social work and sociology? Should we think and care at all?

How do we explain this strand of sociological social work?

The boundaries of 'sociology' and 'social work' were far less sealed than we have been likely to assume, thus making questions of the kind encountered here more 'reasonable'. This has often been presented as an early lack of clarity about the 'real' difference between the fields. Even Queen tended to this position. But several of the themes – the idea of the case study and case work; the relation between the person and the environment; the implications for methods of inquiry – continue to be as much sociology as social work.

It is also striking that social work was seen as interesting to a significant number of prominent sociologists. We have not looked at the sociologists who thought this to be so – e.g. MacIver, Chapin and Greenwood. Chapin (and Queen) used their Presidential addresses to the American Sociological Association to deal with issues that demonstrate the centrality of such concerns to their core thinking. There was movement between the two domains without it being seen as due to charity workers gaining sociological enlightenment. The Chicago influence is central, although it is not easy to be exact on this. Possibly we should think of Chicago sociology as illustrating a shared set of values, visions and ideas that influenced both sociologists and social work (cf. Burrow 1970; Abrams 1982). Recognising divergent visions within social work, and reading social work in the light of history, as Queen would have us do, yields a lost image of what once was found plausible in terms of the interrelation of science, reform, community and social work intervention.

Why did it drift into relative obscurity?

The answer to this question is not clear. There seems to have been no sense of or apparent effort on the part of these people to develop and maintain a shared identity and community, which made consolidation and progress less likely. They were probably marginal to the professional enterprise within social work. There is an interesting moment in Bartlett's interview that appears to reinforce the suggestion referred to below that Burgess withdrew from his efforts to find common cause with social workers. 'I wish now I had kept in touch with Professor Burgess'. She had told him what she hoped to do in social work and he had asked her 'Do you think you are going to get the quality of people in social work who can do this kind of thinking?' 'Of course he was quite right' was her pointed comment almost half a century later.

In addition, the largely hidden history of the relationship between the two university departments at Chicago – inasmuch as it included poor relations – could only have suffocated any enterprise. Despite the fact that the rise to influence of Robert Park and Burgess heralded a transition to a commitment to defining sociology as a science and one in some ways free from an earlier reformist agenda, Burgess worked hard to find social work interesting, and probably only gave up in the 1930s in the face of persistent indifference on the part of the senior members of the social work community (cf. Shaw 2009). To give just one illustration, Burgess sat on a group set up by one of the main national bodies dealing with standards for training for social work – a group that also included Stuart Queen. It ran for almost three years between 1931 and 1933. There is a letter dated 8 March 1933 in the Special Collections from Frank Bruno of George Warren Brown School at Washington University, St Louis.[17] Burgess had clearly written with advice and had suggested borrowing from other professions, but it looks like that had met with a negative response 'because of the feeling that was often taken they have little or nothing to do with social work' (Bruno).

The centrifugal potency of the psychodynamic movement in social work also played its part in suppressing sociological social work. From influential people like Virginia Robinson, there was an element of almost personal hostility. Robinson, in an influential book (Robinson 1930), dismissed Mary Richmond in personalised terms, referring to 'Miss Richmond's point of view that a family situation or an individual can only be understood as it is understood in a social setting' (46), and bemoaning that she is 'concerned entirely with the situational aspects of a family problem' (47).[18] She implies she thinks this a 'feeble foundation' leaving the relationship on a 'friendly, naïve, unanalyzed basis' (48, 50). When she turns to Ada Sheffield she pours vitriol. She criticises her diagnostic conclusions as resting on 'the assumption of vague, undefined social norms and upon a psychology of "sentiments" equally vague and confused' (63), and accuses her of being as subjective as the position she criticises such that she 'loses sight of, obscures and confuses the behaviour behind the term'. She rejoices that 'Happily there was no crystallisation at this level of development in social case work' (64). 'The problem is externalised and causes are located in the environment' (183) is how she describes 'the sociological phase' in social work's development.

This open attack gained force from a limitation in some of the sociological social work. Bartlett adopted life histories for her thesis with Burgess. 'He later asked me to talk to a group of the social agency heads in terms of what I had found' though she laments as others did the lack of sociological concepts she could use, and how psychoanalytical thinking did seem to offer concepts for use. But 'it did throw social work too much toward the one-to-one work ... That's one thing, if social science had come along more quickly with concepts that were more relevant to our work we could have taken hold of them' (Department of Sociology. Interviews with Graduate Students. Special Collections).

From the 'opposite' direction, the radicalism of Saul Alinsky in Chicago meant that the gentler political identity of Clifford Shaw's community intervention model came under threat. Sam Kincheloe recalls 'Saul Alinsky was using the University of Chicago Settlement as a whipping boy, just as, in a way, Shaw started out that way, in order to get the loyalty of the local people. They set it off against somebody else'.[19]

In what ways does it matter?

I have reasoned that the work of the Youngs, Sheffield, Bartlett and to a significant degree Queen, Burgess, Shaw and others, was premised on a fruitful but never fully realised relationship between 'sociology' and 'social work'. The significant minority of engaged sociologists lost interest or were discouraged by the apparent indifference (even hostility) of others in both domains. There were other fields to plough, and other battles to fight. Social work – at least as represented by the majority of Deans of social work schools – was heavily preoccupied with identity building (cf. Abbott 1931).

We can hear echoes down the line some 80 or 90 years later. The loss was a heavy one. Conjunctions between the largely forgotten heritage of Chicago social work and sociology allow a less 'pre-tuned' discussion of what the respective fields may consist, and how practitioners of either might pursue their profession. In Foucault's terms (e.g. Foucault 2002), this project is about examining the discursive traces left by the past in order to write a 'history of the present'. In other words, looking at history as a way of understanding the processes that have led to what we are today. Trying to capture overall the significance of her time at Chicago, Bartlett concluded

> I think the major thing was the broadening out which I needed from casework. Now it would have come later, but I don't think I would have gone into social work in the same way. It's rather a vague contribution but very important to me. And then understanding both in relation to things like case study and all and then in relation to the basic thinking about social phenomena and then the discipline of thinking before you act. Now all these things I honestly think I would not have got if I had gone on straight in social work, and just taken their own course later. I'm very grateful and thankful that I could be at the University of Chicago ... at the time when this kind of change in thought and thinking about people was in the air. (Department of Sociology. Interviews with Graduate Students. Special Collections)

On handling difference, Queen reminds that listening is as important as talking and of not falling into the trap of thinking 'wisdom consists in agreeing with *us*, that cooperation means doing what *we* want, that failure to accept *our* judgment involves a moral or intellectual defect, that opposition to *us* constitutes persecution of the righteous' (Queen 1949, 11). His closing exhortation as President of the ASA was

> let us neither hide away in an ivory tower nor sally forth with the idea that sociology will save the world. Let us pray that we may be spared both from inferiority feelings and from a Jehovah complex. Let us refrain from playing either with concepts or with unassorted facts. Let us guard against hasty generalisations, but having arrived at legitimate conclusions, let us offer them to the world for whatever they may be worth (12).

Without claiming a naïve possibility of bridging yesterday and today, there are two ways in which some current work seems premised on the assumption that sociologically shaped social work is worth the effort. First, there has been a growth of engagement with history in social work on numerous fronts, and in several different countries. This interest has also been evident in some parts of sociology (e.g. Calhoun 2007; Holmwood and Scott 2014). Second, there are those who would argue the value of crafting a sociological social work (e.g. Shaw 2011b; Dunk-West and Verity 2013). While I resist any prescriptive list, the immediate consequences of such a position would play out in the nature of social work practice and the place of social work within the university.

Disclosure statement

No potential conflict of interest was reported by the author.

Notes

1. Branco et al. have initiated interesting work on Richmond and Addams. http://translate.google.co.uk/translate?hl=en&sl=es&u=http://www.readperiodicals.com/201,101/2584917641.html&prev=search.
2. Addams was rarely among the visiting lecturers on the social service programmes and seems to have turned down an invitation to join the staff of the Sociology Department.
3. There were other sociologists whose work calls for attention, for example Robert MacIver (who wrote about social work, MacIver 1931), Stuart Chapin (who worked with Stuart Queen and authored major contributions relevant to the field, Chapin and Queen [1937] 1972), and Greenwood. He and Chapin both wrote about sociology in ways that spoke to an applied agenda, for example through experimental designs (Chapin 1936; Greenwood 1945).
4. http://wc.rootsweb.ancestry.com/cgi-bin/igm.cgi?op=GET&db=ernstm&id=I04925.
5. I do not know when she died but she is described in the Carey interviews for his 1975 book as 'very ill now' by Fay Karpf. University of Chicago. Special Collections. Department of Sociology. Interviews with Graduate Students of the 1920s and 1930s. Box 1, Folder 12.
6. http://special.lib.umn.edu/findaid/xml/sw0133.xml#a2. A brief illustrated life can be found at http://www.nycommunitytrust.org/Portals/0/Uploads/Documents/Harriett%20M.%20Bartlett.pdf.
7. By 'objectively' Young, as with most of her contemporaries, meant something broader than later meanings, using it more or less as equivalent to 'scientifically'.
8. Cooley's terms, who was often seen as arguing in ways that were akin to G.H. Mead.
9. Knowing Young's regard for Burgess, it is hard not to hear echoes of Burgess own arguments about social work records (Burgess 1928; see Shaw, forthcoming-b, for a discussion).
10. Unfortunately, I have not been able to locate any significant archive of Shaw's papers.
11. Mead had lectured to the School of Civics and Philanthropy in Chicago ten years before she wrote her book.
12. The whole of the following is taken from her interview with Carey. University of Chicago. Special Collections. Department of Sociology. Interviews with Graduate Students of the 1920s and 1930s. Box 1, Folder 4.

13. She may be referring to more measurement and evidence-based positions that were to develop subsequently. She refers later to how 'after that period the drive to become scientific moved in the direction of following the methods of the physical sciences'.
14. He actually said 'husband'.
15. University of Chicago. Special Collections. Department of Sociology. Interviews with Graduate Students of the 1920s and 1930s. Box 1, Folder 21.
16. University of Chicago. Special Collections. Department of Sociology. Interviews with Graduate Students of the 1920s and 1930s. Box 1, Folder 9.
17. Burgess, Ernest. Papers. Addenda [Box 204, Folder 20]. Special Collections Research Centre, University of Chicago Library. Training standards.
18. It is interesting that more recent critiques of Richmond have been on the grounds that she advocated an individualising medical model. Robinson was not the only contemporary to view matters differently. Young makes the same connection, although appreciatively (Young 1935), when she draws on both Burgess and Richmond saying that they are 'perhaps complementary' (106). See also Oakley (2014, 252–253) for an interesting comment on how Charlotte Towle viewed Richmond.
19. University of Chicago. Special Collections. Department of Sociology. Interviews with Graduate Students of the 1920s and 1930s. Box 1, Folder 13. Saul Alinsky (1909–1972) was a community activist and organiser, active from the 1930s through to the 1960s, initially in Chicago and latterly more widely. His best known book is *Rules for Radicals*.

References

Abbott, E. A. 1931. *Social Welfare and Professional Education*. Chicago: University of Chicago Press.
Abbott, A. 1995. "Boundaries of Social Work or Social Work of Boundaries?" *The Social Service Review* 69: 546–562.
Abrams. 1968. *The Origins of British Sociology 1834–1914*. Chicago: University of Chicago Press.
Abrams, 1982. *Historical Sociology*. Ithaca, NY: Cornell University Press.
Burgess, E. W. 1928. "What Social Case Records Should Contain to Be Useful for Sociological Interpretation." *Social Forces* 6: 524–532.
Burgess, E. W. 1930. "The Cultural Approach to the Study of Personality." *Mental Hygiene* 14: 307–325.
Burrow, J. W. 1970. *Evolution and Society*. Cambridge: Cambridge University Press.
Calhoun, C., ed. 2007. *Sociology in America: A History*. Chicago: University of Chicago Press.
Chambon, A. 2012. "Disciplinary Borders and Borrowings: Social Work Knowledge and Its Social Reach: A Historical Perspective." *Social Work and Society* 10. http://www.socwork.net/sws/article/view/348.
Chapin, F. S. 1936. "Social Theory and Social Action." *American Sociological Review* 1: 1–11.
Chapin, F. S., and S. A. Queen (1937) 1972. *Research Memorandum on Social Work in the Depression*. New York: Arno Press.
Deegan, M. J. 1986. "The Clinical Sociology of Jessie Taft." *Clinical Sociology Review* 4: 30–45.
Denzin, N. K. 1997. *Interpretive Ethnography*. Thousand Oaks, CA: Sage.
Dunk-West, and F. Verity. 2013. *Sociological Social Work*. Aldershot: Ashgate.
Foucault, M. 2002. *The Archaeology of Knowledge*. London: Routledge.
Greenwood, E. 1945. *Experimental Sociology: A Study in Method*. New York: King's Crown Press.
Höjer, S., and Dellgran. 2014. "Academization of Social Work in Sweden and China." *China Journal of Social Work* 6: 344–352.
Holmwood, J., and J. Scott, eds. 2014. *The Palgrave Handbook of Sociology in Britain*. London: Palgrave.

Kemp, S., J. Whittaker, and E. Tracy. 1997. *Person-environment Practice: The Social Psychology of Inter-personal Helping*. New York: Transaction Books.

Lee, R. 2004. "Recording Technologies and the Interview in Sociology, 1920–2000." *Sociology* 38: 869–889.

MacIver, R. M. 1931. *The Contribution of Sociology to Social Work*. New York: Columbia University Press.

Oakley, A. 2014. *Father and Daughter*. Bristol: Policy Press.

Park, R. E. 1924. "The Significance of Social Research in Social Service." *Journal of Applied Sociology*, May–June, 263–267.

Platt, J. 1994. "The Chicago School and Firsthand Data." *History of the Human Sciences* 7: 57–80.

Queen, S. A. 1922. *Social Work in the Light of History*. Philadelphia, PA: Lippincott.

Queen, S. A. 1928. "Round Table on the Case-study Method of Sociological Research." *Proceedings of the American Sociological Society* 22: 225–227.

Queen, S. A. 1949. "Social Research and Social Practice." *The Mid-west Sociologist* 12: 13.

Queen, S. A. 1981. "Seventy-five Years of American Sociology in Relation to Social Work." *The American Sociologist* 16: 34–37.

Reckless, W. C. 1928. "Suggestions for the Sociological Study of Problem Children." *Journal of Educational Sociology* 2: 156–171.

Reckless, W. C. 1929. "A Sociological Case Study of a Foster Child." *Journal of Educational Sociology* 2: 567–584.

Reid, W. 1998. *Empirically-supported Practice: Perennial Myth or Emerging Reality? Distinguished Professorship Lecture*. New York: State University at Albany.

Robinson, V. 1930. *A Changing Psychology in Social Case Work*. Chapel Hill: University of North Carolina Press.

Shaw, C. 1966. *The Jack-roller*. Chicago: Chicago University Press.

Shaw, I. 2007. "Is Social Work Research Distinctive?" *In Social Work Education* 26: 659–669.

Shaw, I. 2009. "Rereading The Jack-roller: Hidden Histories in Sociology and Social Work." *Qualitative Inquiry* 15: 1241–1264.

Shaw, I. 2011a. "Social Work Research: An Urban Desert?" *European Journal of Social Work* 14: 11–26.

Shaw, I. 2011b. *Evaluating in Practice*. Aldershot: Ashgate Publications.

Shaw, I. 2014. "Sociology and Social Work. In Praise of Limestone?" In *The Palgrave Handbook of Sociology in Britain*, edited by J. Holmwood and J. Scott, 123–154. London: Palgrave.

Shaw, I. 2015. "The Archaeology of Research Practices: A Social Work Case." *Qualitative Inquiry* 21 (1): 36–49.

Sheffield, A. E. 1920. *The Social Case History: Its Construction and Content*. New York: Russell Sage Foundation.

Sheffield, A. E. 1922. *Case-study Possibilities, a Forecast*. Boston, MA: Research Bureau on Social Case Work.

Sheffield, Ada E. 1937. *Social Insight in Case Situations*. New York: Appleton-Century.

Thrasher, F. M. 1927. *The Gang: A Study of 1313 Gangs in Chicago*. Chicago: University of Chicago Press.

Thrasher, F. M. 1928a. "The Study of the Total Situation." *Journal of Educational Sociology* 1: 477–490.

Thrasher, F. M. 1928b. "The Study of the Total Situation." *Journal of Educational Sociology* 1: 599–612.

Thrasher, F. M. 1928c. "How to Study the Boys' Gang in the Open." *Journal of Educational Sociology* 1: 244–254.

Wirth, L. 1931. "Clinical Sociology." *American Journal of Sociology* 37: 49–66.

Young. E. F. 1925. "The Social Base Map." *Journal of Applied Sociology*. Jan.–Feb., 202–206.

Young, V. 1928. "Should Case Records be Written in the First Person?" *The Family* 11: 153–154.

Young, V. (1928) 1929. "Sociological Concepts as an Aid to Social Work Analysis." *Social Forces* 7: 497–500.

Young, V. 1932. *The Pilgrims of Russian Town*. Chicago, IL: University of Chicago Press.

Young, V. 1935. *Interviewing in Social Work: A Sociological Analysis*. New York: McGraw Hill.

Young, V. 1942. *Scientific Social Surveys and Research*. New York: Prentice Hall.
Young, Pauline V., and E. F. Young. 1928. "Getting at the Boy Himself: Through the Personal Interview." *Social Forces* 6: 408–415.

Archives

University of Chicago. Burgess, Ernest. Papers Special Collections Research Center, University of Chicago Library.

University of Chicago. Office of the President. Records, Special Collections Research Center, University of Chicago Library.

University of Chicago. Department of Sociology. Interviews with Graduate Students of the 1920s and 1930s. Special Collections Research Center, University of Chicago Library.

The other Chicago school – a sociological tradition expropriated and erased

Michael Seltzer and Marit Haldar

Faculty of Social Sciences, Oslo and Akershus University College of Applied Sciences, Oslo, Norway

> Occupying a central place in the creation myth of sociological science is the world's first sociology department at the University of Chicago: a faculty hosting reform-minded men developing theories focused on process and change – especially involving immigrants and other poor urban dwellers. A special concern for these theorists was with investigating, measure and solving social problems of the city. The legend tells that these men relied for data collection on the women of Hull House, who then were launching social work projects among the poor. We challenge this long dominant tale with a subversive story about the theoretical and methodological achievements of these women. A central focus in our account is on dissimilarities between theories stressing individual agency promoted by the men of the department and theories of social structure as well as methods for measuring inequality and its consequences developed by these pioneering women of American social science. We conclude by pointing out that their long ignored theoretical understandings of the structural sources of human pain have particular relevance in today's world.

Introduction

This historical review of the literature focuses on the interplay of theory and praxis in the formative years of sociology and professional social work in the USA. Our goal here is a twofold one. Primarily, we wish to examine these often-intertwined histories in relation to long-standing debates in the social sciences about the role of structure and agency in society. In so doing, we wish to show how a handful of women living at Hull House and researching the lives of their neighbours in the slums of the world's fastest growing city came to develop understandings of how social structure, especially its class dimensions, orchestrated and to a great degree determined life in society. Conversely, we wish to show that a group of men – usually referred to as the Chicago school – living and working at some distance from the same slums came to develop opposing understandings emphasizing the role of individual agency in determining many aspects of life in society. Their belief in the capacity for individuals to act autonomously little influenced by social structure was a key element in the Chicago school's model of a society otherwise shaped by 'natural' cycles of conquest and submission, ecological niches and social Darwinist dynamics involving competition, conflict and survival of the fittest. Our second goal of this review is to show how subsequent history has treated the theoretical and methodological accomplishments of Hull House's women. Building on the historical research of Mary Jo Deegan, Linda Gordon, Patricia Lengermann, Irene Levin and Gillian Niebrugge-Brantley, we wish to show how Hull House's sociological achievements have been expropriated and erased by the Chicago school and later chroniclers of its history. We conclude this review of history by assessing how well the sociological theories and methods developed by the women of this other Chicago school have stood the test of time.

The starting point for our review is Chicago of the 1890s where a small bible school began transforming itself into the University of Chicago, thanks to millions of dollars awarded it by John D. Rockefeller. Owing to well-funded recruitment, Albion Small established what proclaimed itself in 1892 as the world's first sociology department. In addition to founding *The American Journal of Sociology,* Small recruited W.I. Thomas, Robert Park, Ernest Burgess and other men to the faculty. This group that came to be known as the Chicago school devoted themselves during the following three decades to theoretical work and research focused primarily on the city and its explosively growing immigrant working class (Bulmer 1981, 1984; Faris 1967; Plummer 1997; Turner 1988). These men made great use of data about these newcomers provided them by a group of women living and working at Hull House, a cluster of buildings in the slums of west Chicago providing a range of services to poor immigrant workers and their families living in the immediate neighbourhood.

This institution, established in 1889 by Jane Addams and Ellen Gates Starr, was inspired by Toynbee Hall, a settlement house in London earlier visited by Addams and Starr. Unlike Toynbee Hall's staff of 'university men', Addams envisaged Hull House as a 'community of university women' (Polikoff 1999, 55). This institution soon attracted a number of socially privileged women holding advanced degrees in economics, political science, law, medicine and other professions rarely open to women in the Victorian age. In researching the living and working conditions of their immigrant neighbours, these women launched groundbreaking quantitative and qualitative studies employing field observations, interviews, questionnaires, participant observation, as well as analyses of diaries, court records, personal voting records and budgets (Lengermann and Niebrugge-Brantley 1998, 243–250).

While the literature contains many descriptions of the Chicago school, relatively few of these have much to say about its relationship with Hull House and the empirical work carried out by these women (e.g. Dentler 2002, 18–19; Hassencahl 1993, 3–4; Stolley 2005, 235). Typically, these accounts tell of harmonious bonds existing between the women of Hull House and the men of the sociology department in the following manner:

> In the early years of the Chicago school, no invidious distinctions were made between the applied sociology pursued by Addams and the Hull House residents and the academic research of the first generation of university of Chicago sociologists. Indeed, the groups had a close working relationship, grounded in personal friendships, mutual respect and shared social philosophies.(Harkavy and Puckett 1994, 304)

We propose here an alternative account drawing from a number of revisionist histories of this relationship (Deegan 1988; Gordon 1991, 2014; Lengermann and Niebrugge-Brantley 1998; Levin 2000, 2011; Reisch and Andrews 2001). In addition, our framing focuses on the differences between how these women and men in Chicago dealt theoretically with the relationship of structure and agency. Though long discussed with diverse phraseologies by classic sociological theorists, this relationship described by Margaret Archer ' as the basic issue of modern social theory' (1988, ix) was famously presented by C. Wright Mills as one involving the contrast between 'issues' of social structure and 'troubles' of individuals (1959).

The main contention of our historical review is that individual agency featured strongly in the theoretical understandings of social life developed by the men of the Chicago school. Their emphasis was on the capacity of the individual to make choices and to act independently of social structure. This manifested itself in two conceptual forms: in one, persons chose to act in accordance with the different racial/ethnic 'temperaments' they possessed, while in the other, individuals chose to act in accordance with how they defined the situations they encountered. These choices, however, took place in the few tiny interstices left open to individuals in organic-like societies understood by the Chicago sociologists as largely shaped by various 'natural' processes of competition, conflict and domination. The social Darwinist ideas informing their theories figured centrally in their programmes for transforming oppressed, unruly and potentially dangerous immigrant workers and their offspring into Americanized workers obedient to industrial discipline and social subordination. Children from immigrant families were specially targeted for these programmes since the sociologists viewed it as imperative for the survival of the American way of life to prevent these youngsters from learning parental ways of life 'below our cultural level' (Thomas, Park and Miller 1921, 198).

Opposing these understandings were structural theories borrowing in part from the writings Friedrich Engels and Karl Marx but developed mainly by the Hull House residents themselves in the course of their pioneering empirical work documenting the lives of the poor and the powerless (Reisch 1998; Reisch and Andrews 2001). The direct knowledge gained by these women through empirical investigations of 'socially produced human pain' led them to advocate reforming as well as radically changing with the collective agency of the working class and its allies, those economic and political structures, impacting so destructively on the lives of so many (Lengermann and Niebrugge-Brantley 1998, 247). With their methods and emphasis on transforming social structure, the Hull House women established what Feagin later described as the 'countersystem' tradition of American sociology (2001, 6–7).

Living on a powder keg in the fastest growing city in the world

All these developments took place in the fastest growing city in the world. From 1850 to 1890, Chicago's population exploded from 30,000 to 1000,000 making it the fifth largest city in the world. Nearly 80% of its population at that time were either foreign born or children of immigrants (Grossman, Keating, and Reiff 2005, 962). Mainly from eastern, central and southern Europe, these immigrants were predominantly peasants funnelled into the horrible working and living conditions of emergent industrial capitalism (Brecher 1972, 1999, 2014; Schneirov, Stromquist, and Salvatore 1999). Given the wretchedness of their working and living conditions and the massive economic downturns of the 1890s, this period witnessed waves of strikes sweeping across the country. At that time, the number of conflicts between rich and poor was unequalled by any country in the world (Schneirov 1998). Immediately prior to the establishment of the University of Chicago, striking train workers in Chicago destroyed 700 railroad cars; 10,000 demonstrators marched in support of the strike and 14,000 militia troops arrived in the city to suppress the strike. The ensuing battle led to the loss of 13 lives and serious injuries inflicted on more than 50 of the strikers and demonstrators (Brecher 2014, 92–93).

Iron-fisted responses by capital to worker militancy in Chicago and elsewhere led to establishing and strengthening of state militias, private armies and the erection of fortress-like arsenals in the centres of American cities. As an afterthought, some industrialists established the Social Science Association. This group's official goal was 'to treat wisely the great social problems of the day' and this came to influence greatly what has been described as the individualizing agenda of the world's first sociology faculty – the need for corporate-liberal control of the disorganization creating individual crises in society (Schwendinger and Schwendinger 1974, 476–489, 371–382). As urged by W.I. Thomas, then a key member of the faculty, personal agency was a key component in planning strategies for controlling societal problems: as he put it, 'the best course that students can follow is to keep individual crisis constantly in mind' (1909, 22).

The first sociologists: men of privilege sharing small town values and morals

This interest in social control reflects in many ways the remarkably similar backgrounds of the first academic sociologists in the USA as shown in a number of studies (Collins and Collins and Makowsky 2010; 1998; Schwendinger and Schwendinger 1974; Smith 1965). None were foreign born and most were middle-aged or older and had ancestors from the British Isles. Nearly all had been born and raised in rural America. If not born on farms, they came from small towns. Their families invariably were members of the petit bourgeois and their fathers, if not ministers, were likely to be merchants, lawyers, physicians and well-to-do farmers. Many of these early sociologists shared backgrounds in organized protestant religions and some, like small, were either ordained or educated as ministers.

With these backgrounds and their funding by financial elites, it is not surprising what constituted the 'great social problems of the day' for these men. After growing up as relatively privileged members of small and socially stabile communities where everyone usually knew their place, they viewed Chicago's slums filled with foreigners as disordered, dangerous places teeming with perils and vices (Collins and Makowsky 1972; 73). For Robert Park, Small's successor, the city from his social Darwinist perspective appeared as a jungle-like site of fierce competition for space and resources between various species as he sometimes put it. Their conflicts, he claimed, followed a cyclical pattern of invasion, penetration and competition culminating in victory for one of the antagonists (Park 1967). A central component in Park's theory of individual agency took form in his notion of 'temperament'. For decades, the thousand-page textbook *Introduction to the Science of Sociology* (1921) he co-authored with Ernest Burgess introduced beginning students to Park's concept of temperament with the following description:

> The temperament of the Negro, as I conceive of it, consists in a few elementary characteristics determined by physical organizations and transmitted biologically. These characteristics manifest themselves in a genial, sunny and social disposition, in an interest and attachment to external physical things rather than subject states and objects of introspection, in a disposition for expression rather than enterprise and action.(136)

Elaborating on this understanding in a manuscript entitled 'unpublished notes on the Negro', Park provided additional details about the temperament of men and women:

Man has got what he wanted by tackling things; going at them directly. The Negro and the woman have got them by manipulating the individual in control.(quoted in Stanfield 1985, 53)

As we shall see in discussing his views of immigrants, hierarchies of temperament ranging from inferior to superior were central to Park's theorizing about 'most primitive' Negroes and Jews as well as the 'most sophisticated Teuton and Latin' ([1918] 1950, 264). Further elaborating about the temperament of the American Negro, Park claimed that such a person was:

> by natural disposition ... neither an intellectual or idealist, like the Jew; nor a brooding introspective, like the East Indian nor a pioneer and frontiersman, like the Anglo-Saxon. He is primarily an artist, loving life for its own sake. His métier is expression rather than action. He is, so to speak, the lady among the races.(Park [1918] 1950, 280)

While the women of Hull House documented in painstaking detail the appalling conditions of slum life for working class families and linked these to their lack of economic and political power, Park and several of his associates viewed the misery and viciousness of slum life as resulting from the shared temperament of those choosing to live there. This particular understanding of individual agency was a key argument in *The City* (1925) where the positioning of the poor and oppressed in urban space was not linked to structures of economic and political power operative in capitalist society, but instead to the temperament of the slum dweller. In that volume, Park, Burgess and McKenzie argued that the city's population 'tends to segregate itself, not merely in accordance with its interests, but with its tastes or temperaments' (43). While recognizing the wretchedness of the slum, Park and his associates argued that individuals would not be living there unless their temperaments 'were perfectly fit for the environment in which they are condemned to exist' (45).

An alternative view of urban life shared by the women of Hull House

Rather than seeing their slum neighbourhood as a social Darwinist jungle filled with persons little influenced by the power disparities of social structure but condemned by their temperaments to choose to live there, the women of Hull House viewed it as an extraordinary spatial niche. This space served two main functions: one providing many services to their oppressed and impoverished neighbours and the other emancipating them from the class and gender norms locking privileged and educated women into prison-like married domesticity of the Victorian age (Gordon 2014; Prochaska 1980). For women prevented by gender norms from practicing their professions, Hull House and similar settlement houses of that time provided opportunities for them to use their talents in forging careers as researchers, political activists, lobbyists, factory inspectors and related occupations. They did this while providing their neighbours with support, space and material resources for kindergartens, medical services, trade union meetings and a host of activities (Gordon 2014; Karger 1988; Lengermann and Niebrugge-Brantley 1998; Reisch and Andrews 2001 28–30).

Sociologically, Hull House was perhaps most significant as the birthplace of groundbreaking empirical research documenting the conditions of life in the neighbouring slums (Deegan 1988; Levin 2011). In order to work effectively to change the existing economic and political system, these women collected data to provide knowledge for improving poor people's lives. Their research was guided by a shared set of deep convictions that 'that the chief problem for amelioration during their time was inequality' (Ritzer 2011, 205). Paradoxically, their data collecting appeared to represent the lone point where their interests intersected with the concerns of the faculty's men. This possibility, however, was blocked by the sociologists' attitudes of patriarchal privilege. As shown by Lengermann and Niebrugge-Brantley (1998), the men of the department 'regarded empirical studies as "women's work"'(243). Quantitative work was farmed out – as Gordon (1991) put it – to 'lower-status workers – at Hull House, initially led by one pioneering researcher, Florence Kelley' (26).

Often considered as the founder of radical social work, Kelley studied law, worked with Friedrich Engels and translated his German manuscript into *The Conditions of the Working Class in England in 1844*. She introduced Marxist literature to Hull House and helped shape what became known as the 'general social theory' advocating transforming economic, political and social structural formations with the collective agency of the working class and identifying:

> economic class position as the main variable explaining ... human misery ... unfettered capitalist greed as the primary cause of that misery, and labor organization and legislation as critical to worker emancipation. (Lengermann and Niebrugge-Brantley 1998, 242)

Kelley and Ellen Gates Starr, co-founder of Hull House, both became members of the Socialist Party (Reisch and Andrews 2001, 16–17). According to a recent study, these two women 'embraced Socialism as the way to redress the poverty and inequality they saw as caused by unregulated industrialization' (Jimenez et al. 2014, 66). Using methods incorporating ideas from Engels' Manchester study as well as survey techniques from Booth's studies of London's working class, Kelley and her research group amassed a gigantic database about various aspects of the lives of slum dwellers. They then presented their findings in the form of a groundbreaking report in the history of social science entitled *Hull House Maps and Papers*. This book combined analyses of research findings with essays and used transparencies and maps in 24 different colours to provide a detailed sociological mapping of the backgrounds and wages of every household in the 19th ward (Residents of Hull-House 1895). In addition to describing interview schedules and other data-gathering methods, their report documented the incidence of child labour in the district and mapped the location of each of the ward's many taverns, brothels and garment producing sweatshops (Gordon 2014; Lengermann and Niebrugge-Brantley 1998, 244–250). As emphasized by Levin (2011)and Levin and Trost (2005, 36), this study may be understood as representing a pioneering project of action research in sociology's history.

Despite their vast research experience, hundreds upon hundreds of publications and part-time teaching activities at the University of Chicago, the sociology department never offered fulltime employment to any of Hull House's women including Edith Abbott who for seven years taught statistics to the department's students. Linda Gordon has argued that 'the development of the entire modern field of social work ... was shaped by the refusal of the university of Chicago sociology department to hire Edith Abbott or Sophonisba Breckinridge'(1991, 169). Excluded from full time employment, Abbott and Breckinridge carried out many field studies (Wade 1964, 168–171). Working alone and collaborating with other Hull House residents, they produced scores of empirical reports (see, for example, Abbott 1910, 1924, 1936; Abbott and Breckinridge 1917; Breckinridge and Abbott 1911).

Perhaps the most important theoretical concept emerging from their book researching the home lives of juvenile delinquents was contained in a key passage declaring that 'There is scarcely a type of delinquent boy who is not associated with others in his wrong doing' (1912, 35). According to Schwendinger and Schwendinger (1997, 12–13), attributing juvenile crime to the social structure of the peer group represented an 'epistemological break' with the then hegemonic theory of individual agency attributing the choice by a youngster to commit delinquent acts to her/his personality damaged by childhood experiences, shaped by frustrated desires and infected by various forms of behavioural pathologies. Clearly, this theoretical shift did represent a major advance in the development of criminology, but the Schwendingers mistakenly credit this to Frederic Thrasher whose book *The Gang: A Study of 1313 Gangs in Chicago* (1927) was published 15 years after Breckinridge and Abbott's groundbreaking presentation of their structural theory of delinquency. Thrasher's book contains hundreds of footnotes but only two refer to Breckinridge and Abbott's book, which is also accorded a single mention in the book's selected bibliography (536). Interestingly, Thrasher is still celebrated as a key theorist and pioneering ethnographer of the Chicago school (Faris 1967; Hannerz 1980; Skolnick 1992, 110), but few of his admirers have questioned whether any fieldworker would be capable of carrying out in-depth ethnographic studies of a handful of gangs, let alone thirteen hundred of these groups.

Yet, in relation to the development of social work education, Abbott and Breckinridge's structural understandings of society came to have a significant role in their establishment of the first coeducational school of social work in the USA. In her study of America's first coeducational schools of social work, Shoemaker (1998) pointed to Abbott and Breckinridge's success in creating a faculty resistant to many powerful forces bent upon making individual casework the basis of social work. This was in keeping with Edith Abbott's disdain for casework narrowly focused on the personal agency of the individual client. One former student remembered Abbott comparing casework to 'bailing out the ocean with a spoon' (Taylor 1977, 83). In describing Abbott's advocacy of shifting the focus of social work away from the psychic life of the client towards actions involving changing social structures and institutions causing human pain, Costin (1983) observed that:

> For her, reality was in the objective environment of the client, in the crowded homes and workplaces of adults and children, in the jails, the inadequate schoolrooms, and the hospital wards they inhabited. Reality for the poor and disadvantages and handicapped was reflected in rates of unemployment, in the punitive environment of relief offices, and in the incidence of infant mortality.(105)

Men of the department: individual agency and the need for control

Such ideas about societal reform and were anathema to Chicago's sociologists who defined their discipline's main goal as one of discovering ways to control the city's masses of exploited workers at a time of labour militancy and strike waves (Schwendinger and Schwendinger 1974, 116–121). In spelling out the anti-reformist agenda of the department, Small (1898) made clear that:

> Radical error and persistent confusion would be forestalled, if students could be familiar from the start with the fact that sociology is not, first and foremost, a set of schemes to reform the world.(113)

Robert Park, Small's successor, was even more forceful in trying to purge all ideas of reform from students. Despite stories about his support of Jane Addams and other women of Hull House, there is very little evidence backing these claims. On the contrary, Park denounced them as 'damned do-gooders' (Lengermann and Nebrugge-Brantley 1998,

15–18; Raushenbush 1979, 96). There was no hiding, as Deegan (1988) points out, Park's 'strong rhetoric against social reform' (159). As Harvey (1986) has noted:

> Park was notorious for his vehement verbal attacks on students who professed an interest in social reform, and is said to have commented that Chicago had suffered more at the hands of 'Lady reformers' than from gangsterism.(196)

As Deegan (1988) has pointed out, Park's intense dislike of social reform – and especially Hull House – had much to do with his hostility towards women as intellectuals as well as his fears of losing financial support from powerful elites (162). Kurtz (1984) has argued that the department's opposition to reformist programmes grew out of the belief about the 'naturalness' of cycles of competition, conflict and domination in society coupled with a strong conservative bias defending the workings of the capitalist economy (28–29). As noted by Feagin (2001), while Park and his colleagues 'frequently researched various forms of urban "disorganisation," ... they rarely analysed deeply the harsher realities of social oppression – especially gender, class and racial oppression – in the development of cities' (8). This was evidenced by the world's first funded sociological research project led by Thomas. It was financed by the then immense sum of fifty thousand dollars donated by a wealthy woman frightened of what newspapers called 'Polish crime' represented by acts of 'violence from otherwise stolid and acquiescent men from Poland working in Chicago's factories' (Collins and Makowsky 1972, 159).

This project, eventually resulting in the co-authored four volumes of *The Polish Peasant in Europe and America* (1918–1920), was much influenced by Thomas' theory of four wishes (1923). He claimed that wishes, respectively, for new experience, security, recognition and mastery directed the choices for action by the individual. These wishes, together with a concept of temperament not unlike that employed by Park, occupied a central place in his theory of individual agency. As Thomas put it in the second volume of this massive work, 'We may call temperament the fundamental original group of attitudes of the individual as existing independently of any social influences' (Thomas and Znanieki [1918] 1958, 1844). The third and final component of his theory of agency was that of the definition of the situation positing 'If men define situations as real, they are real in their consequences'. Thomas and his wife, Dorothy, formally introduced this construct in a book about teaching the unruly pupil to adjust to school (Thomas and Dorothy 1928; 572). It was later reworked by others to include social structural dimensions. Prominent among these later modifications of the Thomas Theorem were ideas advanced by George Herbert Mead (see, for example, Levin and Trost 2005 as well as the notion of the self-fulfilling prophecy developed by Robert Merton (1948). As Musolf pointed out in his largely sympathetic discussion of the concept of defining the situation in relation to theories of personal agency in everyday life:

> Thomas does not emphasize the social influences on one's definition of the situation. Instead, his emphasis is that because one can define situations, one is not totally determined by the social structure or the existential surround.(2003:58)

Popkewitz (2000) has observed that this individualizing nature of the definition of the situation is heavily psychological and much in tune with present-day ideologies of self-help stressing 'the inner capabilities of the individual' as an administrator of 'personal development, self-reflection, and the inner, self-guided moral growth' (148). Much influenced by Thomas's ideas about defining situations, his colleagues Park and Miller advocated similar programmes of moral self-control among the children of immigrant workers who were to be encouraged to reject the cultures of their parents and to define their situations in accordance with standards of behaviour of middle class America. As social Darwinists, Park and Miller viewed these programmes of Americanization as crucial to the survival of their way of life. They declared:

> We have on our hands this problem we are importing large numbers of aliens, representing various types, in the main below our cultural level .... we must make the immigrants a working part in our system of life, ideal and political, as well as economic, or lose the character of our culture. Self-preservation makes this necessary. (Park and Miller 1921, 264)

Not surprisingly because of their own religious backgrounds but somewhat paradoxically given their prejudices, Park, Thomas and their associates saw the religion of immigrants – especially Catholicism and its armies of parish priests – as allies in helping the foreign worker to become Americanized (Thomas and Znaniecki *IV*, 103–120; *V*, 67–92; 1918–1920). As Aronowitz (1973) has observed, the Catholic Church in the USA and elsewhere long generated educational systems for training authority-oriented and well-disciplined workers. The church, he observed, traditionally took:

> an explicitly anti-radical stance. The church worked among trade unionists of the Catholic faith to prevent the formation of socialist and labor parties, arguing that such organizations as the IWW were godless and unworthy of worker affiliation ... Church doctrine interpreted 'the dignity of labor' to mean that the worker should be satisfied with his station in life. (168–169)

Woman of Hull House: sociology as a tool for solving problems of social structure

In contrast to the warm relationship between the Catholic hierarchy and the sociology department, this same hierarchy often represented by Mother Cabrini constantly attacked Jane Addams and others at Hull House for their 'radical' views (Reisch and Andrews 2001, 31; Sennett 2003, 131–132). As a striking contrast to the harsh programmes of Americanization demanding that immigrant youngsters reject the cultures of their parents, these women advocated processes of dual enculturation. At a time when charity workers and early day social workers joined Park and other sociologists in demanding that immigrants abandon their cultures and become 'civilised' (Chambon 2013), the Hull House women argued instead for what a century later would be described and honoured as 'celebrations of the Other' (Sampson 1993). Jane Addams proclaimed immigrant cultures to be valuable correctives and critiques of the materialism of 'tin finish' American culture (1902, 21). She described as 'stupid' demands that immigrants and their children abandon their cultures, which in her view clearly had great potentials for enriching American ways of life (1907, 45). In contrast to the various regimens demanding 'Anglo conformity' (Gordon 1964, 79) from immigrants and their offspring in the early twentieth century, Addams together with the:

> Abbotts and Breckinridge valued the individual cultures and customs of the various immigrant groups. Grace Abbott, especially, wanted the newcomers to stamp their contribution to American life with the national individuality they brought from their homelands. (Costin 2003, 71)

In countering what Addams (1914, 231–258) described and discussed as 'ethnic self-hate' among the children of immigrants required by their schools to become

Americans, Hull House initiated various programmes and exhibitions aimed at helping these youngsters to appreciate that their parents were bearers of cultures worthy of respect (Addams 1904; 272; Gordon 1995, 85).

In contrast to Hull House's positive view of the benefits of biculturation, Park saw only pathology. The results of the individual 'striving to live in two diverse cultural groups' was' ... to produce an unstable character' (1928, 88). Ignoring the class-defined benefits of learning two cultures simultaneously then customary among wealthy children in the USA receiving education in French schools, Park claimed that the same processes among immigrants and Afro-Americans resulted in 'spiritual instability, intensified self-consciousness, restlessness, and malaise' (89). In keeping with the thrust of his psychological framing of personal agency among these individuals, Park – later joined by his student Everett Stonequist (1937) – argued that such doubly enculturated persons had to adopt one or the other of the two cultures – preferably the American one adjudged always by Park as superior to all others – if they wished to escape these forms of psychological problems.

For Park and Burgess, the profit motive rather than the ability to navigate within multiple cultures was that which most benefits the individual and society as a whole. In their introductory sociology text (1921), they elaborated on the 'naturalness' of social Darwinist competition and profit-influenced personal agency by declaring that 'competition invariably tends to create an impersonal social order in which each individual, being free to pursue his own profit .... inevitably contributes ... to the common welfare' (507).

Here, too, the residents of Hull House held a diametrically opposed view of the workings of the capitalist economic order. As documented by Lengermann and Niebrugge-Brantley (1998), rather than devoting themselves to constructing organic and mechanical models of urban life replete with individualized wishes, interests, definitions of situations and racially and sexually stereotyped temperaments, the women of Hull House started with empirical data and built upwards:

> Their typical mode of analysis is to begin from the condition of human pain, analytically as well as sympathetically described, moving to show both its causes in social structure and its consequences for the large community and society. (245)

It seems natural at this point to ask why the understandings of these women differed so greatly from the men of the sociology department since all shared remarkably similar privileged class positions, small town upbringings and educational backgrounds. One possible reason may involve differences in the kinds of experiential knowledge about the city possessed by these two groups. With the exception of Thomas who did work in Chicago's Polish neighbourhoods, there is little evidence that his colleagues had similar lengthy face-to-face contacts with immigrant workers and other slum dwellers. A review of Park's writings, for example, provides little evidence of urban fieldwork despite his boast: 'I have actually covered more ground tramping about in cities in different parts of the world than any other living man' (cited in Madge 1962, 89).

In contrast, everyday interactions with their neighbours were central to the lives of Hull House residents. Reflecting on five years of experience running the medical clinic for slum families she established while living at Hull House, physician Alice Hamilton told of learning there to fear the police after witnessing them murder innocent workers. She recalled that experiences in providing medical aid to slum dwellers during those years made her realize 'how deep and fundamental were the inequalities in our democratic country' (1943, 75). Deegan (1988) has suggested that a closely related factor accounting for the different views of these women and men of the department was a one well known in the history of social sciences. Lodged in their offices at the university, the male sociologists had little to no direct experience of the everyday lives of those experiencing these inequalities. Housed in comfortable academic surroundings, they viewed at a safe distance the data collected by the Hull House residents as *ends*, rather than means. On the other hand, the women of Hull House regarded data collected in face-to-face encounters with the oppressed as *means* for initiating, directing and transforming the existing social order (33). Employing a gendered understanding of the contrast between these two perspectives, Lengermann and Niebrugge-Brantley (1998) argue that the experiences of these women living and working with the poor and the oppressed led them to develop a special kind of consciousness much like that which has developed along similar lines and for similar reasons among contemporary feminist scholars. Both groups, they emphasize, share a deep set of convictions that:

> theory and research should be empirically grounded and empowering of the disempowered, that the correct relationship between researcher and subject is one of mutuality of recognition ... and that social analysis should build from situated accounts to a general and critical theory of society. (20)

Finally, perhaps the simplest explanation for the striking contrast between the views of these women and the men of the sociology faculty comes from Henri Bergson's well-known epistemological argument that there exist only two ways of acquiring knowledge: 'The first implies that we move around the object; the second, that we enter it' (1999, 21).

A history lost, stolen and purposely erased

In concluding this historical review, it is necessary to address perhaps the greatest injustice done to the groundbreaking methodological and theoretical work done by the women of this other Chicago School. Though often given rightful credit for their roles in establishing professional social work, a reading of contemporary introductory sociology textbooks easily reveals just how effectively these women and their accomplishments have been purged from the history of the discipline. Despite efforts in recent decades to restore their heritage, the tale still dominating the literature is one celebrating Park, Thomas and other men of the Chicago School as those singlehandedly responsible for transforming armchair social philosophy into a science of sociology based on empirical research and evidence-based theories. However, as Deegan (1988), Levin (2011) and Platt (1996) have documented, Park and other of his colleagues effectively erased many of the sociological contributions of Hull House women, expropriated others for themselves and then proclaimed themselves the founders of urban sociology. As Deegan (1988) has strongly emphasized, *Hull-House Maps and Papers* stands alone as a pioneering template for subsequent sociological research and theory but it was quite literally 'erased from the annals of sociology' (55). Similarly, Park and Burgess make no mention of the hundreds of research reports as well as the scores of articles in *The American Journal of Sociology* authored by Hull House residents in the their *Introduction to the Science of Sociology* (1921). This textbook contains a single short sentence about Jane Addams and makes exactly two small references to her writings. The invisibility of Addams and her colleagues from histories of the Chicago School continues through recent times as evidenced by Tomasi's book-length chronicle containing a single phrase informing readers that 'several studies of slums, immigrants and other aspects of urban life had been carried out at Hull House' (1998, 91) and Bulmer's history with a lone reference to Hull House research (1984, 89).

In the most recent edition of his monumentally detailed description of sociological theories, George Ritzer (2011) had this to say about the deletion of the theoretical and methodological achievements of the women of Hull House from the history of sociology:

> That they are not today known or recognized in conventional histories of the discipline as sociologists or sociological theorists is a chilling testimony to the power of gender politics within the discipline of sociology and to sociology's essentially unreflective and uncritical interpretation of its own practices. Although the sociology theory of each of these women is a product of individual theoretical effort, when they are read collectively, they represent a coherent and complementary statement of early feminist sociological theory .... As the developing discipline of sociology marginalized these women as sociologists and sociological theories, it often incorporated their research methods into its own practices, while using their activism as an excuse to define these women as 'not sociologists.' Thus they are remembered as social activists and social workers rather than sociologists. (2011, 205–206)

As Gordon (1991) has argued, central among the greatest distortions of the pioneering sociological work carried out by these women was the oft-repeated fiction that 1927 marked the introduction by W. F. Ogburn of the quantitative research tradition of Chicago sociology. The second major distortion was that while women traditionally have been sociology's 'soft' qualitative investigators, men have been its 'hard' quantitative researchers (26). In arguing against this particular fiction about who pioneered quantitative research in Chicago, Delamont (2003) observed that:

> under Park ... women were despised for their demographic and survey work. Then, when quantitative methods rose in the discipline, they become associated with the elite work done by men. (92)

Despite the claims of those still championing the Chicago school, there are few sociologists today supporting its social Darwinist views of society or downplaying, like Thomas, structural influences on the individual's definition of the situation. Similarly, millions of mentally stable bicultural women and men in today's multicultural world disprove Parks prediction of the mental disorders destined to develop among them. Likewise, few today take seriously the notion that individual agency in the form of temperament accounts for the spatial organization of cities into slums, shantytowns, gentrified neighbourhoods, gated communities and luxurious high-rise enclaves. Though it is beyond the scope of this historical review, it is obvious that few cities today conform to the model of the organically evolving city comprised of five concentric zones proposed by Park and Burgess. Their predictions of the prosperity always to be found in the outer zones of the city are today negated in third world cities edged by thousands upon thousands of favelas, *bidonvilles* and shantytowns as well as by the impoverished residents of the suburbs of Paris and other cities in Europe. In the final analysis, we would argue that there is little of substance remaining after the contributions of Hull House wrongly attributed to the Chicago school have been reclaimed. Shorn of these appropriated accomplishments and outdated trappings, the heritage of the Chicago school is not particularly noteworthy. As summarized in Collins and Makowsky's recent assessment of western sociology:

> .... the principal shortcoming of the Chicago school turned out to be the thinness of its theorizing, and this in the end was to be its downfall. It has since lapsed into a

pre-occupation with statistical methods and description, in the virtual absence of explanatory theory. (2010, 164)

Perhaps the only lasting theoretical achievement attributed to the Chicago school is that of symbolic interactionism developed by George Herbert Mead, a professor teaching in the department of philosophy at the university. Though he was a personal friend of Thomas and many sociology students at the University of Chicago attended Mead's lectures on social psychology, he was like his friend and colleague, John Dewey, only a peripheral member, of the Chicago school. In Lewis Coser's major study of central sociological theorists, he points out that:

> Something of a myth seems to have spread recently, namely, that the members of the department of sociology formed a unified Chicago school of social psychology around the person of Mead. This was not the case. For example, although both W. I. Thomas and Robert Park held Mead in high regard, the former pretended not to understand him and the latter claimed not to have read much of his work. While it is easy to conclude retrospectively that Mead should have had a special appeal for sociologists, in fact, the only major link between Mead and the sociology department was Ellsworth Faris, Mead's former student now teaching in that department. (1977, 345)

While the question of Mead's membership in the Chicago school is a contentious one, it is clear that he had strong ties to Hull House where he served for years as its secretary. (Lewis and Smith 1980)

The legacy of the other Chicago school

While there is much indicating that the theories of the Chicago school have not weathered the test of time, it seems reasonable to ask how the theories of the other Chicago school have fared. As earlier described in this historical review, the hallmark of the sociology developed by the Hull House women was to begin with empirical descriptions of conditions of human suffering and then to identify the sources of this misery in the structural arrangements of class society and finally to advocate changes in these configurations for improving or eliminating the causes of such pain. If we take these structural understandings as a point of departure and examine a number of major sociological works of recent years, it is uncanny how prescient these women were in their theorizing and research. It is a remarkable testimony to the strength of their achievements that we today witness a host of major studies replicating their understandings of the power of structures in determining the lives of society's members. We find their ideas reproduced in Richard Wilkinson and Kate Pickett's detailed studies cataloguing the range of somatic and psychic maladies produced by social inequality (2009); in Robert Putnam's recent accounting of the devastating ways inequality impacts on impoverished American youngsters (2015); in the mammoth investigation of the misery and suffering produced by structural arrangements in France and the United States carried out by Pierre Bourdieu and his team of associates (2002); and finally in Göran Theborn's recent analyses of lethal social structures in today's world in the study he chillingly titles *The Killing Fields of Inequality* (2013). All of these carefully researched, highly detailed and in many respects monumental works presenting structural explanations for much of the misery experienced by so many today fit neatly into the theoretical and research template pioneered by the women of Hull House. All of these contemporary researchers, like their predecessors a century ago in Chicago, begin with empirical identification and measurement of diverse forms of human suffering and inequality and then trace their links to the structural arrangements of society. In so doing, these recent large-scale investigations showing the social structural causes of human suffering in today's world represent in many ways living memorials testifying to the quality of the sociological theories and methods pioneered and developed more than a century ago by the women of the other Chicago school.

Acknowledgment

We wish to thank Linda Gordon, Florence Kelley Professor of History at New York University, who so generously shared with us her immense store of knowledge of the women of Hull House.

References

Abbott, Edith. 1910. *Women in Industry.* New York: Appleton and Company.
Abbott, Edith. 1924. *Immigration Select Documents and Case Records*. Chicago, IL: University of Chicago Press.
Abbott, Edith. 1936. *Tenements of Chicago, 1908–1935*. Chicago: University of Chicago Press.
Abbott, Edith, and Sophonisba Breckinridge. 1917. *Truancy and Nonattendance in the Chicago Schools*. Chicago: University of Chicago Press.
Addams, Jane. 1902. "The New Social Spirit." *National Council of Jewish Women, Proceedings*, 16–22. Chicago: National Council of Jewish Women.
Addams, Jane. 1904. "The Humanizing Tendency of Industrial Education." *Chautauquan* 39 (May): 266–272.
Addams, Jane. 1907. *Newer Ideals of Peace*. New York: Macmillan
Addams, Jane. 1914. *Twenty Years at Hull House*. New York: Macmillan.
Archer, Margaret. 1988. *Culture and Agency: The Place of Culture in Social Theory*. Cambridge: Cambridge University Press.
Aronowitz, Stanley. 1973. *False Consciousness: The Shaping of American Working Class Consciousness*. New York: McGraw Hill.
Bourdieu, Pierre. 2002. *The Weight of the World: Social Suffering in Contemporary Society*. Cambridge: Polity Press.
Brecher, Jeremy. 1972. *Strike!*. San Francisco, CA: Straight Arrow Press.
Brecher, Jeremy. 1999. *Strike!* Revised and Updated ed. Cambridge, MA: South End Press.
Brecher, Jeremy. 2014. *Strike!* Revised and Expanded ed. Oakland, CA: PM Press.
Breckinridge, Sophonisba, and Edith Abbott. 1911. "Chicago Housing Conditions, IV: The West Side ." *American Journal of Sociology* 17 (1): 1–34.
Breckinridge, Sophonisba, and Edith Abbott. 1912. *Delinquent child and the home*. New York: Russell Sage Foundation.
Bulmer, Martin. 1981. "Quantification and Chicago Social Science in the 1920s: A Neglected Tradition." *Journal of the History of the Behavioral Sciences* 17: 312–331.
Bulmer, Martin. 1984. *The Chicago School of Sociology: Institutionalization, Diversity and the Rise of Sociological Research*. Chicago: University of Chicago Press.
Chambon, Adrienne. 2013. "Recognising the Other, Understanding the Other: A Brief History of Social Work and Otherness." *Nordic Social Work Research* 3 (2): 120–129.
Collins, Randall, and Michael Makowsky. 1972. *The Discovery of Society*. New York: Random House.
Collins, Randall, and Michael Makowsky. 1998. *The Discovery of Society*. 6th ed. New York: McGraw Hill.
Collins, Randal, and Michael Makowsky. 2010. *The Discovery of Society*. 8th ed. New York: McGraw Hill.
Coser, Lewis. 1977. *Masters of Sociological Thought: Ideas in Historical and Social Context*. New York: Harcourt, Brace and Jovanovich
Costin, Lela. 1983. "Edith Abbott and the Chicago Influence on Social Work Education." *Social Service Review* 57 (1): 94–111.
Costin, Lela. 2003. *Two Sisters for Social Justice: A Biography of Grace and Edith Abbott*. Urbana-Champaign: University of Illinois Press.

Deegan, Mary Jo. 1988. *Jane Addams and the Men of the Chicago School. 1892–1918.* New Brunswick: Transaction Books.

Delamont, Sara. 2003. *Feminist Sociology.* London: Sage.

Dentler, Robert. 2002. *Practicing Sociology: Selected Fields.* Westport, CN: Praeger.

Faris, Robert. 1967. *Chicago Sociology: 1920–1932.* Chicago: University of Chicago Press.

Feagin, Joe. 2001. "Social Justice and Sociology: Agendas for the Twenty-first Century." *American Sociological Review* 66 (1): 1–20.

Gordon, Milton. 1964. *Assimilation in American Life: The Role of Race, Religion and National Origins.* Oxford: Oxford University Press.

Gordon, Linda. 1991. *Social Insurance and Public Assistance: The Influence of Gender in Welfare Though in the United States, 1890–1935.* Discussion Paper No. 960–91., Institute for Research on Poverty, Madison, WI: University of Wisconsin.

Gordon, Linda. 1995. *Pitied But Not Entitled: Single Mothers and the History of Welfare 1890–1935.* Cambridge: Harvard University Press.

Gordon, Linda. 2014. "Free Space: The Settlement-House Movement", Unpublished Chapter. January 27, 2014, for Forthcoming Book.

Grossman, James, Ann Keating, and Janice Reiff. 2005. *The Encyclopedia of Chicago.* Chicago, IL: University of Chicago Press.

Hamilton, Alice. 1943. *Exploring the Dangerous Trades: The Autobiography of Alice Hamilton, M.D.* Boston, MA: Little Brown.

Hannerz, Ulf. 1980. *Exploring the City: Inquiries Toward an Urban Anthropology.* New York: Columbia University Press.

Harkavy, Ira, and John Puckett. 1994. "Lessons from Hull House for the Contemporary Urban University." *Social Service Review* 68 (3): 299–321.

Harvey, Lee. 1986. "The Myths of the Chicago School." *Quality and Quantity* 20: 191–217.

Hassencahl, Francis. 1993. "Jane Addams." In *Women Public Speakers in the United States, 1800–1925: A Biocritical Sourcebook,* edited by Karlyn Campbell, 1–13. Westport, CN: Greenwood Press.

Jimenez, Jillian, Eileen Pasztor, Ruth Chambers, and Cheryl Pearlman Fuji. 2014. *Social Policy and Social Change: Toward the Creation of Social and Economic Justice.* New York: Sage.

Karger, Howard. 1988. *Social Workers and Labor Unions.* Westport, CN: Greenwood.

Kurtz, Lester. 1984. *Evaluating Chicago Sociology.* Chicago, IL: University of Chicago Press.

Lengermann, Patricia, and Gillian Niebrugge-Brantley. 1998. *The Women Founders: Sociology and Social Theory 1830–1930.* New York, NY: McGraw Hill.

Levin, Irene. 2000. "Forhold mellom sosiologi og sosialt arbeid." [trans. The Relation between Sociology and Social work]. *Sosiologisk Tidsskrift* 8 (1): 61–71.

Levin, Irene. 2011. "Sociology and Social Work in Chicago – An Institutional Division." *Keynote address, International Seminar, Sociology and Social Work,* Lisbon, Portugal, 27 May.

Levin, Irene, and Jan Trost. 2005. *Hverdagsliv og samhandling med et symbolsk interaksjonistisk perspektiv.* [Everyday Life and Interaction in a Symbolic Interactionist Perspective]. Oslo: Fagbokforlaget.

Lewis, David, and Richard Smith. 1980. *American Sociology and Pragmatism: Mead, Chicago Sociology and Symbolic Interactionism.* Chicago, IL: University of Chicago Press.

Madge, John. 1962. *The Origins of Scientific Sociology.* New York: Free Press of Glencoe.

Merton, Robert. 1948. "The Self-Fulfilling Prophecy." *The Antioch Review* 8 (2): 193–210.

Mills, Charles. 1959. *The Sociological Imagination.* New York: Oxford University Press.

Musolf, Gil. 2003. *Structure and Agency in Everyday Life: An Introduction of Social Psychology.* 2nd ed. Lanham,.MA: Rowman and Littlefield Publishers

Park, Robert. 1928. "Human Migration and the Marginal Man." *American Journal of Sociology* 33 (6): 881–893.

Park, Robert. (1918) 1950. "Education in Its Relation to the Conflict and Fusion of Cultures." *American Sociological Review* 13: 38–63. Reprinted in Robert Park, Race and Culture, 261–283. Glencoe, IL: Free Press

Park, Robert. 1952. *Human Communities: The City and Human Ecology.* Glencoe: Free Press.

Park, Robert. 1967. "Human Ecology." In *Robert Park on Social Control and Collective Behavior,* edited by Ralph Turner, 69–84. Chicago: University of Chicago Press.

Park, Robert, and Ernest Burgess. 1921. *Introduction to the Science of Sociology.* Chicago: University of Chicago press.

Park, Robert, and Herbert Miller. 1921. *Old World Traits Transplanted*. New York: Harper and Brothers.
Park, Robert, and Florian Znaniecki. 1918–1920. *The Polish Peasant in Europe and America: Monograph of an Immigrant Group*. Boston: Robert Badger The Gorham Press.
Park, Robert, Ernest Burgess, and Roderick McKenzie. 1925. *The City: Suggestions for Investigation of Human Behavior in the Urban Environment*. Chicago: University of Chicago press.
Platt, Jennifer. 1996. *A History of Sociological Research Methods in America*. Cambridge: Cambridge University Press.
Plummer, Ken. 1997. *The Chicago School: Critical Assessments*. London: Routledge.
Polikoff, Barbara. 1999. *With One Bold Act: The Story of Jane Addams*. New York, NY: Boswell Books.
Popkewitz, Thomas. 2000. "Reform at the Social Administration of the Child: Globalization of Knowledge and Power." In *Globalization and Education: Critical Perspectives*, edited by Nicolas Burbules and Carlos Torres, 157–186. London: Routledge.
Prochaska, Frank. 1980. *Women and Philanthropy in Nineteenth Century England*. Oxford: Clarendon Press.
Putnam, Robert. 2015. *Our Kids – The American Dream in Crisis*. New York: Simon and Schuster.
Rausenbush, Winifred. 1979. *Robert E. Park: Biography of a Sociologist*. Durham, NC: Duke University Press.
Reisch, Michael. 1998. "The Socio - Political Context and Social Work Method, 1890–1950." *Social Service Review* 72 (2): 161–181.
Reisch, Michael, and Janice Andrews. 2001. *The Road Not Taken: A History of Radical Social Work in the United States*. New York, NY: Brunner-Routledge.
Residents of Hull-House. 1895. *Hull-House Maps and Papers: A Presentation of Nationalities and Wages in a Congested District of Chicago, Together with Comments and Essays on Problems Growing Out of the Social Conditions*. New York: Thomas Crowell.
Ritzer, George. 2011. *Sociological Theory*. New York: McGraw-Hill.
Sampson, Edward. 1993. *Celebrating the Other: A Dialogic Account of Human Nature*. London: Harvester Wheatsheaf.
Schneirov, Richard. 1998. *Labor and Urban Politics: Class Conflict and the Origins of Modern Liberalism in Chicago, 1864–97*. Urbana : University of Illinois Press.
Schneirov, Richard, Shelton Stromquist, and Nick Salvatore, eds. 1999. *The Pullman Strike and the Crisis of the 1890s: Essays on Labor and Politics*. Urbana: University of Illinois Press.
Schwendinger, Herman and Julia Schwendinger. 1974. *Sociologists of the Chair. A Radical Analysis of the Formative Years of North American Sociology (1883–1922)*. New York: Basic Books.
Schwendinger, Herman, and Julia Schwendinger. 1997. "When the study of delinquent groups stood still: In defense of a classical tradition." *Critical Criminology* 8 (2): 5–38.
Sennett, Richard. 2003. *Respect in a World of Inequality*. New York: W.W. Norton.
Shoemaker, Linda. 1998. "Early Conflicts in Social Work Education." *Social Service Review* 72 (2): 182–191.
Skolnick, Jerome. 1992. "Gangs in the Post-industrial Ghetto." *The American Prospect* 8 (Winter): 109–120.
Small, Albion. 1898. "Seminar Notes: The Methodology of the Social Problem. Division I. The Sources and Uses of Material." *American Journal of Sociology* 4 (3): 113–144.10.1086/ajs.1898.4.issue-1
Smith, Dusky. 1965. "Sociology and the Rise of Corporate Capitalism." *Science and Society* 29: 1–18.
Stolley, Kathy. 2005. *The Basics of Sociology*. Westport, CN: Greenwood Press.
Stonequist, Everett. 1937. *The Marginal Man*. New York: Scribners.
Taylor, Eleanor. 1977. "The Edith Abbott I Knew." *Journal of the Illinois State Historical Society* 70: 178–184.
Theborn, Göran. 2013. *The Killing Fields of Inequality*. Cambridge: Polity Press.
Thomas, William. 1909. *Sourcebook for Social Origins*. Chicago, IL: University of Chicago Press.
Thomas, William. 1923. *The Unadjusted Girl with Cases and Standpoint of Behavior Analysis*. Boston, MA: Little Brown.

Thomas, William, and Dorothy Thomas. 1928. *The Child in America: Behavior Problems and Programs*. New York: Knopf.

Thomas, William, Robert Park, and Herbert Miller. 1921. *Old World Traits Transplanted*. New York: Harper.

Thomas, William, and Florian Znaniecki. 1918–1920. *The Polish Peasant in Europe and America. Monograph of an Immigrant Group. Volumes I, II, III, IV and V*. New York: Alfred Knopf.

Thomas, William and Florian Znaniecki. (1918) 1958. "Life Record of an Immigrant – Introduction" *Part IV. The Polish Peasant in Europe and America*: Volume II. 1831–1914. New York: Dover Publications.

Thrasher, Frederic. 1927. *The Gang: A Study of 1,313 Gangs in Chicago*. Chicago: University of Chicago Press

Tomasi, Luigi. 1998. *The Tradition of the Chicago School of Sociology*. Aldershot: Ashgate.

Turner, Jonathan. 1988. "The Mixed Legacy of the Chicago School of Sociology." *Sociological Perspectives* 31 (3): 325–338.

Wade, Louise. 1964. *Graham Taylor: Pioneering for Social Justice – 1851–1938*. Chicago, IL: University of Chicago Press.

Wilkinson, Richard, and Kate Pickett. 2009. *The Spirit Level: Why Equality is Better for Everyone*. London: Penguin.

The theoretical foundation of social case work

Siri Fjeldheim, Irene Levin and Eivind Engebretsen

Faculty of Social Sciences, Department of Social Work, Child Welfare and Social Policy, Oslo and Akershus University College of Applied Sciences, Oslo, Norway

Social work is often defined as a practical field with limited theoretical contributions as opposed to sociology that is perceived as theoretical. As a consequence, social work's own researchers often tend to search outside their profession to find its scientific basis. Hence, social work's own theoretical contributions have often been overlooked, diminished or even perceived as non-existent. In this article, we turn to one of social work's founding mothers, Mary Richmond (1861–1928) and one of her most important texts, *What is Social Case Work?* (1922). Our aim is to show the theoretical contribution of her text, and thereby to highlight certain theoretical developments within social work itself. Through a hermeneutically close reading, we challenge some traditional and dominant interpretations positioning Richmond's texts within pathological and individualistic perspectives. We demonstrate how the two key concepts 'personality' and 'man and his environment', together with the model of social case work, reflect a dynamic view of social interactions in which the individual is inextricably bound together with its social surroundings.

Introduction

Social work is often defined as a practical field with limited theoretical contributions as opposed to sociology that is perceived solely as a theoretical field. As a consequence, social work's own researchers often tend to search outside their profession to find its scientific basis, as has been highlighted by Payne (1991), Hutchinson and Oltedal (1996) and Meeuwisse, Sune, and Swärd (2006). In some ways, this has proved to be a good strategy. Theories developed within other traditions undoubtedly have contributed to understandings of practical as well as theoretical positions in social work. However, this has led to many situations where social work's own contributions have been overlooked, diminished or even perceived as non-existent.

Our goal in this article is to highlight certain theoretical developments within social work itself, and our focus will be on the theoretical foundation of one of the canonical writings of social work: *What is Social Case Work?* (1922) by Mary Richmond (1861–1928). The book is an important text in social work's early history for its role in contributing to the foundation of the profession's knowledge. However, when *What is Social Case Work?* was first published, the book received a half-hearted reception from social workers and many were critical to Richmond's lack of psychoanalytical insight (Fischer 1970, 22). This lack of interest is still mirrored in contemporary texts. Through a hermeneutically close reading of *What is Social Case Work?*, our aim is to show that the theoretical contributions made by this book have long been overlooked or ignored in many assessments of Richmond's writings. We hope thereby to challenge some traditional and dominant interpretations of her texts. Our main concern here is answering the question: How does Richmond define the theoretical foundation of social case work?

There are several reasons for choosing *What is Social Case Work?* for closer study. Firstly, in many respects, the history of social work remains largely untold, which has had serious consequences for the construction of social work (Burnham 2011, 5; Timms 1997, 723). As Richmond herself succinctly put it: '… a profession which did not know its own history, which was indifferent to the memory of the men and women responsible for its making, would still be a shambling and formless thing' (Richmond 1930, 556). Secondly, very few have taken on the tasks of conducting closer readings and analyses of Richmond's books and as a result, the impact of her work is often unclear (Pittman-Munke 1985, 160). Finally, *What is Social Case Work?* became much less influential than her previous book *Social Diagnosis* (1917). In that volume, Richmond presented a thorough description of social diagnosis as a method for investigating the person and his social environment as a prerequisite for social treatment (Richmond 1917, 51). Social diagnosis, however, is only one part of the case work process. It says little about the theories and models underpinning Richmond's conceptualization of the social case work process as a whole. In writing *What is Social Case Work?*, Richmond aimed to clarify the whole case work process and place social diagnosis in a proper perspective (Pumphrey 1957, 402). In the following, we first present relevant research, followed by our theoretical framework for the article. We then turn to our analysis of the book and present two basic ideas underlying the text, supplemented by a demonstration of how two of Richmond's main concepts are shaped by these basic ideas. We conclude with a presentation of her model of social case work.

What happened to theory within social work?

Social work – a 'borrowing field'?

The search for a strong theoretical base has been a continuing theme throughout the history of social work practice (Turner 1996, 6). Several authors have addressed the question of whether social work is a science or just a practical profession. In Rogowski's description of 'the rise and the fall of the profession of social work', he states '[T]he importance of theory in examining the development of social work cannot be overstated' (Rogowski 2010, 10). This understanding is a representative one, though few writers have been as explicit as Rogowski.

Brante (2003) attempted to determine the scientific position of social work by carrying out interviews with 15 professors of social work at Swedish universities. One of his main research concerns involved the question of whether there existed a paradigmatic work in the profession. In order to assist his informants, he introduced to them several examples of paradigmatic works in other fields – such as Marx, Darwin, Durkheim, Weber and Parsons. None of the professors in his sample included any canons from social work in answering this question, and Brante's conclusion was that there were no paradigmatic works in social work. In discussing these findings, he mentioned that they could be related to the backgrounds of the professors since most of them were trained in sociology and psychology, while only five had social work backgrounds. In his study, Brante made no reference to Richmond or other important contributors in social work such as Octavia Hill, Henrietta and Samuel Barnett, and Alice Salomon. He does mention Jane Addams, but only as an example named by one informant, and he makes no use of her in his analysis. Brante depicts social work as a new scientific field as a reason for why these professors were not familiar with the paradigmatic works of the profession. By situating social work as a profession emerging in the development of the welfare state, Brante effectively excluded the early history of the profession (Brante 2003, 133–134).

Another position adopted towards theories in social work involves defining social work as a 'borrowing field'. Within this view, social work is considered to use theories; however, they do not originate from social work itself, but are 'borrowed' from other disciplines, such as psychology, sociology or social policy. Soydan's (1993) book on the history of ideas in social work refers to social work as a borrowing field characterized by the import of theories and methods for analysis from other disciplines. This does not mean that he is unaware of social work's own contributions through its founding mothers like Richmond and Addams. Soydan employs a perspective focused on the individual and the society, but he dichotomizes these and then asks what is sick – the individual *or* the society? According to Soydan, social work has been overly interested in the individual at the expense of the society. He sees Richmond as a representative of the individual while describing Addams as a representative of those focusing on the society. His position is a rather common one, but from our perspective, this kind of dichotomizing does not fit when we closely examine Richmond's writings. Soydan's position fails to grasp the dual focus of social case work dealing with *both* the individual *and* the society. As van Wormer has emphasized, it is precisely this attention to the person as well as the situation that creates the special character of social work (van Wormer 2002, 24).

The perception of being a borrowing field has followed social work for many years. Already in 1960, Holter mentions what she viewed as social work's 'handicap' in lacking its own theoretical foundation in her article: 'Sosialarbeiderens yrkesrolle'[1] published in the very first issue of the journal of social science in Norway.[2] Dahle (1992) later challenged Holter's position by pointing out that nearly all disciplines may be perceived as borrowing from others. Medicine is a typical example since it draws from a range of theories such as chemistry, biology, psychology and so on. However, being a borrowing field has not influenced medicine's reputation in the same negative way as it has for social work. As Dahle pointed out, when borrowing theories, social work becomes 'less of everything', while medicine becomes 'more of everything' (Dahle 1992). The implication of being a borrowing field is thus not unique to social work. The diffusion of theoretical concepts is a process shared by all disciplines. Even traditional disciplines like sociology and psychology borrow from other disciplines, such as history and philosophy (Levin 2004).

Questions of how theories relate to social work are not new, and they have often been raised from outside as well as inside the field itself. One familiar dichotomization of theory and practice defines social work as *either* solely practical *or* as solely borrowing its theories from others. One consequence of such reasoning is to situate the theoretical outside the discipline and social work thus ends up being 'only' practical. Whether social work is defined as theoretical or not, this kind of reasoning easily leads to the loss of potential contributions and perspectives coming from within social work itself. This clearly has consequences for what Cornell sees as social work's '… dual focus on both individual assistance and social reform' (Cornell 2006, 50). These and related questions posed here are connected, as we shall show, to Richmond's theoretical contributions. But before moving on to our analysis, let us turn our attention to some traditional interpretations of social case work in a historical context.

Previous research on Mary Richmond

Interpretations of Richmond's texts vary in accordance with the interpreters perspectives and have changed over time, mirroring the changes in the sociocultural contexts of which interpretations are a part. As we have noted, different views and interpretations on Richmond's texts have been offered. However, one of these particular narratives has been a dominant and long-standing one. During the 1930s and 1940s, casework gradually became a form of therapy, heavily influenced by psychoanalytic theory. Turner explains: '... it was during the 40s that the four concepts of casework, psychodynamic theory, psychotherapy and diagnosis came to be seen as a unified concept, and a shift in social casework can be seen, from person and situation to person only' (Turner 2002, 10–11). When many social workers in the 1970s took a stand against the medical model and what they feared was unreasonable categorizing, their position involved rejecting the Freudian and diagnostic school then associated with Richmond (Turner 2002, 20). Her theoretical contributions, earlier interpreted within a sociological or multi-theoretical perspective, then became described as pathological and psychiatric.

The medical and individualistic interpretations of her writings have remained a dominant narrative up to the present day. Contemporary interpretations has often lumped Richmond's theory of social case work together with the psychoanalytic tradition. These understandings, however, have ignored major differences between her writings about social case work and psychodynamic traditions in social work. In this way, Richmond got caught up in the 'psychoanalytic sweep' found in later interpretations (see for instance Pozzuto and Arnd-Caddigan 2008, 62). Such an interpretation of her work is not the only one offered, but it is of special importance owing to the dominant picture it provides of social case work and its base of knowledge in contemporary social work literature.

Many social work researchers refer to Richmond and her publications. Interestingly, little turns up when searching for the book's title *What is Social Case Work?*, except Richmond's own book. However, many books and articles refer to *Social Diagnosis* (1917) as well as other aspects of her life and career. Of special interest has been whether the positioning of her work was within social or natural sciences or interactional or pathological perspectives. Typical are the many differing interpretations of her theoretical and scientific approaches. Rather than a single dominant description, there exists a collection of differing and often opposing understandings of her work. Thus, for one author, Richmond was ahead of her time (Montalvo 1965, 104) but for another, she was antiquated (Berelman 1968, 395). She was involved in social reform (Agnew 2004; Murdoch 2007; Pittman-Munke 1985, 164; Soydan 1993, 89–94) and she did not care about social reform (Soydan 1993, 91). She believed that the individual was the 'sick' element that needed to be fixed and adapted to society (Soydan 1993), but also she had genuine insights into the complex duality of person and society (Cornell 2006). She was part of the diagnostic/Freudian school of thought (Kokkinn 2005), and she was opposed to Freud, and sociological or interactional in her approach (Berelman 1968, 399; Fischer 1970, 20; Murdoch 2007). All these conflicting opinions are in and of themselves reason enough for justifying the need for a detailed examination of her actual text. To our knowledge, such a close reading has not been done yet.

In the next section, we will explain our theoretical approach and what we have done in order to highlight her theoretical contributions.

Theoretical approach

We have used several of Gadamer's hermeneutical key principles, such as the hermeneutic circle and history of effects, as a basis for our detailed examination of Richmond's texts. Through a way of reading the whole text and its parts, described as the hermeneutic circle, Gadamer explains how understanding of meaning gradually evolves as a result of a dialogue between the text and its reader (Gadamer 2010, 329). The history of effects literally describes the effects, or the trails, the text leaves behind (Gadamer 2010, 381). This represents one way of describing how Richmond's text lives on (or not) in contemporary literature, and how her ideas are seen as transferred through tradition, through a complex intertextual system, where she figures as a reference as well as a silent voice in other texts (Engebretsen 2005, 43). References to Richmond's work are involved in an intertextual pattern that affects how social workers today conceive of social work's base of knowledge. Gadamer insisted that these effects of the text or the tradition that it creates are important keys to interpretation. However, he also emphasized the importance of confronting the 'effects' of the text with the text itself through careful reading. Although the reception of Richmond's text is a resource in the interpretation, it is also a possible source of misreading. The hermeneutical circle is about comparing 'established readings' of the text, i.e. our expectations, with what the text actually says (the textual elements) in order to revise the standard interpretation.

Hence, to gain a deeper understanding of *What is Social Case Work?*, we have subjected it to a series of close readings. A first cover-to-cover read-through has given us a general overview and knowledge of its structure and content. Later readings of the book have further contributed to a deepened understanding of the text and the interconnections between the texts as a whole related to certain chapters, paragraphs, expressions and concepts. Throughout these readings, we have posed two main analytical questions to the text: How are processes and changes expressed? and How does Richmond present her position on the relation between the individual and his surroundings? Such hermeneutic readings have the potential for nuancing traditional interpretations of Richmond's theories of social case work, for challenging hegemonic narratives, and for illuminating early contributions that might have been overlooked or misinterpreted. Our main aim throughout these readings has been to gain a deeper and more accurate understanding of the knowledge base of social work.

In the following, we will make a three-step presentation of our findings. First, we introduce two *basic ideas* fundamental to Richmond's theoretical framings of social case work. Next, we illustrate the roles played by *two key concepts* in her understandings of the basic tasks of the discipline. And finally, we present her model of social case work and show how it includes these basic ideas and key concepts.

Two basic ideas in social case work: processes and human interdependence

Richmond's text builds upon a foundation of two basic ideas of *processes* and *human interdependence*. Processes, according to Richmond, stem from the fact that: '... the human mind is not a fixed and unalterable thing … it is a living, growing, changing, highly suggestive thing …' (Richmond 1922, 131). The person's life is not static, but constantly in movement. Moreover, this process of change is not autonomous, but dependent on other human beings and social contexts – it evolves around human interdependence. As she puts it: '… a human being's knowledge of his very self is pieced together laboriously out of his observations of the actions and reactions of others' (Richmond 1922, 129).

Processes and human interdependence are interlinked categories, but while processes highlight movement and change, human interdependence emphasizes interactions between persons and their environment. Human interdependence involves social processes, as they explain how people and situations evolve and develop over time in close relation to each other. Richmond's definition of social case work flows out of these two basic ideas: 'Social case work consists of those processes which help develop personality through adjustments, consciously effected, individual by individual, between men and their social environment' (Richmond 1922, 98–99).

Processes and human interdependence are all-embracing ideas in Richmond's theories. These are expressed through her key concepts, such as 'personality' and 'man and his environment' (we will shortly return to these two concepts in more detail). Common to these concepts are the notions that people and their environment are changing all the time and that they are interrelated. With this kind of understanding, Richmond situates herself in the theoretical discussions of her age. James Mark Baldwin and George Herbert Mead, both of whom she refers to in her book, shared a perspective on the individual as constantly changing in close interaction with the social environment (Richmond 1922, 129–131). Like Richmond, these scholars emphasized the interactional and dynamic part of human life as well as how people develop and evolve through social processes.

Earlier interpreters of Richmond's writings, like Muriel Pumphrey, situate Richmond within a multi-theoretical perspective and as being influenced by sociology as well as psychology, psychiatry, medicine, education, philosophy and scientific evolvement (Pumphrey 1957, 405). Berelman, too, albeit somewhat reluctantly, describes Richmond within a sociological tradition, owing to her focus on the individual's relation to society (Berelman 1968, 396, 402). In addition, he presents a common view drawn from the mid-1920s that Richmond's unwillingness to turn to psychoanalysis rendered her old-fashioned and antiquated. That Richmond never included a single mention of Freud's theories in her writings has been noted by a number of writers (Fischer 1970, 22, 26; Walkowitz 1990, 1054). As Berelman puts it:

> … unfortunately, Mary Richmond has become something of an embarrassment to professional social work since it has moved from pre-World War I age of Victorian morality to a post-World War I age of psychoanalytic insight. Mary Richmond was a prude. (Berelman 1968, 395)

While social workers of that time were embracing Freud's psychoanalysis, Richmond was troubled about the psychiatric direction social work was taking (Agnew 2004, 181) and was resolute in her belief that 'the distinct approach of the case worker, in fact, is back to the individual by way of his social environment' (Richmond 1922, 98). With this in mind, let us turn back to her two key concepts to further analyse how these illustrate her understandings of human interdependence and processes.

Two key concepts: 'Personality' and 'man in his environment'
Personality

'Personality' is a key concept in Richmond's theory illustrating in certain respects how she defines the interdependence between people and their context, and how people develop, change and grow through these interactions.

This concept can hold different meanings and understandings. The expression 'the development of personality' (Richmond 1922, 90) is easily associated within a medical model, where the individual is defined as having a problem, or as sick. Framed thusly, the expert helper is the one who diagnoses the individual and decides on a proper treatment. The individual is the one who has to change according to the helper's treatment plan, and to adjust himself to society's demands. Social work textbooks tend to support this view. Both Shulman (1992) and Johnson and Yanca (2004) devote short passages treating Richmond as a historical pioneer operating within an individualistic and pathological framework. Shulman hardly mentions any of her contributions as he takes a stand against the diagnostic school in his interactional approach (Shulman 1992). However, they fail to recognize that Richmond saw diagnosis as a dynamic process related to human interdependence.

When we turn to Richmond's own text, it is clear that her understanding of personality is genuinely *social*. For her, a change of the personality is dependent upon processes between the person and his environment. She defines personality as: '… not only all that is native and individual to a man but all that comes to him by way of education, experience, and human intercourse' (Richmond 1922, 92). Our physical heredity is unalterable and individual, but our social heritage and our environment is personal, and the whole becomes our personality (Richmond 1922, 92). She draws a distinction between individual and personal, where personality is a more inclusive term than the individual. While the individual is restricted to biology, the personal springs from the encounter with society. Thus, the personality is socially constituted: it is the product of the social environment. In addition, while the individual is more static, one's personality is changing all the time (Richmond 1922, 93). These important understandings are all too often overlooked in accounts of Richmond's writings.

Richmond makes the explicit claim that development of the personality is achieved through the client's social relations;

> That field [social case work] is the development of personality through the conscious and comprehensive adjustment of social relationships … The distinctive approach of the case worker, in fact, is back to the individual by way of his social environment. (Richmond 1922, 98)

Personality and change are thus described as conditioned by the environment. By emphasizing the methodological individualism of Richmond, later interpretations have oversimplified her concept of personality and overlooked its fundamentally social character involving interdependent processes between personality and the environment. These interpretations often fail to see that Richmond's focus of interest in social case work is directed to the individual approach, which is not the same as an individualistic approach. Social case work is genuinely social and always about improving social relations (Richmond 1922, 224).

Although the goal of social case work for Richmond is to develop the client's personality, this must not be understood as if social case work happens solely with and through the client. Personality, she emphasizes, is a social process developed through the interaction with the environment (Richmond 1922, 133). To address the personality is for Richmond to address the client, his environment and the relation between them on equal terms. This represents a much more dynamic and social understanding of personality than what is found in the individualistic approach Richmond is often portrayed as advocating. However, Richmond's interactional descriptions of the development of personality still might be questioned. In her definition of social case work, as earlier cited, she writes that: *Social case work consists of those processes which develop personality through adjustments consciously effected, individual by individual, between men and their social environment* (Richmond 1922, 98–99). What exactly does Richmond mean by an adjustment between the person and his environment? Is an adjustment to be understood as a demand for the person to adjust to society – and not the other way around? That is a valid translation of the concept, and how she commonly is interpreted. Still, such an interpretation might also be challenged, by the expression 'between men and their social environment', where Richmond describes an adjustment that indicates a demand for change and adaption on both parts – the individual and the environment. To give a deeper meaning, her definition of social case work must be analysed in conjunction with other paragraphs and chapters, and the text as a whole. Richmond's views expressed throughout the book give further support to an interactional understanding of development of personality through adjustments. Her ideas on human interrelations are inspired by sociological theorists, among them Mead, who described how the societal and the personal are mutually influencing each other, each reflexively producing its effects in the context of the other (Gubrium 2013; Mead 1967). These views challenge certain traditional interpretations of Richmond's theories on social case work as being focused solely on the individual as a person to be fixed and adapted to society.

In order to further understand Richmond's concept of the relation between the person and his environment, we need to study more closely what she actually means by the environment.

Man and his environment

Richmond's concept of the relationship between the individual and the society is defined as the relation between 'man and his environment', today referred to as 'person-in-situation' (Cornell 2006). In her view, the environment is always social, which is shown through the expression 'social environment'. As we learned from *Social Diagnosis* (1917), she includes social in all aspects of the social work field. The 'social' is tied to her main concepts and is an almost ever-present prefix in her writing. When Richmond writes about diagnosis, she emphasizes *social* diagnosis. When she describes the environment, she emphasizes the *social* environment. In so doing, she emphasizes human interdependence – not just the person and not just external factors, but the interwoven relations between them. Richmond's consistent use of the prefix 'social' may also be understood as her attempt to distinguish social work from other fields, such as medicine and psychiatry.

Interventions in the client's environment, or indirect work as Richmond calls it, aim to develop the client's personality and alleviate the difficulties experienced in his social relations (Richmond 1922, 24; Johnson 1999, 323). This kind of work thus entails that the individual(s) involved are still the focus of attention, even when the work is done with or through external sources. Richmond clearly assigns a key role to her concept of indirect work in her theory of social case work (Richmond 1922, 102). However, this concept seems to sometimes be confused with the concept of mass betterment. Mass betterment was a common description in the late nineteenth century for social reform and social action. The mass, or rather groups of people, were the centre of attention for this kind of social work – not individuals one by one (Richmond 1922, 98). Mass betterment was thus a different method within social work concerned with the public, e.g. working towards better housing conditions in neighbourhoods, as opposed to social case work that worked with the individual client or case. An unclear distinction between indirect work and mass betterment might be a factor in disparate interpretations of Richmond's involvement in the environment (e.g. Hutchinson and Oltedal 1996; Soydan 1993). Although Richmond was actively involved in both social reform and social case work, her participation in reform has been given little attention (Murdoch 2007). However, social case work also involved work with the social environment, but through indirect work.

As a distinction has been made between indirect work and social reform, we need to take a closer look at what Richmond means by the social environment. The social environment is difficult to narrow down, since it seems to involve almost anything and anyone concerning the person's well-being. Richmond describes it as '… the exclusion of all those things which have no real influence upon his [the persons] emotional, mental, and spiritual life' (Richmond 1922, 99). What then does she include in the concept? Since indirect work is done to alleviate the client's difficulties through interventions with the environment (Johnson 1999, 323), a number of people, agencies and institutions – and even physical surroundings – might be included. In *Social Diagnosis,* Richmond described those people and institutions most often involved in social case work, such as the family and relatives, physicians, clergymen, public officials, teachers and the workplace (Johnson 1999, 323; Richmond 1917, 1922, 24, 112) – to name but a few.

Richmond also exemplifies what might be included in the social environment through her use of cases. For example, in one of her cases, she describes a young married couple with marital and financial problems referred to the family welfare agency. The couple have a young child and the woman is three months pregnant. They have recently lost their apartment and all their furniture because of their financial situation. The woman lives with her mother while the husband sleeps in a stable. He is described as a man who beats his wife, as well as having a drinking problem. The wife is described as nagging and a bit difficult. The social worker works out a plan with the couple, involving short- and long-term help, for example, financial support and cooperation with a doctor for physical examinations and treatment. A change of environment is recommended, involving staying apart for a while and rest in the countryside. As the treatment goes on, it involves conversations with the couple, further cooperation with doctors, a mental health clinic, different welfare offices, a priest, the husband's workplace and a rural home for substance abusers. Later, a home for the couple is found, the furniture reclaimed and the husband comes temporarily back to work. We see in this case how work with the family and its environment involves a range of contextual factors and how direct work with the client and indirect work with the environment continually interplay throughout the process (Richmond 1922, 51–59).

Richmond's cases and descriptions define the environment as encompassing a wide range of people, institutions and agencies, measures and material things: 'Action ranges from the humblest services, guided by affection, patience, and personal sympathy, to such radical measures as complete change of environment, the organisation of resources where none existed before, and the reknitting of ties long broken' (Richmond 1922, 255–256). The family and relatives hold a special place in social case work as the individual's immediate environment. However, as we have seen, Richmond also includes the broader environment.

Richmond places great emphasis on work with the environment as characteristic of social work: 'The comprehensive, many sided approach through the social environment is peculiarly well adapted to the end which social case work has in view' (Richmond 1922, 111). Indirect work represents an important element in defining social work and assists us in distinguishing social work from other helping professions (Johnson 1999, 332). Other social work researchers also describe social work through the environment as a set of activities distinguishing social work from related fields (Perlman 1957; Saari 2002; Shulman 1992). Yet, the environment often seems to be a difficult and complex field to include in social work theory (Cornell 2006). Moreover, social work researchers are seldom specific about what they actually refer to when writing about the environment. Different concepts are used to describe it including society, context, situation – and environment. All have different meanings and refer to different circumstances. In addition, descriptions of work with the environment often emphasize psychological insights involving people in arrangements of cooperation with their environments – in other words, using the same strategies emphasised in direct treatment of the client (e.g. Hollis 1964; Johnson and Yanca 2004, 263). Specific skills that are needed to do indirect work are thus often left obscured.

We emphasize Richmond's view on contextual factors, because if development of personality depends on human interdependence between the person and his environment, then change is achieved through that person's relation to other people, communities and institutions. We now bring this section to a close with Richmond's description of social case work. This model involves interrelations between four key dimensions and illustrates how processes and human interdependence are integrated into her theories.

Four dimensions of social case work

Four dimensions are involved in and continually interplay throughout the social case work process. These include insight into individuality, insight into the social environment,

Table 1. Mary Richmond's four dimensions of social case work.

	DIRECT SOCIAL WORK	**INDIRECT SOCIAL WORK**
INSIGHTS	Insight into individuality and personal characteristics	Insight into the resources, dangers, and influence of the social environment
	SOCIAL DIAGNOSIS Treatment plan	
ACTS	Direct action of mind upon mind	Indirect action through the social environment.
GOAL	Better adjustment between man and his environment Develop personality	

direct action of mind upon mind and indirect action through the social environment (Johnson 1999, 325; Richmond 1922, 101–102).

This can be illustrated as in Table 1 (Fjeldheim 2013):

Direct social work thus involves both insights and acts. Insight into individuality and personal characteristics is gained through the direct relation with the client, and entails knowledge of the individual's personal and social history. Actions involve different activities together with the client, like assisting him to a doctor's appointment or counselling in family relations.

Indirect social work as well involves a broad spectre of insights and action with and through the person's social environment (Johnson 1999, 323; Richmond 1922, 24). Insights involve knowledge of the resources, dangers and influences of contextual factors (Richmond 1922, 102), for instance a knowledge of organizations' willingness to employ disabled clients. Action might involve reaching an agreement with a particular workplace to hire and facilitate work for a blind client (Richmond 1922, 103–114).

When the social worker has taken down a client's history and gathered all necessary information, she forms a social diagnosis and decides on a treatment plan. On this basis, she acts directly towards the individual, while also acting indirectly in the social environment through other people, institutions and agencies. The aim is improved adjustment, not only for the client, but also for the person *and* the environment (Richmond 1922). As argued earlier, it is important to note that Richmond promotes adjustment 'between men and their social environment'.

All four dimensions of direct work, indirect work, insights and actions need to be included in professional social case work. As Richmond remarks: 'Trained skill was shown in the combination of these itemised acts, which no untrained person, however intelligent, would have achieved' (1922, 102). Richmond points out that social case work requires both insights and actions into both the person and the environment, although she concludes that indirect actions are more exclusive to the field of social work than other approaches (Johnson 1999, 325; Richmond 1922, 110). Indirect action, however, seems to be less theorized, less researched and given little attention in social work literature (Johnson 1999, 325; van Wormer 2002, 23).

Perhaps the most important contribution to the theoretical foundation of social case work in *What is Social Case Work?* is Richmond's insistence on the combination of direct and indirect work throughout the whole case work process as well as her focus on the continuous interplay of insight and action. Her theory of social processes and human interdependence is clearly expressed through the four dimensions of the model: direct work, indirect work, actions and insights. Throughout the social case work process, there is movement and change between the individual and his environment as well as between insights and acts. For Richmond, the person is nothing in himself, but is constantly interacting and changing with the social environment (Richmond 1922, 129).

Strangely, this model seems to be forgotten knowledge. Later it has taken form in diverse definitions, descriptions and formulations that never quite captured the foundation of social work as thoroughly as Richmond did. In the years following Richmond, the influence of psychology led many social work researchers, such as Hamilton (1951) and Hollis (1964), to adopt a strengthened interest in the individual's psyche and emotions as well as a focus on the relationship between the client and the social worker. To a certain degree, social work became for many a set of activities reduced to conversations between the client and the social worker at the social worker's office. The comprehensive approach suggested by Richmond focusing on the client's environment receded into the background. As the border separating social work from psychology became more unclear, understandings of social processes and the interdependence between the person and his environment were diminished.

Conclusion

In this article, our aim has been to bring to light how Richmond defined the theoretical foundation of social case work in *What is Social Case Work?* In so doing, we have hoped to challenge some traditional views positioning Richmond's texts within pathological and individualistic perspectives. Through our readings, we discovered that Richmond's theories were grounded on two main ideas: *processes* and *human interdependence*. These two ideas are expressed in the theories of social case work throughout her book. The two key concepts 'personality' and 'man and his environment', together with the model of social case work, illustrate how social case work for Richmond was to be based upon a dynamic view of social interactions. This perspective sees the individual inextricably bound together with its social surroundings (Richmond 1922, 93). To Richmond, social case work consisted of processes involving several constantly changing and intertwined dimensions. Moreover, these processes were ever dependent on interactions with other human beings.

Few today remember Richmond's theories and philosophy on human interdependence and how her understandings focused on dynamic processes rather than static operations. Over time, Richmond was included in the psychosocial tradition, also referred to as the 'diagnostic school'. Even though the diagnosticians developed many of her ideas and concepts further, there clearly exists a definitive break between Richmond and the psychosocial tradition. The relation between the person and his surroundings, which was Richmond's main concern, was clearly modified by the influence made upon social work by Freudian psychoanalysis. Even though Richmond named her most famous work *Social Diagnosis*, she never called her work diagnostic nor did she include psychoanalysis in her theories. Her theories were explicitly social and relational in their approach, and founded on dynamic processes and human interrelations, rather than intrapsychic inspection. However, social work literature has gradually accepted a static concept of diagnosis and tended to view her theories as directly imported from medicine (Turner 2002).

Many questions raised today concerning the scientific position of social work might be traced back to social work's own history and earlier writings. It is an important task for future research to challenge traditional narratives by conducting studies of social works own classics and canons. If not, important contributions to the profession's theoretical foundation might be overlooked or lost forever.

Notes

1. The professional role of the social worker.
2. Tidsskrift for samfunnsforskning.

References

Agnew, Elizabeth. 2004. *From Charity to Social Work: Mary E. Richmond and the Creation of an American Profession*. Urbana, IL: University of Illinois Press.

Berelman, William C. 1968. "Mary Richmond's Social Diagnosis in Retrospect." *Social Casework*, July: 395–402.
Brante, Thomas. 2003. *Om konstitueringen av nya vetenskapliga fält - exemplet i socialt arbete* [About the Constitution of New Scientific Fields – The Example of Social Work]. Høgskoleverkets rapportserie 2003: 16R.
Burnham, David. 2011. "Selective Memory: A Note on Social Work Histography." *British Journal of Social Work* 41: 5–21.
Cornell, Kathryn L. 2006. "Person-in-situation: History, Theory, and New Directions for Social Work Practice." *Praxis* 6 (Fall 2006): 50–57.
Dahle, Rannveig. 1992. *Å kunne litt av hvert* [Knowing Something About Most Things]. *Nytt om kvinneforskning* 2/92: 16–18.
Engebretsen, Eivind. 2005. "*Barnevernet som tekst – nærlesning av 15 utvalgte journaler fra 1950-og 1980-tallet* [Children's Services as Texts – A Close Reading of 15 Selected Journals From the 1950s and 1980s]. PhD diss." Humanistic Faculty, University of Oslo.
Fischer, Joel. 1970. "Portents From the Past: What Ever Happened to Social Diagnosis?" *International Social Work* 13 (2): 18–28.
Fjeldheim, Siri. 2013. "Fra Richmond til Hollis – en gjennomgang av lærebøker i sosialt arbeid fra 1917 til 1964 [From Richmond to Hollis – A Review of Social Work Textbooks From 1917 to 1964]." Master thesis in social work, Oslo and Akershus University College of Applied Sciences.
Gadamer, Hans Georg. 2010. *Sannhet og metode* [Truth and Method]. Oslo: Pax Forlag.
Gubrium, Erika. 2013. "Poverty, Shame, and the Class Journey in Public Imagination." *Scandinavian Journal of Social Theory* 15 (1): 105–122.
Hamilton, Gordon. 1951. *Theory and Practice of Social Case Work*. New York: Columbia University Press Hollis.
Hollis, Florence. 1964. *Casework – A Psychosocial Therapy*. New York: Random House.
Holter, Harriet. 1960. "Sosialarbeiderens yrkesrolle [The Professional Role of the Social Worker.]" *Tidsskrift for samfunnsforskning* 1 (1): 28–49.
Hutchinson, Gunn Strand, and Siv Oltedal. 1996. *Modeller i sosialt arbeid. Fra ulike røtter til samme felt* [Models in Social Work. From Different Roots to the Same Field]. Tano: Aschehoug.
Johnson, Louise C., and Stephen J. Yanca. 2004. *Social Work Practice – A Generalist Approach*. Boston, MA: Pearson Education.
Johnson Yvonne M. 1999. "Indirect Work: Social Works Uncelebrated Strength." *Social Work* 44 (4): 323–334.
Kokkinn, Judy. 2005. *Profesjonelt sosialt arbeid* [Professional Social Work]. Oslo: Universitetsforlaget.
Levin, Irene. 2004. *Hva er sosialt arbeid* [What is Social Work?]. Oslo: Universitetsforlaget.
Mead, George Herbert. 1967. *Sindet, selvet og samfundet* [Mind, Self, and Society]. København: Akademisk Forlag.
Meeuwisse, Anna, Sunesson Sune, and Hans Swärd. 2006. *Socialt arbete: en grundbok* [Social Work: A Basic Textbook]. København: Natur & Kultur.
Montalvo, Frank F. (1965) 1982. "The Third Dimension in Social Casework: Mary E Richmond's Contribution to Family Treatment". *Clinical Social Work Journal* 10 (2): 103–112.
Murdoch, Allison D. 2007. "Situational Approaches to Direct Practice: Origin, Decline and Re-emergence". *Social Work* 52 (3): 211–217.
Payne, Malcolm. 1991. *Modern Social Work Theory: A Critical Introduction*. Basingstoke: The Macmillan Press.
Perlman, Helen Harris. 1957. *Looking Back to See Ahead*. Chicago, IL: The University of Chicago Press.
Pittman-Munke, Peggy. 1985. "Mary E. Richmond: The Philadelphia Years." *Social Casework: The Journal of Contemporary Social Work*. March: 160–166.
Pozzuto, Richard, and Margaret Arnd-Caddigan. 2008. "Social Work in the US: Sociohistorical Context and Contemporary Issues." *Routledge, Taylor & Francis Group: Australian Social Work* 61 (1): 57–71.
Pumphrey, Muriel W. 1957. "Mary Richmond's Process of Conceptualization." *Social Casework* 38: 399–406.
Richmond, Mary E. 1917. *Social Diagnosis*. New York: Russel Sage House.

Richmond, Mary. 1922. *What is Social Case Work? An Introductory Description.* New York: Russel Sage Foundation.
Richmond, Mary. 1930. *The Long View Papers and Adresses.* New York: Russel Sage Foundation.
Rogowski, Steve. 2010. *Social Work. The Rise and the Fall of a Profession.* Bristol: The Policy Press.
Saari, Carolyn. 2002. *The Environment: Its Role in Psychosocial Functioning and Psychotherapy.* New York: Colombia University Press.
Shulman, Lawrence. 1992. *The Skills of Helping – Individuals, Families and Groups.* Itasca, IL: F.E. Peacock.
Soydan, Haluk. 1993. *Det sociala arbetets idéhistoria* [The History of Ideas in Social Work]. Lund: Studentlitteratur AB.
Timms, Noel. 1997. "Taking Social Work Seriously: The Contribution of the Functional School." *British Journal of Social Work* 27: 723–737.
Turner, Francis J. 1996. *Social Work Treatment. Interlocking Theoretical Approaches.* New York: The Free Press.
Turner, Francis J. 2002. *Diagnosis in Social Work. New Imperatives.* New York: The Howarth Press.
Walkowitz, Daniel J. 1990. "The Making of a Feminine Professional Identity: Social Workers in the 1920s." *The American Historical Review* 95 (4): 1051–1075.
van Wormer, Katherine. 2002. "Our Social Work Imagination." *Journal of Teaching in Social Work* 22 (3–4): 21–37.

Evidence and research designs in applied sociology and social work research

Kjeld Høgsbro

Department of Sociology and Social Work, Aalborg University, Aalborg, Denmark

Today, social work is confronted with a political demand for being evidence-based, and researchers investigating social work practice are discussing the premises of this demand. They are asking if this discussion was substantially different from the one taken more than 50 years ago, and whether it had to be repeated all over again. This article tries to answer this question by reviewing the considerations in the history of applied sociology and its relevance for recent social work research. The ambition of delivering a research that has an impact on social work practice is not unique, neither for the evidence movement nor the practice research tradition we see today. The article reviews statements from Weber to Dorothy Smith and looks at the similar ambitions within the traditions for *Sociological Practice, Clinical Sociology, Urban Anthropology, Social Engineering, Action Research, Formative and Realistic Evaluation and Institutional Ethnography*. Some of these approaches share common roots with Social Work Research in the Chicago milieu of social science in the 1920s and 1930s, and the ambitions and aims are almost identical. The article identifies the more important experiences from the history of applied sociology and discusses its contributions to understanding questions of validity, evidence, methodology, practical relevance of research and scientific legitimacy in the areas of research which aim at contributing to the practical development of social services for marginalized people. By doing this, hopefully the history of applied sociology may prevent deeper mistakes, illusions and misleading in the development of social work research today.

The ambitions of systematic reviews

In a Danish weekly journal, with an influential audience of high officials and decision-makers, the following statement made by the editors was included in one of their special issues in 2005 (Hede and Andersen 2005):

> Remarkable results come from existing evidence-based knowledge. For example, we know that some public interventions are definitely harmful. In other instances, we know of the existence of methods that are much better than the ones we are using. We may find instances where different methods yield similar results, although the choice has been subject to serious professional and political conflicts. Finally and fortunately, we know that in many cases the public services work and indeed work quite well. This is important information if we do not want to destroy a good practice. (Translated from Danish by the author)

The article thus stated that we already had an unambiguous knowledge of what was the best practice in the different fields of social work. Reporters like Hede and Andersen are not supposed to put references into their texts to make it possible to reconstruct the empirical ground of their statements, but to social work researchers it seemed quite unclear what kind of accurate knowledge the article was referring to. Considering all the complex factors influencing social work practice, the statement sounds like a utopia and a vision that seemed quite unachievable. Further reading of the article informs you that this goal is obtained by the production of systematic reviews (SR) based on randomized controlled trials (RCT), and when you dig into the sources of this statement, you find that they stem from a panel of representatives from The Campbell Institute, a couple of politicians and some representatives from organizations of social workers. The rhetoric and illusions of the article was quite typical for that period and these kinds of statements put a considerable pressure on social work practice and social work research in the following years. Thus, the quotation above serves as an ideal point of departure for the discussion in this article. In the international journals, researchers had to defend their theoretical positions in confrontation with this empirical idealism, and practitioners had to defend the relevance of practical experience and knowledge. To some extent, the arguments for this defence can be found in a review of earlier discussions in the tradition for applied social research, which is the aim of this article.

In the discussion between representatives of The Cochrane Collaboration, The Campbell Collaboration and researchers outside these institutions, the researchers were in general more aware of the ambiguities connected to procedures, sampling and theoretical premises for making SR. Both organizations are producing SR of research results made all over the world, and they experience, of course, the uncertainty associated with the procedures of this kind of meta-research. Their reviews mainly include results from RCT, and directors like Iain Chalmers have defended this practice. In Iain Chalmers' polemic quarrel with Martin Hammersley in his article *Trying to do more good than harm in policy and practice* (Chalmers 2003) and Hammersley's *Is the evidence-based practice doing more good than harm* (Hammersley 2005), the basic issue, according to Ian Chalmer as representing the Cochrane Collaboration, was to what extent the researcher is able to manipulate the results whether this is his intention or not. The only fortune of RCT is, according to Ian Chalmers, that no factors, known or unknown can influence the results apart from their random influence on both the intervention group and the control group, and that this influence is defined by exact mathematic methods. Accordingly, Merete Konnerup, representing the SFI Campbell, defines the objectives of the Campbell Collaboration as related to effect studies and defines studies of user influence, implementation, organizational structures and cultures, competences, etc. as being outside the capability of the collaboration. RCT-based meta-analysis thus has to be accompanied by qualitative studies that identify the causes (Konnerup 2005). Thus, it seems rather unclear how and to what extent SR based on RCT studies, which are not accompanied with results from qualitative studies, and the identification of influential contextual factors, can be indicative for practice. Mark Pearsons conclusion to this discussion is that 'there are two questions to be asked. One is related to the question of whether the results determines the practice in an unambiguous way, and the other is related to the validity of meta-analysis based on RCT' (Pearson 2007). Mark Pearson claims that the second issue defines the essential disagreement between researchers, whilst the first question is mostly raised among decision-makers with a lack of knowledge of the premises for social research. What Mark Pearson and Hammersley do not notice is that the core argument in Ian Chalmers article is how RCT as a method neutralize the influence of the idiosyncrasies of the researchers. In this way, rather interestingly, the choice of method referring to validity interferes with premises of governance, which we will come back to.

The validity of RCT's

In answering the question of the validity of RCT's, Mark Pearson claims that there are two basic problems in such an 'empirical pragmatism': the missing focus on the external validity of the investigation and the lack of reflection on the construction of basic categories (diagnostics, treatment, outcome measure) defined outside the review-producing institutions (Pearson 2007).

The first problem seems to be rather simple to explain to a wider audience (Høgsbro 2013). When you select a sample of people (clients, patients, citizens) for RCTs, you have to consider what kind of population the sample represents. When RCT is only testing a biochemical reaction on a certain kind of medicine, the sample of bodies must be regarded as representing human bodies as such. However, when studying the effects of social work, the sample collected in a certain part of New York might not represent anything else. In any case, a complicated theoretical judgment is needed in order to justify a transition of the results to a middle size Danish city. Furthermore, the procedure of controlling the intervention is rather simple when patients are given a pill, however, rather complicated when they are subject to therapeutic intervention, social support or training. Judging what has actually characterized the intervention depends on careful qualitative observations and interviewing including training of staff members in the procedures of the intervention. Furthermore, the construction of an 'ordinary' procedure for the control group might be even more complicated due to the lack of knowledge about such ordinary procedures.

As regard the variety of the results of those RCT's, you never know whether this variety is a result of differences in social context of the different RCT's (milieu, class, urbanization welfare system, etc.). Thus, SR conclusions founded on the average result of these RCT's is more or less a construction of a statistical illusion as Tor-Johan Ekeland puts it (Ekeland 2005). Following his argument, the conclusion is that unless you have valid theoretical arguments for saying that the sample represents social clients in general, and the intervention and constructed 'ordinary service' are in accordance with typical forms of practice, the RCT's are nothing but a sample of case studies referring to different interventions within different contexts.

The second problem, the lack of reflection on the construction and definition of basic categories, is a bit trickier. When investigating, for example interventions aimed at preschool children with autism (Høgsbro 2007), you might find it quite difficult to define autism in an unambiguous way. Are the inclusion criteria for the RCT that the children should have got at diagnosis within the autism spectrum? And then, to what extent are the premises for getting this diagnosis the same all over the world? Or does it depend on specific tests that are contemporarily recognized by the professionals in the field? Moreover, how do different actors understand 'effects'? The public administration might take it for granted that you are researching long-term effects because immediate effects are not relevant to the political decision. However, our repertoire of psychometric tests measuring the immediate effects after 1 year of training does not automatically indicate long-term effects (Sbordone 1998). The entire process of doing RCT's then relies on basic categories defined outside the systematic review, and when comparing the results from different RCT's, we do not know whether schizophrenia, autism, challenging behaviour, homelessness, sexual abuse, delinquency, etc. are defined in the same way all over the world.

Thus, the whole dialogue between researchers and political actors (regardless of their position within the field of general research, primary studies and SR) becomes very complicated when discussing the external validity and relevance of the 'evidence' that should identify 'evidence based practice'.

Furthermore, several other problems were identified in the discussion among researchers between 2000 and 2010:

(1) If it takes 4 years to develop and test a new method for practice and 2 years to make SR, then it will take 6 years before new methods are recognized as 'evidence based'. If practitioners refuse to use methods that are not 'evidence based' or politicians reject these methods, this will seriously delay the development of practice (Levine and Fink 2006).
(2) Different professions are influenced by different frames of references that influence their interpretation and understanding of the implementation of results from SR (Ventimiglia et al. 2000). The evidence movement thus creates a basically new relation between research, practice and common sense that is totally unpredictable (Webb 2001).
(3) The context that dominates SR is related to North American societies, although they pretend to be international (Hansen and Rieper 2009), and combined with a hierarchy of journals for publishing scientific results dominated by North American Journals; this entails the risk of destroying a necessary diversity of welfare systems and social work practice (Burawoy 2005).

The question of risk and trust

When looking at these problems linked to the trust in evidence-based social work at that time, the conclusion must be that several obstacles are blocking the direct way from SR to guidelines for practice. Thus, if references to international SR's are getting more important than references to practical experience, this might threaten the quality of social work. It might further increase the conflict between top-down governance and local professional experience when results from these reviews overrule professional judgment and advice (Börjeson and Johansson 2014). It might also lead to a rather conservative form of practice when new methods are discriminated because they have not yet been approved by SR's. Furthermore, the diversity of social work methods and welfare system might be threatened by North American social work practice that has a longer tradition for RCT studies (Hansen and Rieper 2009).

So why did it actually become so popular between 2000 and 2010? And how did it lead to such widespread illusions that it gathered the strength of a social movement of research institutions, political decision-makers, high officials and representatives of professional organizations (Hansen and Rieper 2009)? And why is it still dominating the discussion today.

After all, the scientific argument against a definite trust in such a 'pragmatic empiricism' is not new; hence, it seems unnecessary to go through these arguments all over again (Simons 2004). However, as mentioned above, the answer might be found in the article of Iain Chalmer who points out that RCT is a method where the results are less influenced by the prejudices of the researchers (Chalmers 2003). According to this statement, its influential position in modern welfare policy might not stem from a 'positivistic' illusion but rather from a political disrespect for researchers as regard research interests and the risk of hidden agendas. Accordingly, it is not a question of meta-scientific premises but a question of political culture or governmentality (Dean 1999).

This leads us to a discussion on the relation between applied sociology and policy-making since its onset at the beginning of the twenties century to its emerging trends of today. The purpose of this study was to identify general traits in the relationship between social research and policy-making that might be relevant to present social work research.

The tradition from Max Weber

Max Weber might have been the first sociologist who tried to define the relation between social science and politics in a way that shows mutual respect and recognition of the differences between the two actors in the development of the modern welfare state (Weber 1904).

To Max Weber politicians define the values of the political development and the goals of this development that should be in accordance with the values. The role of social scientists was then to investigate the coherence between values and goals. They could contribute with discussions on the risk of the unexpected consequences of reaching these goals, and they could contribute with a discussion of the origin of values, alternative values and the expected diversity of values among the citizens. Furthermore, they could contribute to the discussion by identifying the means that might lead to the preferred goals and propose a choice of means with respect to the resources used.

Max Weber's implicit stipulation was that all human action is linked to considerations on aims and means that benefit values and goals, and these considerations may be qualified by scientific methods. As such, he came pretty close to the paradigm of rational choice. This was later explicitly outlined as five phases starting from an identification of social issues to identifying missing knowledge (Lindblom and Cohen 1979; Weiss 1972):

(1) Define goals and values and rank them.
(2) Establish an overview of accessible strategies and methods that can lead to the defined goals.
(3) Establish an overview of possible consequences of alternative strategies.
(4) Investigate the relation between values, goals and consequences of different strategies.
(5) Make choices on qualified and well-informed grounds.

Though Max Weber regarded his own considerations and suggestions as rational and necessary for the development of society, he also concluded that this was not realistic in his own time because of the rather chaotic political conflicts of that time (Weber 1904). So apparently the 'ideal form' of political decisions as an interplay between policy and social research had to wait for a change in political culture that would make such a paradigm more accessible.

In a way, this change in political culture seemed to happen just after the Second World War, when biological approaches to social problems were abolished in political and scientific discussions due to the extreme versions of biological determinism characterizing the Nazi regime (Bauman 1989). Paul Lazersfelt, who invented the term 'social engineering' at a seminar in Oslo in 1948, became one of the leading figures in the development of institutes of applied social research aimed at facilitating the development of a modern welfare state (Lazarsfeld and Reitz 1975). These institutes exerted a remarkable influence on the development of the political strategies of post-war European countries. This might have been caused by the optimistic vision of the modern welfare programme that was intended to eliminate poverty as well as inequality and conflicts under a rationally organized new global order. A programme like this was written by Beveridge in 1942 during the Second World War and spread among the soldiers to gain support to the allied troops as an alternative to the Nazi propaganda and the East Asian Programme of the Japanese Army (Beveridge 1954; Lawrence 1971).

Towards the end of the 1970s, many of the methodologies aimed at giving neutral objective prescriptions for policy-making had been developed. It included demographic surveys of social problems, evaluation methods and experimental research. However, upon reviewing the statements from leading figures in this field, you will find a significantly pessimistic conclusion (Lazarsfeld and Reitz 1975; Lindblom and Cohen 1979; Weiss 1972). Conflicts between political decisions and applied research are stated as related to:

- The unclear expectations of the political actors.
- Ambiguous goals.
- Interest conflicts related to the results and conclusions of evaluations.
- Systematic ignorance as regard unintended consequences.
- The complex character of the intervention due to political interventions in the process.
- Political ambivalence as regard the need for alternative theoretical explanations.
- Interference with common-sense judgment and the hidden agendas of strong social actors.

If this is the general experience from a period normally regarded as being dominated by the ambition of creating a rational approach to social problems, it might challenge the basic premises of Weber's rational ideal form of collaboration between social science and governance. Still, these premises seem to dominate both the paradigm of evidence-based practice and the Practice Research Programme. The Practice Research Programme is characterized by including practitioners in the research process (Austin, Fischer, and Uggerhøj 2014). They are supposed to participate in the discussion when defining the basic issues of the research, when it comes to the analysis and interpretation of data and when it comes to the conclusion. The evidence movement gave authority to results from international SR's and the Practice Research Programme involved the idea that systematic dialogue between researchers and practitioners during the research process would lead to unambiguous rational solutions (Konnerup 2005; Uggerhøj 2014).

In the 1970s, the tradition for social engineering was criticized within the sociological community for being too closely related to strong political interests and for ignoring the influence of fundamental conflicts in society. A new trend was to be born in applied sociology; it aimed at supporting a 'bottom-up' development of society involving social actions of suppressed and marginalized groups (Burawoy 2005). In a certain way, this trend was in accordance with the mobilization and self-organized initiatives of the minority groups of these years; sexual minorities, the disability movement and movements among indigenous people (Thomas 2007). In the wake of this development, the social engineering tradition met its alternative in the form of 'sociotechnics' (Høgsbro et al. 2009; Podgórecki 1996). Mainstream quantitative social research strategies was modified by mixed method approaches, and researchers like Donald Campbell found it necessary to supply quantitative data with qualitative research methods, dialogues with practitioners, historical records and ethnography (Campbell 1978). Evaluation research was developed into formative evaluation, empowerment evaluation and even constructivist evaluation (Fetterman, Kaftarian, and Wandersman 1996; Guba and Lincoln 1989). With reference to the terminology of practice research today (Uggerhøj 2014), you may define this movement as a movement away from 'research on practice' towards 'practice research', in which differences of interests and rationalities were recognized as a premise for the dialogue between researchers and different actors within the field.

Clinical sociology, sociological practice and sociotechnics

Two traditions from the Chicago School in the 20s seemed to benefit from this development and enjoyed a kind of revival. These were sociological practice and a tradition for clinical sociology (Fritz 1991; Høgsbro et al. 2009).

Simultaneously with social work, clinical sociology was born around the sociological milieu of the University of Chicago in the 1920s (Fritz 1991). It was born with much of the same intensions as the social work tradition but with a clear sociological profile that differed from the more cross-disciplinary and to some extent psychoanalytical profile of the social work research and practice (Levin 2004). Clinical sociology focused on practical intervention in family problems and problematic interactions in organizations. The aim was to clarify the problems and offer the actors a sociological understanding of the conflicts enabling them to look at the interaction from the perspectives of the different actors involved. By doing this, it aimed at reaching to some kind of peace-making solution to the benefit of everyone involved (Fritz 1991). The theoretical references for the interventions were drawn from the general knowledge of normative conflicts and social roles of Durkheim and Simmel, with a special reference to symbolic interactionism. This might be regarded a more holistic approach to understanding human conflicts than that of the psychoanalytical approach. The difference between clinical sociology and sociological practice is not easily defined; however, to some extent, the tradition of sociological practice was addressing the more macro-sociological levels and dealt with the general services offered to certain categories of people and marginalized local communities, whilst clinical sociology was intervening in the specific problems of families and organizations and mediating directly in conflicts between individuals (Høgsbro et al. 2009). When combining mediation and sociological theory and method, these programmes seem quite close to Practice Research as it is presented today in the Helsinki Statement (Austin, Fischer, and Uggerhøj 2014).

The first systematic courses in clinical sociology were established in the 1920s (Fritz 1991) in a sphere of optimism about constructing a modern world based on more scientific approaches to understanding human beings. At the same time, the concentration of poverty and the new social problems of the larger metropolises such as Chicago was a challenge which these sociological milieus had to address (Hannerz 1980). Still, it must be taken into consideration that the hegemonic approach at that time, with a considerable influence on social policy, was the biological and partly racist approach to understanding poverty and ethnic conflicts (Bauman 1989; Koch 1996). In the wake of this reference and the uprising of national conservatism in the thirties, the influence of modern sociology was generally marginalized.

This picture changed after the Second World War (Lazarsfeld and Reitz 1975), and this might be interpreted as a result of the catastrophe of extreme eugenics and the new global order following the dissolution of European colonies. It gave way to the macro-sociological research of the conditions of the citizens, and the experiences of group dynamics among soldiers during the Second World War gave way to micro-sociological studies (Lazarsfeld and Reitz 1975). Even critical sociological theory became established and was integrated in social work research (Adorno 1957). Although different levels of sociology were represented, focus still seemed to centre around quantitative surveys supporting the general level of bio-politics (Dean 1999; Lazarsfeld and Reitz 1975). There might have been two reasons for this. One of these is that this design seemed to be less influenced by the prejudices of the researcher, as mentioned earlier with reference to Ian Chalmers. The other is that access to new technologies, in this case computer technologies and statistics developed in the 1930s, created an optimism about the possibility of gaining direct access to information that had been out of reach until this point (Lazarsfeld and Reitz 1975).

Thus, in a way, the more micro-sociological approaches to social intervention, such as clinical sociology and sociological practice, were overshadowed by the macro-sociological quantitative survey tradition that became an integrated part of the nation building following the Second World War (Høgsbro et al. 2009).

During the 1970s, however, this changed. The tradition of social engineering that had been part of the nation building process of the 1950s and 1960s was criticized for contributing to a top-down implementation of rational governance and ignoring the general conflicts in the population (Burawoy 2005; Høgsbro et al. 2009; Podgórecki 1996). Furthermore, it had contributed to the suppression of groups among people with disabilities and mental illnesses that were merely regarded as subjects to normalization on the premises of the hegemonic standards of society (Thomas 2007). The civil rights movements of the 1960s paved the way for recognizing forms of suppression linked to stigmatization, discrimination and marginalization of minority groups (Høgsbro 2012). In the wake of these movements, many other minority groups were mobilized. Minority groups such as sexual minorities, people with disabilities and the new feminist movement now focused first and foremost on the cultural premises for the suppression of rights (Smith 2006). Concordantly, the focus of applied social research changed. Sociologies referring to the works of Michel Foucault and Erving Goffman now developed a kind of symbiosis with these movements (Thomas 2007). On the one hand, these movements used them as a theoretical reference, since they questioned the 'natural' order of norms and values, emphasized the de-construction of discourses on which society was founded and revealed the strategies people had to follow and submit to when they did not fit into these systems (Foucault 1980; Goffman 1963). On the other hand, the movement might have contributed considerably to the exposure of these theoretical approaches. Had it not been for the civil rights movement, you might even ask whether Foucault and Goffmann had been so well-known today.

During this period, sociologists such as Adam Podgorecky, who still kept on elaborating on Webers profound stipulations and the whole idea of contributing to rational decision-making, transformed the ideas from the social engineering tradition into a concept of sociotechnics. Sociotechnics emphasized the values of different groups, the more critical analysis of these values and the process of implementing research that involved the people on the ground. It became a concept for a bottom-up support to suppressed and marginalized groups, and it supplied them with sociotechnics that enabled them to develop strategies for integrating into society on their own terms

(Podgórecki 1996). Hence, his programme shared two ambitions with the programme for Practice Research today: the involvement of people on the ground and the respect for the academic premises for doing research (Uggerhøj 2014).

During the 1980s and 1990s, the traditions of sociotechnics, sociological practice and clinical sociology collaborated even closer with respect to their international organization and its American journals. It developed a tradition for employing mediation for trying to solve conflicts between citizens before they were brought to court, and they engaged in the process of 'glocalization' emphasizing projects and mobilizing resources in local communities that were in the risk of being deserted under the influence of global competition (Høgsbro et al. 2009). This was a period dominated by a political focus on user influence, the empowerment and mobilization of grass-roots organizations and the role of peer groups in the rehabilitation of marginalized individuals, and as such it formed a new kind of governmentality which used empowerment technics as instruments in the construction of coherence on a national as well as a global level (Høgsbro 2012). The traditions thus became part of a new regime (Dean 1999).

Now more than 100 years after Weber wrote his thesis, the conclusion of this author is that political decision-makers at first hand refuse to acknowledge results that do not fit into their basic conception of social reality. After some years, an accumulation of research results and theoretical discussions will influence and change the political frames of references, their conception of social phenomena and political philosophy (Burawoy 2005). However, the final result is unpredictable and sometimes surprising.

With respect to this conclusion, the strength of the Practice Research programme is that, through its dialogues and learning processes (Uggerhøj 2014), it produces local stakeholders that become political actors defending the results and knowledge born in the collaboration between researchers and practitioners. The weakness might be that the whole integrated research process might sustain and reproduce social discourses and idioms that are regarded as common sense at the time of the research.

The rise of New Public Management and the evidence movement

The emphasis on direct dialogue and collaboration between researchers and local actors seemed to disappear at the end of the 1990s (Høgsbro 2012). The goals of the nation building process were restricted to a much more narrow focus on global competition and the integration of marginalized groups on the labour market (Pedersen 2011). Critical questions on the premises of hegemonic cultural values and its stigmatizing effects were downplayed. Furthermore, a more individualistic neoliberal view on human nature, as rationally optimizing the person's gain of social relations, had led to a stronger focus on economic motivations for being on the labour market. An old notion of the existence of a poverty culture that was kept into an alliance with welfare professionals, who made them stay on social benefits, was revitalized as a theory explaining the marginalization of specific groups (Prince 2001). This idea originated from discussions among conservatives in USA in the early 1950s, but it had receded to the background during a period in which the hegemonic discourse focused on the social reasons for marginalization and poverty and saw the development of social work and social services as means of breaking the cruel circle of powerlessness. The Reagan administration changed this situation and the idea of social workers forming an alliance with their clients was revived in a fusion with critical left wing discourses on stigma and professional suppression (Dean 1999; Prince 2001). In an extreme version of this discourse, you may encounter concepts such as 'welfareaholics' which refers to social benefits as if it was a kind of substance abuse. In the more gentle Scandinavian versions, professional discourses were seen as stigmatizing the clients and keeping them in a passive role (Järvinen and Mik-Meyer 2003).

Along with the concepts for governance belonging to New Public Management (NPM), the approach to understanding social problems and the dilemmas of social work was restricted to finding simple indicators for measuring labour market effects of different concepts for social intervention and for getting accurate and unambiguous evidence for the effectiveness of these interventions. Furthermore, the research should distance itself from practical knowledge. From this point of view, the weakness of the programme of Practice Research is that the results of the research will raise the suspicion that it is being influenced by the interest in expanding the social services as shared by social work researchers, social workers and clients. This is where the 'evidence movement' gains its relevance.

When reviewing the statements of both politicians and social scientist, it seems unrealistic to expect that the politicians should interfere in the discussion on scientific methods. Our interpretation of the discourses and their context more or less leads us to conclude that in fact they do not care. They only demand that researchers come up with some level of agreement on what is regarded as 'best practice', based on methods that deliver simple, unambiguous measures that are not influenced by the interests of professional groups and local organizations. The producers of SR based on RCT have offered such a service. If this is not possible, the whole construction of a NPM approach to social work is seriously threatened. And what comes next – does an alternative to NPM exist today? This is exactly the 'governmentality' that the Practice Research Programme is up against.

Addressing structures and factors

The discussion on evidence-based social work raised the question of whether we really had to repeat meta-scientific arguments all over again, and when reviewing the methodological discussions in relation to applied sociology, experimental social research as well as surveys and evaluation research it is reasonable to conclude that: yes, we did. Not so much because the methodological considerations had not been adequately formulated before 1980, but because the complex political dynamics around social research seem to have been forgotten in recent methodological discussions.

However, there is an institutional aspect to this question that we still need to understand: NPM has reduced the role of user organizations from partners in the process of defining the problem and constructing the services to the role of critical users who can support the government in identifying the service with the best effect on the integration of people on the labour market (Høgsbro 2012). NPM has restricted the critical analysis of professional systems to its technics and ethics. Understanding the contexts for both social workers and users of social services simply seems too complicated to be integrated in the recommendations to the politicians. However, somehow reality contradicts this reduction of the complexity (Börjeson and Johansson 2014). We have to address the black box of effect evaluations. We need to address the factors in the life-world of social clients and find out what is limiting their access to social relations and participation instead of merely restricting it to labour market connections that might be more influenced by the state of the market than influenced by the client's personal initiatives. We have to investigate the whole process of the contact between citizens and social services and identify possible systematic obstacles which might render it difficult for the users to get access to help. We have to identify the factors in the organization of social work and the collaboration between different agents that make the total structure difficult to access and comprehend for both users and professionals.

In the entire field of social work research, SRs based on RCTs only represent a marginal contribution to our necessary knowledge of social work, and from this point of view, practice research has something to offer. However, other designs taken from the richness of applied sociology might be relevant as complementary approaches. Seen from the perspective of practice research, they are closer to the concept of 'research on practice' (Uggerhøj 2014); however, this is due to other virtues that might be a fortune in certain contexts.

Realistic evaluation and institutional ethnography

With respect to the conclusions above, the investigation of the structures and factors which underlie social work practice demands complex designs, and during the last 10 years, two traditions, with references to applied sociology, have been developed and spread globally as designs that are able to meet these challenges. One of these is realistic evaluation as defined by Pawson and the other is institutional ethnography as defined by Dorothy Smith (Pawson and Tilley 1997; Smith 2005).

Realistic evaluation seeks to identify a solution mediating between the acknowledged scepticism about definite values and problem definitions and a need for unambiguous recommendations (Pawson and Tilley 1997). The objectives of the programme are to investigate the definition of the problems and the construction of goals and means in its totality as a social process that includes different actors and different discourses interacting with the social context of the intervention. As such it aims at widening the scope of the evaluations to a broader sociological investigation, including not only an empirical report of identified effects but also an identification of the mechanisms of action and the relation between intervention and context.

Institutional ethnography draws on the tradition for interpretive approaches to ethnography (Geertz 1973) which draw on the hermeneutic tradition from Gadamer (1989) combined with the structuralistic approach of Levi-Strauss (1963). Initially, these were formulated by Clifford Geertz in his essays from 1973 and later represented by Hammersley and Atkinson (Geertz 1973; Hammersley and Atkinson 2007). This ethnographic tradition has been merged with the concept of 'life-world' taken over from modern phenomenology represented by Alfred Schutz (Schutz and Luckmann 1989). With its ambition of investigating the conflicts between users and professionals in the institutional settings of the welfare system, the theoretical approach is rather similar to Habermas' considerations in *The theory of communicative action* from the 1980s (Habermas 1981).

In her book from 2005, the intentions of Dorothy Smith is to pave the way for a sociology that starts from the everyday lives of people seriously investigating their experiences and knowledge and from this point on to expand the research to include the more distant and trans-local factors that influence their situation (Smith 2005). She criticizes traditional mainstream sociology for hastily jumping to a conclusion on the situation of people with reference to sociological theory of the situations of different categories of people (Classes, milieus, etc.). Moreover, when they are actually engaged in the revelation of a real life situation, they reach a premature conclusion on how the *system* influences this situation. Dorothy Smith wants to apply an ethnographic approach throughout her research investigating exactly how the system works. She wants to identify the specific institutional setting, its professional discourses and regulating text that frames the everyday actions of professionals and users. By doing this, she wants to expand the knowledge of the actors involved and widen their horizons with knowledge of what is going on at trans-local levels. By accumulating the results from such institutional ethnographies, she wants to approach a more accurate knowledge of how modern institutions work.

Compared with the recent programmes of Practice Research, both traditions are closer to 'research on practice' (Uggerhøj 2014). The explicit reason for this is that the approaches use the 'otherness' of the researcher as a special strength just like other ethnographic approaches do. The aim of Institutional Ethnography is to identify mechanisms, problematics and 'trans-local' factors that are hidden from the perspective of the practitioners and users; partly because they are buried under a layer of premises that are taken for granted and partly because these factors are linked to actors, dynamics and processes beyond the 'horizon of the life-world' of the local actors.

Conclusions

The review of the history of applied sociology shows a richness of methodological experiences and considerations from using different designs and advanced discussions on the relation between applied research, professional practice and political decisions. Instead of ignoring these experiences and starting from the bottom, social work research should learn from these discussions. How are we doing research that has a social impact on practice and what do we become a part of when we are doing it. In a concentrated form, the history of applied social research shows that:

(1) Almost any question as regard the relation between theory, research and practice has been raised and discussed within different contexts throughout history. This creates a rich material of possibilities for combining designs in different ways when research is addressing the issues and problematics of different actors.
(2) The relation between social research and political decisions is complicated. You may never expect political decisions to follow recommendations unambiguously. You must expect that political decision-makers refuse to acknowledge results that do not fit into their basic conception of social reality.
(3) Over time social research will contribute to the change of political frames of references and their conception of social phenomenon and political philosophy, partly as a support to current social movements. However, it will end up integrating results from social research in an unpredictable and sometimes astonishing way.
(4) Throughout its history, Applied Social Theory has been influenced by political mainstream discourses in its scope, its basic understanding of its role and its choice of methods and designs. One has to acknowledge and be aware of this influence.
(5) Recent discussions on evidence-based practice and practice research include elements that may be traced back to former discussions within applied social research. It is urgent to consider the strands of these discussions if we do not want to 'do it all over again'.

Understanding the history of applied social research helps us recognize which type of political wave we are recently experiencing. It helps us to understand the 'trans-local' factors that influence the collaboration between practitioners, users and researcher. This is important if we do not want to get caught in a political web reproducing recent political discourses and restricted premises for doing social work research. It helps us keeping a distance to recent political premises for social work research by giving us a rich repertoire of designs and theoretical approaches, and this is important whenever social work practice is being confronted with new challenges.

Disclosure statement

No potential conflict of interest was reported by the author.

References

Adorno, T. W. 1957. "Sociologi og empirisk forskning [Sociology and Empirical Research]." In *Det videnskabelige perspektiv* [The Scientific Perspective], edited by L-H. Schmidt, 291–312. Copenhagen: Akademisk Forlag.
Albæk, E. 1988. *Fra sandhed til information – evalueringsforskning i USA – før og nu* [From Truth to Information – Evaluations i USA in the Past and Today]. Copenhagen: Akademisk forlag.
Austin, M. J., M. Fisher, and L. Uggerhøj. 2014. "Helsinki Statement on Social Work Practice Research." *Nordic Social Work Research* 4: 7–13.
Bauman, Z. 1989. *Modernity and the Holocaust*. Oxford: Blackwell.
Beveridge, J. 1954. *Beveridge and His Plan*. London: Hodder and Stoughton.
Börjeson, M., and K. Johansson. 2014. "In Search for a Model for Knowledge Production and Practice Research in Swedish Social Work." *Nordic Social Work Research* 4: 70–85.
Burawoy, M. 2005. "For Public Sociology." *American Sociological Review* 70: 4–28.
Campbell, D. 1978. "Qualitative Knowing in Action Research." In *The Social Contexts of Method*, edited by P. Brenner and M. Brenner, 184–209. London: Croom Helm.
Chalmers, I. 2003. "Trying to do More Good than Harm in Policy and Practice: The Role of Rigorous, Transparent, Up-to-Date Evaluations." *The Annals of the American Academy of Political and Social Science* 589: 22–40.
Dean, M. 1999. *Governmentality – Power and Rule in Modern Society*. London: Sage.
Ekeland, T.-J. 2005. "Kvalitetssikring eller instrumentalistisk fejlgreb." [Obtaining Quality or an Instrumental Failure.] *Social Kritik* 17 (102): 34–47.
Fetterman, D. M., S. J. Kaftarian, and A. Wandersman. 1996. *Empowerment Evaluation – Knowledge and Tools for Self-Assessment & Accountability*. London: Sage.
Hansen, H., and O. Rieper. 2009. "The Evidence Movement: The Development and Consequences of Methodologies in Review Practices." *Evaluation* 15 (2): 141–163.
Foucault, M. 1980. *Power/Knowledge – Selected Interviews and Other Writings 1972–1977*. London: Harvester Press.
Fritz, J. M. 1991. "The Emergence of American Clinical Sociology." In *Handbook of Clinical Sociology*, edited by H. M. Rebach and J. G. Bruhn, 17–30. London: Plenum Press.
Gadamer, H.-G. 1989. *Truth and Method*. London: Sheed & Ward, The Crossword Publishing Company.
Geertz, C. 1973. *The Interpretation of Cultures – Selected Essays by Clifford Geertz*. New York: Basic Books.
Goffman, E. 1963. *Stigma. Notes on the Management of Spoiled Identity*. New Jersey, NJ: Prentice Hall.
Guba, E. G., and Y. S. Lincoln. 1989. *Fourth Generation Evaluation*. Newbury Park, CA: Sage.
Habermas, J. 1981. *Theorie des Kommunikativen Handelns* [Theory of Communicative Action]. Frankfurt am Main: Suhrkamp Verlag.
Hammersley, M. 2005. "Is the Evidence-based Practice Movement Doing More Good than Harm? Reflections on Iain Chalmers' Case for Research-based Policy Making and Practice." *Evidens & Policy* 1 (1): 85–100.

Hammersley, M., and P. Atkinson. 2007. *Ethnography – Principles in Practice*. 3rd ed. New York: Routledge.
Hannerz, U. 1980. *Exploring the City. Inquiries Toward an Urban Antropology*. New York, NY: Columbia University Press.
Hede, A., and D. Andersen. 2005. *Virker velfærden? – Et debatoplæg om evidens og velfærd*. [Does the Welfare Work? A Discussion Paper on Evidence and Welfare]. København: Mandag Morgen.
Høgsbro, K. 2004. "Procesevaluering." [Proces Evaluation.] In *Håndbog i Evaluering*, edited by O. Rieper, 66–80. København: AKF.
Høgsbro, K. 2007. *ETIBA – en forskningsbaseret evaluering af rehabiliterings – og træningsindsatsen for børn med autisme* [ETIBA – A Research Based Evaluation of the Rehabilitation and Training of Preschool Children with Autism Spectrum Disorders]. Copenhagen: AKF.
Høgsbro, K. 2012. "Social Policy and Self-help in Denmark – A Foucauldian Perspektive." *International Journal of Self Help & Self Care* 6 (1): 43–64.
Høgsbro K. 2013. "Evidenslogik og praktisk erfaring indenfor rehabilitering." [The Logic of Evidence and Practical Experiances from Rehabilitation Programs.] In *Handicapforståelser*, edited by I. S. Bonfils, B. Kirkebæk, L. Olsen, and S. Tetler, 119–134. København: Akademisk Forlag.
Høgsbro, K., H. Pruijt, N. Pokrovsky, and G. Tsobanoglou. 2009. "Sociological Practice and the Sociotechnics of Governance." In *The New ISA Handbook of Contemporary Sociology: Conflict, Competition, Cooperation*, edited by A. Denis and D. K. Fishman, 42–57. London: SAGE/ISA.
Järvinen, M., and N. Mik-Meyer. 2003. *At skabe en klient – institutionelle identiteter og socialt arbejde* [Creating a Client – Institutional Identities and Social Work]. København: Hans Reitzel.
Koch, L. 1996. *Racehygiejne i Danmark 1920–56* [Eugenics in Denmark 1920–56]. København: Gyldendal.
Konnerup, M. 2005. "De gode viljers utilstrækkelighed – virkning, evidens og socialt arbejde." [The Limits of the Good Will – Impact, Evidens and Social Work.] In *Empiri, Evidens, Empati – Nordiska Röster om Kunskapsutvikling i Socialt Arbejde*, edited by S. Ljunggren, 116–135: Copenhagen: NOPUS.
Lawrence, P. 1971. *Road Belong Cargo – A Study of the Cargo Movement in the Southern Madang District of New Guinea*. London: Butler & Tanner.
Lazarsfeld, P. F., and J. G. Reitz. 1975. *An Introduction to Applied Sociology*. Oxford: Elsevier.
Levin, I. 2004. *Hva er Socialt Arbeid* [What is Social Work]? Oslo: Universitetsforlaget.
Levine, R., and M. Fink. 2006. "The Case Against Evidence Based Principles in Psychiatry." *Medical Hypotheses* 67: 401–410.
Lévi-Strauss, C. 1963. *Structural Anthropology*. Middlesex: Basic Books.
Lindblom, C. E., and D. K. Cohen. 1979. *Usable Knowledge – Social Science and Social Problem Solving*. London: Yale University Press.
Pawson, R., and N. Tilley. 1997. *Realistic Evaluation*. London: Sage.
Pearson, M. 2007. "Systematic Reviews in Social Policy: To go Forward, Do We First Need to Look Back?" *Evidens & Policy* 3 (4): 505–526.
Pedersen, O. K. 2011. *Konkurrencestaten* [The Competitive State]. København: Hans Reitzels Forlag.
Podgórecki, A. 1996. "Sociotechnics: Basic Concepts and Issues." In *Social Engineering*, edited by A. Podgórecki, J. Alexander, and R. Shields, 23–57. Ottawa, ON: Carleton University Press.
Prince, M. 2001. "How Social is Social Policy? Fiscal and Mardet Discourse in North American Welfare States." *Social Policy and Administration* 35 (1): 2–13.
Sbordone, R. J. 1998. "Ecological Validity: Some Critical Issues for the Neuropsychologist." In *Ecological Validity of Neuropsychological Testing*, edited by R. J. Sbordone and C. J. Long, 15–41. New York, NY: St. Lucie Press.
Schutz, A., and T. Luckmannn. 1989. *The Structures of the Life-world*. Evanston, IL: Northwestern University Press.
Simons, H. 2004. "Utilizing Evaluation Evidence to Enhance Professional Practice." *Evaluation* 10 (4): 410–429.
Smith, D. 2005. *Institutional Ethnography – A Sociology for People*. Toronto: AltaMira.

Smith, D. 2006. *Institutional Ethnography as Practice*. Toronto: Rowman & Littlefield.

Thomas, C. 2007. *Sociologies of Disability and Illness*. New York, NY: Palgrave-Macmillan.

Uggerhøj, L. 2014. "Learning from Each Other: Collaboration Processes in Practice Research." *Nordic Social Work Research* 4: 44–57.

Ventimiglia, J. A., J. Marschke, P. Carmichael, and R. Loew. 2000. "How do Clinicians Evaluate their Practice Effectiveness? A Survey of Clinical Social Workers." *Smith College Studies in Social Work* 70: 287–306.

Webb, S. A. 2001. "Some Considerations on the Validity of Evidence-based practice in Social Work." *British Journal of Social Work* 31: 57–79.

Weber, M. 1904. "Die 'Objectivität' Sozialwissenschaftlicher und Sozialpolitischer Erkenntnis [The Objectivity of the Realization of Social Research and Social Policy]." In *Max Weber. Udvalgte Tekster*, edited by H. Andersen, H. H. Bruun, and L. B. Kaspersen, 65–127. København: Hans Reitzels Forlag.

Weiss, C. H. 1972. *Evaluation Research – Methods of Assessing Program Effectiveness*. Englewood Cliffs, NJ: Prentice-Hall.

The help system and its reflection theory: a sociological observation of social work

Werner Schirmer and Dimitris Michailakis

TEFSA Platform for Theory-Driven Research, Department of Social and Welfare Studies, University of Linköping, Norrköping, Sweden

> The relation between sociology and social work is analysed in this article as a relation between observer and object of observation. As a theoretical framework, we use Luhmannian systems theory, according to which modern society is characterised by functional differentiation, that is a horizontal structure of function systems such as polity, economy, education, science, law, etc. Each of these fulfils a particular function for society. One such system is the help system, referring to social services and their practice. Its societal function is the management of inclusion/exclusion and social integration. Function systems contain what Luhmann calls 'reflection theories', which are associated with specific academic disciplines (such as the political system/political theory/political science or the education system/pedagogical theory/educational science). Although their basic operations are linked to science (research, theories and methods, publications), reflection theories are part of their system; their function is to reflect on the unity and meaning of the function system. This article argues that the discipline of social work serves as the reflection theory for the help system. A solid reflection theory in the help system is important in order to define guiding criteria for professional ethics to be used in social services. The lack of an adequate reflection theory can lead to the intrusion of ideologies that are inappropriate to the logic of the help system, such as New Public Management or administrative technocracy, which might threaten the integrity of the help system.

Introduction

In this article, we discuss the relation between sociology and social work as a relation of subject and object, or observer and observed. In particular, we make use of Niklas Luhmann's theory of social systems (Luhmann 2012, 2013) as a framework to observe the discipline of social work. From this perspective, we present a description of social work which may seem unfamiliar and will most likely differ from typical state-of-the-art descriptions provided by the discipline itself. Having said that, we claim that it offers insights that are nevertheless highly relevant to social work.

According to Luhmann's theory, the primary structure of modern society is *functional differentiation*, that is a horizontal differentiation form of function systems such as the polity, economy, religion, science, etc. each fulfilling a particular function for society. Another such system is the *help system*. This system refers to social work practice and largely coincides with the social services. Its societal function is the management of inclusion/exclusion.

Function systems contain what Luhmann calls 'reflection theories', which are associated with specific academic disciplines (such as the political system/political theory/political science or the education system/pedagogical theory/educational science). This article argues that the discipline of social work serves as the *reflection theory for the help system*. Although their basic operations are linked to science (research, theories and methods, publications), reflection theories are part of their system; their function is to reflect on the unity and meaning of the function system. An elaborated reflection theory in the help system is important in order to define guiding criteria for professional ethics to be used in social services as well as for the socialisation of future professional social workers. The lack of an adequate reflection theory can lead to the intrusion of ideologies that are inappropriate to the logic of the help system, such as New Public Management, which might threaten the integrity of the help system.

The structure of the article can be summarised as follows. The section 'Functional differentiation' gives a brief outline of Luhmann's theory of functionally differentiated society. Following a suggestion by systems theorist Dirk Baecker (1994), The section 'Society's help system' illustrates that within the Luhmannian framework the practice and professional activities of social work can be understood as a function system, namely the system of social help, or *help system*. Drawing on the work of another systems theorist, André Kieserling (2004), we will state in The section 'Reflection Theory' that function systems often host their own academic discipline, which not only is associated with science but mainly works as a *reflection theory* for its own function system. The section 'The Discipline Social Work as a Reflection Theory of the Help System' brings these different pieces together and provides some reasons for the main argument of this text that the discipline of social work is the reflection theory of the help system. The final section, Implications and Added Value for Social Work, discusses the added values of such a view of social work and some implications for both social work theory and practice.

Functional differentiation

The concept of 'functional differentiation' (Luhmann 2013) denotes the idea that the primary structure of modern society is characterised by the differentiation of a number of specialised communication systems such as the economy, the polity, science, education, religion, medicine, arts, the media and, as will be shown in the next section, the help system. These systems are called function systems because they each fulfil a particular function for society as a whole. The term function refers to the solution of a specific problem, for example, the societal problem of scarcity that is solved by the function system of the economy, the problem of collective decision-making that is solved by the political system or the problem of knowledge that is solved by the scientific system.

The idea of functional differentiation has its predecessors in classics of social theory such as Durkheim's social division of labour, Simmel's description of intersecting social circles, Weber's characterization of modern society as a polytheism of value spheres, Parsons' differentiation of four function systems in the AGIL scheme and Habermas' differentiation of lifeworld and the function systems of the capitalist economy and political administration. What these early and later classics have in common is that they understand society as a differentiated entity. Luhmann's theory continues the tradition of differentiation theory but breaks with these approaches insofar as he does not put individuals (or actions as in the case of Parsons and Habermas) at the centre of social analysis but rather *communication* (Luhmann 1995). For Luhmann function systems are thus communication systems, and the structural characteristic of modern society is the differentiation of self-referentially closed and autonomous (with respect to their rationality) communication systems. In other words, economic communication is differentiated from scientific, political, religious and other forms of communication.

Because they focus on their specific societal reference problem, function systems have developed particular rationalities and specialised modes of observation. In this way, they can decode the enormous, historically unprecedented complexity of modern society into a small slice of social reality. Function systems reduce complexity in their environment into spheres of relevance with the help of guiding distinctions, so-called binary codes such as payment/no payment for the economic system, true/false for science, immanent/transcendent for religion or lawful/unlawful for the legal system. These codes are the lenses through which function systems observe social reality, and each one does so in its specific, unique way. For the economic system, the world appears as a collection of commodities to be purchased for a price; for science, the world appears as a collection of research objects to be analysed and studied; for the legal system, the world appears as a matter of balancing potential mutually conflicting interests. While the binary codes provide the function systems with a tool to view the world in a particular way, they cannot see what their unique perspective does not allow them to see. An economic system has no sensitivity to the truthfulness, legality, aesthetic attractiveness or sacredness of objects – only to their price and corresponding profit expectations.[1]

As a structure of society, functional differentiation therefore implies a multitude of observing systems; it implies that there is neither a unity nor a congruence of perspectives (Luhmann 1989, 2013) and that there is no Archimedean standpoint from which the perspective of one function system could provide an overview of social reality in a comprehensive way that is universally valid and binding for all. Every function system has its blind spots, and as a consequence, no function system is more or less accurate in its descriptions than the others.

There is also another aspect of function systems that is of particular interest for this article: being communication systems, function systems are not constituted by human beings. However, they make use of individuals in a specific way that Luhmannian sociologists call *inclusion* (Schirmer and Michailakis 2015). Social systems include human beings in their operations as carriers of function-specific professional roles that function systems require in order to execute their respective functions: politicians in the polity, traders in the economy, priests in religion, doctors in medicine, lawyers and judges in the legal system, teachers in the education system, etc. Furthermore, each function system includes individuals through complimentary layman roles such as voters, consumers, believers, patients, defendants and students.

Inclusion is a universal normative claim of function systems not to exclude anybody (Bommes and Scherr 2000b; Luhmann 2013): from a function system's perspective, nobody should be excluded from the economy, education, political participation, religion, healthcare, etc. However, empirical reality shows that in a significant number of cases, functional differentiation leads to cumulative exclusions of individuals (Luhmann 2005 [1995]).[2] Social exclusion has been recognised as a paramount social problem that requires a solution on a societal level. This is the function of a relatively newly differentiated function system: the help system.

Society's help system

This section argues that there is a function system centred on social help. This argument was first brought forward by Luhmann scholar Dirk Baecker (1994) and since has been supported and to some extent developed by other authors in the German literature (Fuchs 2000; Hillebrandt 2010; Merten 2000) and Scandinavian literature (Andersen 2003, 2006; La Cour 2002; La Cour and Højlund 2008; Moe 2003; Nissen 2005). To begin, we need to distinguish this kind of help from the broader concept of help in everyday life. The help system refers to the *organised help that is provided by social work, that is public and private social services* for people identified by the system as *needy*. By way of its professionalisation, help through social work becomes a reliably expectable benefit.

As a structure of mutual expectations (between the provider and the receiver), help has a different role in modern society than it had in archaic and stratified societies. In archaic societies, help was organised through unspecified reciprocity: anybody could help anybody else and expect future help as a quid pro quo without specifying the kind, time and range. Stratified societies based help on moral and religious imperatives of charity and expectations of rewards for generosity in the afterlife (Luhmann [1973] 2005, 176). Both of these pre-modern societies depended on help as a key structural element. Historically, the help system as it has evolved in the Western world has its roots in Christian charity ('feeding the poor') and pedagogy, which themselves are built upon religious/moral ideas. However, since modern functionally differentiated society cannot be integrated by religious or moral catch-all formulas (let alone by reciprocity), other forms of help are needed (Luhmann [1973] 2005, 181). Not only is help by the help system differentiated from everyday, non-organised help by its relation to social exclusion (in contrast to helping friends with moving). It is also differentiated from charity (giving a coin to a beggar) by a formalisation of the relation between helpers and helped as well as the criteria for execution of the help provided. Accordingly, the take-off towards differentiation as a function system goes hand in hand with the development of a professional knowledge base, professional craftsmanship and professional ethics.

Nowadays, we can note that the help system has been differentiated as a function system in its own right. More concretely, the help system creates its distinct sphere of meaning and observes (i.e. distinguishes and selects events from its environment by means of) the code *help/not help* (Baecker 1994). Help communication communicates about deficit compensation (ibid., 99), and logically, this means that help is selected where the omission of help (*not help*) might have been possible (see also Moe 2003, 16). Empirically, it is organisation systems of the social services that need to decide whether particular individuals are recognised as cases eligible for help, or no (more) help (Baecker 1994, 99, 105).

The function of the help system needs to be understood in the context of functional differentiation and the ways function systems include and exclude (see previous section). As Luhmann noted in an influential essay (Luhmann [1995] 2005), it is particularly the frequently occurring circumstance of cumulative exclusions from one system to the next that cause major problems for individuals: without inclusion in a political system there is no legal support; without education there is exclusion from the economy. Mass exclusion is a subsequent problem (*Folgeproblem*) of functional differentiation, and the system of social help is a functional reaction to this subsequent problem. Some authors (Baecker 1994; Fuchs 2000; Sommerfeld 2000) therefore speak of social help as a *secondary* function system (see also La Cour and Højlund 2008). The help system identifies, addresses and strives to solve the effects of social exclusion that cannot be taken care of by the standardised support of the welfare state (political system). Its societal function can be described as 'management of social exclusion' (Scherr 1999; Schirmer and Michailakis 2015; see also Wirth 2009; Bommes and Scherr 2000b). Exclusion management can take on the forms of exclusion prevention, inclusion mediation or exclusion administration, depending on the clientele and their case-specific situations. While exclusion prevention deals with people threatened with exclusion from one or more social systems (for example, working people addicted to stimulants or alcohol), inclusion mediation is intended for temporarily excluded people to process their 'includability', that is attractiveness to other social systems through education, therapy, etc. (examples are refugees, long-term unemployed persons, or people who recently experienced a crisis), and finally, exclusion administration focuses on cases whose regular inclusion in other social systems is 'beyond hope' (such as people with severe mental illness).

Exclusion management as the function of the help system takes place on an individual level. Social work organisations become active when individuals are excluded or threatened by exclusion from function systems that are vital for social existence (the economy, polity, education, healthcare, etc.). While, for example, homelessness may be the result of housing and social policy, economic recession, oversupply in the labour market, etc., the social services do not change social structures but support those people afflicted by these structures. Instead of reforming housing policy or labour markets, social services provide help for homeless individuals in terms of improving their includability.

While managing individuals' problems regarding exclusion from other systems, the help system includes these individuals as 'clients'. Client is the complimentary role of the help system (like the consumer in the economy or the voter in the polity); the social worker is the performance (professional) role. So for individuals whose inclusion in other systems is at stake, the help system provides for 'substitutional inclusion' (Baecker 1994, 103; Bommes and Scherr 2000a, 76); that is, inclusion as a client is a substitute for 'regular' inclusion in other systems. This kind of inclusion is meant to be temporary until it is no longer necessary (which would indicate a successful social work intervention). The help system can work on the includability of its clients but cannot include them in other systems (Fuchs 2000, 161; Wirth 2009, 414); inclusion in those systems is up to the systems themselves.

To the extent that social help is an autonomous function system and not simply an auxiliary agent for the welfare state or the legal system, the help system itself – that is, its code, programmes and reflection theories (see below) – determines what/who is a case for social help and what/who is not. Therefore, it can primarily focus on helping, and not merely on the normalisation of 'deviant' cases. The latter, often brought forward as a criticism against social work (not least by Habermas 1992), is the result of confusing a function system's function (solving a problem for society) and its performance (providing support for other function systems). While the function of exclusion management aims at society (and its members) as a whole, the supposed effects of the help provided for the function systems differ from system to system. The economic system requires competent and reliable workers, the education system requires pupils who can sit still and refrain from disturbing the class, the political system requires 'good citizens' who do not threaten the public order – to name but a few of the performances of the help system, that is, its specific contribution to other function systems.

Reflection theory

The previous section showed that, according to Luhmannian sociology, the activities of the social services could be understood as being subject to a societal function system, just like the economy, polity, science, etc. This section presents an argument mainly developed by Luhmann scholar André Kieserling (2004), namely that most (though not all) function systems have their own academic disciplines,[3] which in systems theory are called *reflection theories*.[4] Economic theory is the reflection theory of the economy; political theory is the reflection theory of the polity; pedagogy is the reflection theory of the education system, theology is the reflection theory of the system of religion. In the next section, we will argue that the academic discipline of social work is the reflection theory of the help system. Before moving on, we need to explain the concept of reflection theory in more detail.

On the one hand, reflection theories usually consider themselves to be *scientific disciplines*. Reflection theories are, like any other academic discipline, represented by professorships and university departments which include the right of examination and promotion; they guide and carry out research with the help of scientific methods of data collection and data analysis; furthermore, they have publication outlets with peer review and impact factors.

On the other hand, reflection theories have a specific relation towards their function systems; more precisely, they are what systems theorists call *self-descriptions* of the function systems. In contrast to outside descriptions (*Fremdbeschreibungen*), which can afford to formulate more or less critical views of the system – think of a Marxist critique of the market economy – self-descriptions are compelled to be more loyal to their system (see Kieserling 2004, 49, 88). As Kieserling (ibid., 58) argues, the *raison d'être* of reflection theories is to reflect on and positively evaluate the code and societal function of their function system. In other words, reflection theories have an affirmative nature regarding their function system: legal theories appraise the law, economic theories endorse markets and rationality; political theories usually esteem the state or equivalent forms of governance. Negative evaluations of (and even indifference towards) the function would instead cause irritation rather than appreciation within the function system. Imagine a theology that challenges the existence of divine, transcendent beings, a philosophy of science that denies interest in knowledge or truth, a pedagogical theory that questions the possibility of changing individuals by means of teaching.

While theories in purely scientific disciplines submit to the code of true/untrue (Luhmann 1990), reflection theories also align with the code of their function systems (Kieserling 2004, 64). That means that they are more restricted in terms of choice of and attitudes towards research topics than, say, a sociological description. Research informed by reflection theories must satisfy claims of usefulness for their respective function systems. In order to be intelligible by the practitioners of the respective system (judges, priests, pedagogues, social workers, etc.), reflection theories strive for a semantic unity of plausibility and evidence (ibid., 59). They cannot simply convey research findings that contradict the plausibilities and values within their function systems. Kieserling argues straightforwardly that reflection theories are part of their function systems, rather than of the function system of science. From a systems-theoretical perspective, reflection theories then appear as internal subsystems of the function systems. Whereas a function system differentiates itself from its societal environment (polity and society, education and society, religion and society, help system and society – with society always being the environment, but a different one for each function system), a reflection theory differentiates itself from the practice of its own function system (political theory and political practice, pedagogic theory and pedagogic practice, theology and religious practice, social work theory and social work practice).

Reflection theories consider the practices of their function systems (help, teaching, preaching), while *reflection theories as practices themselves* take on the practice forms of science, that is conducting and publishing research; finding and producing knowledge. From the viewpoint of the reflection theory, this internal differentiation appears as tension between theory and practice or knowledge production and knowledge application (Kieserling 2004, 72). By associating themselves with science, reflection theories legitimise their own status within their function systems. Associating themselves with their function systems, they might assert their usefulness in solving societal reference problems and develop self-descriptions based on both scientific truth and community benefit. Both associations are necessary especially because reflection theories are in charge of educating, training and socialising future practitioners in their professional fields: lawyers and judges require training in law, priests in theology, physicians in medicine and social workers in social work.

One last note on reflection theories is necessary. As already Luhmann ([1972] 2014) noted, function systems do not just host one reflection theory but several of them. Economic theory, political theory, theory of law, for instance, all consist of many different schools (or sub-theories) each competing with the others for the status of the most adequate descriptions in and of their field. So, while Keynesianism and neo-classic economic theory have differing views on how economic policy should look like, they are both part of 'the' reflection theory of the system of economy.[5] The same is valid for realist and idealist theories of international politics, which strongly disagree on how to achieve security from potential enemies but share the view that security is a key goal of political theorising, which makes them reflection theories of the system of politics. Similar examples can be found for the reflection theories of other function systems.

The discipline social work as a reflection theory of the help system

If we bring together the different strands of theorising presented in the previous sections (society as differentiated in function systems, each hosting a reflection theory and social help as a function system), we can argue that the academic discipline of social work is the reflection theory of the help system. In this section, we will provide some arguments to support our claim. Reflection theories convey positive attitudes towards the function of their host system in society, which makes them basically (though not always explicitly) normative. As is true of the help system itself, help is also considered to be something good by the discipline social work. Accordingly, good help (in line with professional ethics) is better than less good help; omission of help where help is possible is the worst alternative – unless in the paradoxical case of help to self-help by ceasing help efforts, which in turn could be a particular method of providing help.

This has become very obvious in the debates for and against *evidence-based practice* (Bergmark, Bergmark, and Lundström 2011; Gambrill 1999; Otto, Polutta, and Ziegler 2009; Soydan 2012; Webb 2001). Whatever side the debaters are on, they always argue for improving the quality of help. Depending on the side, the 'good practice' can be achieved either by usage of the 'best evidence available' (Sackett et al. 1996) or by protecting professional discretion against manualization and bureaucratization (Harris 1998; Webb 2001). What the debaters all have in common is that each claims to represent the 'better practice', thus the better help. By contrast, a sociological analysis might be interested in how different ways of defining what 'good' practice is vary across eras, across countries, across observers and stakeholders, across scholarly paradigms, etc. It is important to note that sociological analysis is neither constrained by the imperatives and normativity claims of the help system, nor forced to take sides.

Since a reflection theory is a subsystem of its hosting function system, it tends to submit to the host system's code rather than to that of science. Sometimes there can be an outright contradiction between what is scientifically true and what is in line with the semantics of 'help', and in such situations, reflection theories support what is plausible in their function system. For example, one hardly finds academic social work texts that make use of evolutionary psychology to explain gender or power differences, or neuroscience to explain deviant behaviour, despite the fact that there is abundance of scientific evidence (Pinker 2002), sometimes even acquired with the 'gold standard' of randomised controlled trials. Similarly, statements that question the benefits of social equality would hardly be welcome in social work journals, not even when tying them to facilitation of decision-making (think not just of the military but of any organisation consisting of more than one member) or to the sociological fact that even the most democratic societies are highly stratified in order to function properly (who is going to do the low status jobs?). The implications of such findings would be unacceptable for academic social work because they would contradict professional values and be irreconcilable with human justice. One last and obviously most controversial example is prostitution. In social work, it is widely treated as a social problem that requires remedies, particularly because it is regarded as an engine for human trafficking, slavery, gender oppression, etc. Without legitimising prostitution the tiniest bit, non-normative and non-obvious,[6] research could examine the stabilising functions of prostitution for marriage (Davis 1937). We do not aim to defend such research but use it as evidence for the argument that there are simply some things that could be studied in the social sciences but which one simply cannot consider in social work and still expect to remain a respected member of the discipline's community.

The key to understanding all of this is that – in contrast to science, where truth and verifiable knowledge are the reference problem – social work takes sides with the marginalised, the poor, the deprived, the victims of oppressive structures, etc. and aims to promote social change to their benefit. Scholarly social work conducts research and writes for their benefit (Ife 2012), either directly by advocating their interests or indirectly by informing and educating those who work to help them. As a result, social work follows the imperatives that prevail within the function system of help, not in that of science.

There is substantial overlap between science-oriented communication and social work communication (what is 'good' help can also be true, and vice versa), but in potential cases of conflict, the help code is superior to the scientific code in social work. As shown in the previous section, this is neither a peculiarity of social work nor is it a weakness – it is simply a structural characteristic of a reflection theory (more on this in the next section).

While most of the scholarly practice taking place in the context of academic social work (conducting research, publishing, grant applications, PhD supervision, etc.), there is always the – sometimes latent, often manifest – link between academic practice and professional practice (Parton 2000). Whatever academics write is almost always expected to have some relevance to practice in some way. This is important for the legitimacy of the reflection theory in its function system; likewise, this legitimacy is underpinned by attempts to connect the methodologies of the reflection theory more closely to the scientific canon, as can be seen in recent debates about whether social work is or should be a science (Brekke 2012, 2014; Merten, Sommerfeld, and Koditek 1996; Staub-Bernasconi 2007). On the other hand, however, the functional differentiation between the reflection theory and the professional activity is an explanation of what is often complained to be a suboptimal relation between theory and practice (Michailakis and Schirmer 2014).

Reflection theories tend to overstate the impact they have (or ought to have) on society and other function systems. For example, in textbooks one often reads that social work has the mandate to solve social problems and promote social change (see e.g. Healy 2001; Staub-Bernasconi 2007). Certainly, there is no doubt that social workers in their daily work deal with social problems and their consequences, and the more they consider themselves as social *pedagogues* (particularly in continental Europe), they engage in social change by educating and helping to empower their clients. However, it would be easy to argue that social problems are solved and social change is achieved by other systems than the help system. Economists might claim that capitalism and the liberalisation of markets have reduced global poverty and raised global living standards; scientists might claim that their innovation and advances have facilitated a more comfortable lifestyle, survival, longevity, mobility and communication; politicians (as well as administrators and planners) might claim that their political programmes have provided for inclusion, equality, employment, etc. We should mention in particular social mass movements such as the bourgeois movement (French Revolution), labour movement (welfare state), suffragettes (women's political inclusion) and various minority movements which, at least on the macro-level, forced dominant classes, power structures or discourses to give way, thereby enabling change. From this ad hoc comparative perspective, one might wonder why social work should be the engine of social problem-solving and social change. Our position is not to question the efforts and successes of social work on behalf of this – quite the contrary. Our argument is rather that reflection theories typically overestimate the function and its positive effects on society as a whole, and social work (being the reflection theory of the help system) does not differ in this respect from other reflection theories of other function systems.

Put roughly, while liberal economists think more market is good for society and that social problems are the result of too little market, political theorists in contrast believe that more governance is good for society while social problems are the effect of too little governance, that is, too much laissez-faire towards other systems. In a similar vein, social work scholars assume that because there is too much injustice in the world, more help (understood as motivation, activation, empowerment, illumination, solidarity, equality) is needed to solve the problems. What all these views have in common is that the source of the problems is considered to be outside the function system while the solution is to be found inside it.

Implications and added value for social work

The presented argument is built consistently within in the framework of Luhmannian systems theory. Such a point of departure has its advantages as well as limitations. However, in order to evaluate these, the measure is not of positivist–objectivist kind in terms of which framework is closer to 'objective truth' than others but it is a heuristic one: what insights does a certain framework allow us to see, and what practical value does it have? The Luhmannian approach neither provides insights into how to improve social work practice, nor does it provide (normative) accounts on what 'good practice' is. The argument of this article is a sociological one, but it offers at least threefold added value for social work, both in terms of discipline and practice. Considering the discipline social work as a reflection theory provides new answers to old questions in the self-reflection of the help system: (1) the identity question, (2) the question of academization/scientification and (3) the question of the relation between theory and practice.

(1) The identity question is as old as the professional practice itself: What is social work about? What are its unity (what is common to all social workers) and its difference (what is genuine about social workers in comparison with psychologists, psychiatrists, nurses, pedagogues, sociologists)? Similarly, the academic discipline is torn by its uncertain identity: whether it ought to be a science-based action theory to guide practitioners (Brekke 2014; Miller 2001; Obrecht 1996), a critical social science of social problems and social change (Dominelli 2002; Fook 2002) or even a 'discipline without qualities' as Kleve (2007) suggests in allusion to Robert Musil's famous novel. The sociological answer to the identity question, based on Luhmannian systems theory, is twofold: first, there is the help system, which as a function system of society fulfils an exclusive function (exclusion management) in an autonomous way. With its focus on help, this system offers a perspective on society and social problems that is distinct from that of other professions and other function systems. Second, if we locate the discipline of social work as a subsystem within the help system, the identity problem looks less severe because, as a reflection theory, its tasks and its exclusivity (in contrast to neighbouring disciplines) are given by the functional logic of the help system. Obviously, being classified as a reflection theory, this does not entail any kind of degradation – that is, that social work was not (yet) good enough to meet the requirements of being a full-fledged and fully respected science (whatever that might be). On the contrary, reflection theories are crucial to their function systems for boundary management. They are important gatekeepers for fending off intrusions by other function systems (not least those of the economy, politics and positivist science) that tend to impose their own codes on the logic of the help system. This has become an issue in particular in the context of outsourcing formerly public social services to the private sector. Private social care organisations (unless they are NPOs) strive for economic profit. The 'good help' then becomes relegated to an interchangeable means of profit, not an end in itself as the professional ethics of the help system would require (see Gethin-Jones 2012). A reflection theory needs to formulate principles and programmes to safeguard the fulfilment of the societal function of its system. Similarly, the recent rise of New Public Management, which has gained in popularity among welfare administrators who are looking for ways to reduce costs and maintain a belief in the efficiency increases that NPM keeps promising, could be interpreted as a failure of social work to focus too much on the competition with other research disciplines and too little on defending the integrity of the function system. This leads us to the second point.

(2) Similarly to the identity question, the aspiration towards academization and scientization is also almost as old as the profession itself. While academization, that is the establishment of the discipline at universities, is useful in terms of legitimising the systems-internal differentiation between practice and reflection theory, the aspiration of scientization runs contrary to the *raison d'être* of the discipline. We certainly do not question the necessity of a (interdisciplinary) scientific foundation for the knowledge base of social work professionals. However, we argue that attempts to completely

transform social work into an empirical science – be it bio-psycho-social natural-science-style positivism or a sociology of inequality and social problems – would imply abandoning the reflective function it has for the help system. The more social work turned into a positivist natural science, the more it would find evidence and contribute to its own knowledge base but the less it would be able to interpret and normatively evaluate the meaning of all this evidence for practitioners, who not only need to follow programmes but, at least equally important, attach meaning to it. This meaning can only come from the help system itself. If, on the other hand, social work tried to turn into an empirical science of social inequality and social problems, the more difficult it would be to remain distinct from sociology. The latter situation has led some commentators to reject the necessity of social work in the first place (for a Swedish case see Börjeson cited in Brante 1987, 41), arguing that the discipline should be abolished because it could not keep up with sociology. We find that such statements miss the point completely because sociology cannot replace social work, for the simple but nonetheless intricate reason that social work as reflection theory has a different function than a (purely) scientific discipline. While both sociology and social work make statements about inequality and social problems, the associated meanings are completely different (a matter of truth or a matter of help and assistance).

(3) Finally, regarding the discipline social work as a reflection theory of the help system gives a new interpretation to the enduring conflict between theory and practice. In our view, the often observed dysfunctional or problematic 'transfer' from theory/research to practice is based on misleading expectations. As a reflection theory, the usefulness of practice lies scarcely in empirical findings and their translation into concrete guidelines for practitioners. Quite the contrary – most practitioners do not want to sacrifice their professional discretion; they consider social work as an art rather than as assembly line work in the best Taylorist-Fordist sense. The usefulness of the "theory" comes to the fore especially in the education of future social work practitioners. In their training, they learn not just a lot of facts and practical methods. A key function of training is socialisation in the core values, creation of meaning and provision of a normative compass for what "good practice' is. Similarly, with its academic practice (papers, books, lectures, etc.) as reflection theory, the discipline social work can prevent hardened professional practitioners from turning into cynics over their long career when they constantly have to deal with interprofessional, political or client-related obstacles.

One last thought on the relation between theory and practice – as academic practice, a reflection theory entails the conduct of research, both empirical and theoretical. While this kind of research aligns itself with the scientific system (true/false), it is subject to the code of its function system (help/not help), which means that both topics and approaches are restricted, as is argued in the section Reflection Theory. To maintain its internal differentiation from professional practice, a reflection theory as academic discipline requires a certain amount of relative autonomy from professional practice. The discipline itself does not practice help; it researches, publishes, debates. On the other hand, the relative autonomy needs to be mutual. Subordination of one to the other (when the discipline prescribes how practitioners should do their work, or vice versa, when practice defines what research the discipline needs to conduct) is dysfunctional for the system itself. Relative autonomy should not be confused with autarchy, as both are parts within and are oriented towards the same function system. In this regard, they share the same identity.

Notes

1. This is, of course, different for organisation systems and for individuals, which/who have the ability to change perspectives and have to adjust to multiperspectivity.
2. As has been pointed out by some authors (Nassehi and Nollmann 1997; Schirmer and Michailakis 2015), it is less the universalistic semantics of function systems than the restrictive membership practices of organisations that are the key engines of exclusion.
3. Academic discipline refers to a system of concepts and methodological rules employed in the endeavour to interpret and explain phenomena that result in a specific body of knowledge. Disciplinary knowledge is hosted in academic departments.
4. On the concept of reflection theory, see also the works of Roar Hagen (2006), 169–192.
5. We thank one of the anonymous reviewers for this example.
6. In the sense of Randall Collins' non-obvious sociology (Collins 1982).

References

Andersen, Niels Åkerstrøm. 2003. *Borgerens kontraktliggørelse* [The Contractualization of the Citizen]. Kopenhagen: Hans Reitzels Forlag.

Andersen, Niels Åkerstrøm. 2006. *Partnerskabelse* [Partnerships]. Copenhagen: Hans Reitzels Forlag.

Baecker, Dirk. 1994. "Soziale Hilfe als Funktionssystem der Gesellschaft." [Social Help as Function System of Society] *Zeitschrift für Soziologie* 23 (1):93–110.

Bergmark, Anders, Åke Bergmark, and Tommy Lundström. 2011. *Evidensbaserat socialt arbete: Teori, kritik, praktik* [Evidence-based Social Work: Theory, Critique, Practice]. Stockholm: Natur & Kultur.

Bommes, Michael, and Albert Scherr. 2000a. "Soziale Arbeit, sekundäre Ordnungsbildung und die Kommunikation unspezifischer Hilfsbedürftigkeit." [Social Work, Secondary Order Building and the Communication of Unspecific Needs of Help.] In *Systemtheorie Sozialer Arbeit* [System Theory of Social Work], edited by Roland Merten, 67–86. Opladen: Leske & Budrich.

Bommes, Michael, and Albert Scherr. 2000b. *Soziologie der sozialen Arbeit, Eine Einführung in Formen und Funktionen organisierter Hilfe* [Sociology of Social Work]. Beltz Juventa: Weinheim, Basel.

Brante, Tomas. 1987. "Sociologiska föreställningar om professioner." [Sociological Images of Professions.] In *Den Sociologiska Fantasin – teorier om samhället* [The Sociological Phantasy – Theories of Society], edited by Ulla Bergryd, 124–154. Stockholm: Raben & Sjögren.

Brekke, John S. 2012. "Shaping a Science of Social Work." *Research on Social Work Practice* 22 (5): 455–464.

Brekke, John S. 2014. "A Science of Social Work, and Social Work as an Integrative Scientific Discipline: Have We Gone Too Far, or Not Far Enough?" *Research on Social Work Practice* 24 (5), 517–523.

Collins, Randall. 1982. *Sociological Insight. An Introduction to Nonobvious Sociology.* New York: Oxford University Press.

Davis, Kingsley. 1937. "The Sociology of Prostitution." *American Sociological Review* 2 (5): 744–755.

Dominelli, Lena. 2002. *Anti-oppressive Social Work Theory and Practice.* Hampshire: Palgrave MacMillan.

Fook, Jan. 2002. *Social Work: Critical Theory and Practice.* London: Sage.

Fuchs, Peter. 2000. "Systemtheorie und Soziale Arbeit." [Systems Theory and Social Work.] In *Systemtheorie Sozialer Arbeit* [Systems Theory of Social Work], edited by Roland Merten, 157–175. Opladen: Leske & Budrich.

Gambrill, Eileen. 1999. "Evidence-based Practice: An Alternative to Authority-based Practice." *Families in Society: The Journal of Contemporary Social Services* 80 (4): 341–350.

Gethin-Jones, Stephen. 2012. "Outcomes and Well-Being Part 2: A Comparative Longitudinal Study of Two Models of Homecare Delivery and their Impact upon the Older Person Self-reported Subjective Well-being. A Qualitative Follow up Study Paper." *Working with Older People* 16 (2): 52–60.

Habermas, Jürgen. 1992. *The Theory of Communicative Action Vol. 2. Lifeworld and System: A Citique of Functionalist Reason*. Cambridge: Polity press.

Hagen, R. 2006. *Nyliberalismen og samfunnsvitenskapene. Refleksjonsteorier for det moderne samfunnet* [Neoliberalism and the Social Sciences. Reflection Theories for Modern Society]. Oslo: Universitetsforlaget.

Harris, J. 1998. "Scientific Management, Bureau-Professionalism, New Managerialism: The Labour Process of State Social Work." *British Journal of Social Work* 28 (6): 839–862.

Healy, Lynne. 2001. *International Social Work: Professional Action in an Interdependent World*. Oxford: Oxford University Press.

Hillebrandt, Frank. 2010. "Hilfe als Funktionssystem für Soziale Arbeit." [Help as Function System for Social Work.] In *Grundriss Soziale Arbeit* [Compendium Social Work], edited by Werner Thole, 235–247. Wiesbaden: VS-Verlag.

Ife, Jim. 2012. *Human Rights and Social Work. Towards Rights-based Practice*. 3rd ed. Cambridge: Cambridge University Press.

Kieserling, André. 2004. "Die Soziologie der Selbstbeschreibung: Über die Reflexionstheorien der Funktionssysteme und ihre Rezeption der soziologischen Theorie." [The Sociology of Self Description. On the Reflection Theories of Function Systems and their Reception of Sociological Theory.] In *Selbstbeschreibung und Fremdbeschreibung. Beiträge zur Soziologie soziologischen Wissens* [Self Description and Other Description. Contributions to the Sociology of Sociological Knowledge], edited by André Kieserling, 46–108. Frankfurt/Main: Suhrkamp.

Kleve, Heiko. 2007. *Postmoderne Soziale Arbeit. Ein systemtheoretisch-konstruktivistischer Beitrag zur Sozialarbeitswissenschaft* [Postmodern Social Work. A Systems-Theoretically-Constructivist Contribution to Social Work Science]. Wiesbaden: VS-Verlag.

La Cour, Anders. 2002. *Frivillighedens pris: en undersøgelse af Niklas Luhmanns teori om sociale systemer og dens anvendelse på området for frivilligt socialt arbejde* [The Price of Voluntariness: An Examination of Niklas Luhmann's Theory of Social Systems and its Application to the Field of Voluntary Social Work]. Copenhagen: Copenhagen University.

La Cour, Anders, and Holger Højlund. 2008. "Voluntary Social Work as a Paradox." *Acta Sociologica* 51 (1): 41–54.

Luhmann, Niklas. 1989. *Ecological Communication*. Chicago, IL: University of Chicago Press.

Luhmann, Niklas. 1990. *Die Wissenschaft der Gesellschaft* [The Science of Society]. Frankfurt/Main: Suhrkamp.

Luhmann, Niklas. 1995. *Social Systems*. Palo Alto: Stanford University Press.

Luhmann, Niklas. 1973 [2005]. "Formen des Helfens im Wandel gesellschaftlicher Bedingungen." [Forms of Helping in the Course of Changing Social Conditions.] In *Soziologische Aufklärung 6* [Sociological Enlightenment 6], edited by Niklas Luhmann, 167–186. Wiesbaden: VS-Verlag.

Luhmann, Niklas. 1995 [2005]. "Inklusion und Exklusion." [Inclusion and Exclusion.] In *Soziologische Aufklärung 6* [Sociological Enlightenment 6], edited by Niklas Luhmann, 226–251. Wiesbaden: VS-Verlag.

Luhmann, Niklas. 2012. *Theory of Society*. 1vol. Palo Alto: Stanford University Press.

Luhmann, Niklas. 2013. *Theory of Society*. 2vol. Palo Alto: Stanford University Press.

Luhmann, Niklas. 1972 [2014]. *A Sociological Theory of Law*. edited by Martin Albrow. Oxon: Routledge.

Merten, Roland. 2000. "Soziale Arbeit als autonomes Funktionssystem der modernen Gesellschaft? Argumente für eine konstruktive Perspektive." [Social Work as Autonomous Function System of Modern Society? Arguments for a Constructive Perspective.] In *Systemtheorie sozialer Arbeit* [Systems Theory of Social Work], edited by Roland Merten, 177–204. Opladen: Leske & Budrich.

Merten, Roland, Peter Sommerfeld, and Thomas Koditek. 1996. *Sozialarbeitswissenschaft – Kontroversen und Perspektiven* [Social Work Science – Controversies and Perspectives]. Neuwied: Luchterhand.

Michailakis, D., and W. Schirmer. 2014. "Vad händer när teori och praktik i socialt arbete integreras?" [What Happens If Social Work Theory and Practice are Integrated?]. *Socialvetenskaplig tidskrift* 21 (2): 127–141.

Miller, Tilly. 2001. *Systemtheorie und soziale Arbeit. Entwurf einer Handlungstheorie* [Systems Theory and Social Work. Sketch of an Action Theory]. Stuttgart: Lucius & Lucius.

Moe, Sverre. 2003. *Den moderne hjelpens sosiologi. Velferd i systemteoretisk perspektiv* [Sociology of the Modern Help. Welfare from a Systems-Theoretical Perspective]. Sandnes: Apeiros Forlag.

Nassehi, Armin, and Gerd Nollmann. 1997. "Inklusionen. Organisationssoziologische Ergänzungen der Inklusions-/Exklusionstheorie." [Inclusions. Organization-sociological Amendments of the Inclusion-/ExclusionTheory.] *Soziale Systeme* 3 (2): 393–411.

Nissen, Maria Appel. 2005. "Behandlerblikket." [The Caring View] PhD Thesis, Institut for Sociale Forhold og Organisation, Aalborg universitet.

Obrecht, Werner. 1996. "Sozialarbeitswissenschaft als integrative Handlungswissenschaft. Ein metawissenschaftlicher Bezugsrahmen für eine Wissenschaft der Sozialen Arbeit." [Social Work Science as Integrative Action Science. A Meta-scientific Frame of Reference for a Science of Social Work.] In *Sozialarbeitswissenschaft – Kontroversen und Perspektiven* [Social Work Science – Controversies and Perspectives], edited by Roland Merten, Peter Sommerfeld, and Thomas Koditek, 121–183. Neuwied: Luchterhand.

Otto, Hans-Uwe, Andreas Polutta, and Holger Ziegler, eds. 2009. *Evidence-based Practice – Modernising the Knowledge Base of Social Work*. Barbara Budrich: Opladen & Farmington Hills.

Parton, Nigel. 2000. "Some Thoughts on the Relationship between Theory and Practice in and for Social Work." *British Journal of Social Work* 30 (4): 449–463.

Pinker, Steven. 2002. *The Blank Slate. The Modern Denial of Human Nature*. New York: Penguin.

Sackett, David L, William M. Rosenberg, J. Gray, R. Brian Haynes, and W. Scott Richardson. 1996. "Evidence Based Medicine: What It Is And What It Isn't." *BMJ: British Medical Journal* 312 (7023): 71–72.

Scherr, Albert. 1999. "Transformations in Social Work: From Help Towards Social Inclusion to the Management of Exclusion." *European Journal of Social Work* 2 (1): 15–25.

Schirmer, W., and D. Michailakis. 2015. "The Luhmannian Approach to Exclusion/Inclusion and Its Relevance to Social Work." *Journal of Social Work* 15 (1): 45–64.

Sommerfeld, Peter. 2000. "Soziale Arbeit als sekundäres Primärsystem und der 'very strange loop' sozialarbeiterischer Profis." [Social Work as a Secondary Primary System and the Very Strange Loop' of Social Work Professionals.] In *Systemtheorie Sozialer Arbeit* [Systems Theory of Social Work], edited by Roland Merten, 115–136. Opladen: Leske & Budrich.

Soydan, Haluk. 2012. "Understanding Social Work in the History of Ideas." *Research on Social Work Practice* 22 (5): 468–480.

Staub-Bernasconi, Silvia. 2007. *Soziale Arbeit als Handlungswissenschaft: systemische Grundlagen und professionelle Praxis – Ein Lehrbuch* [Social Work as Action Science: Systemic Basics and Professional Practice – A Textbook]. Bern: Haupt.

Webb, Stephen A. 2001. "Some Considerations on the Validity of Evidence-based Practice in Social Work." *British Journal of Social Work* 31 (1): 57–79.

Wirth, Jan. 2009. "The Function of Social Work." *Journal of Social Work* 9 (4): 405–419.

Why social work and sociology need psychosocial theory

Elizabeth Frost

Department of Health and Applied Sciences, University of the West of England, Bristol, UK

> Sociology and social work as disciplines have, over the last decades, had an, at best, ambivalent relationship. Whereas branches of sociology, such as symbolic interactionism, have produce theory of immense use to social work, for example the concept of 'stigma' and work in the field of identity, others are harder to utilise and indeed can seem to be antithetical to building social work theory for practice. Both structuralist and post-structuralist paradigms have been criticised for this latter difficulty. This paper argues that the current cross-disciplinary developments integrating scholars concerned with theory, research and practices, from within sociology, psychoanalysis, psychology, social policy and social work, with the academic and practice discipline of psychosocial studies, offers a way forward. The theory, the paper suggests, from psychosocial studies, allows a re-analysis of some of the impasses in applying post-structural sociological theory to essentially modernist projects such as social work. It also bridges traditional academic/practice divides such as the role of the 'knower' in relation to the 'known' and elucidates an agenda for research practices and methodologies which harness sociological and social work ontologies.

Introduction

Over the last two decades, a substantial body of UK literature and research has been generated in the social sciences to form an emerging discipline called psycho-social or psychosocial studies (the hyphen is part of a complex debate, and used by some and not others). From within the disciplines of sociology, psychology, social policy, psychotherapy, psychoanalysis and social work a academic grouping, recently designated 'The Association For Psychosocial Studies' in the UK, has configured across these subject boundaries and across research and practice (see e.g. Hoggett 2001; Cooper and Lousada 2005; Bainbridge et al. 2007; Walkerdine and Jimenez 2012). In social work, a renewed interest in the application of psychoanalytic and psychodynamic thinking to practise and research has emerged, for example in work on relationship-based practice (Trevithick 2003; Ruch 2012) on child protection (Ferguson 2005) and on suicide (Briggs 2008).

This paper aims to consider how the psychosocial theory emerging contemporarily from within sociology and related disciplines can bridge the traditional divide between sociology and social work and address some of the problems for each in their theoretical relationships with the other. The contrast between contemporary psychosocial thinking and the much criticised forms of psychodynamic and psychosocial casework in social work, as practised in 1960s and 1970s (Hollis 1965) will be underscored.

The article initially explores what contemporary psychosocial studies is (and is not), how and where it is being developed and what some of its themes are now. Next, it establishes a focus on the relationship between sociology and social work, from Marxism through to post-structuralism, and considers how particularly the latter has exacerbated divisions between these two disciplines. The example of identity is used to illustrate how psychosocial theory can improve this. The paper considers some of the shared concerns of both sociology and social work, particularly identity and reflexivity, and considers the role of psychosocial thinking in supporting and advancing this mutual engagement. Finally, the paper considers the frequently divisive area of research and presents an example of psychosocial research which integrates sociological and social work concerns, practices and approaches: in other words how the psychosocial can advance relevant and theoretically rigorous knowledge production for both of these disciplines in a mutually inclusive process.

What is psychosocial theory now?

'Psychosocial' in itself is a slippery term, having been used in slightly different ways in different disciplines, so to 'clear the decks' of potential misunderstandings, it seems worth briefly establishing what it is not, before considering its specific contemporary usage under discussion in this paper.

In the 1960s and 1970s in the UK, the USA and parts of Europe, it was fairly ordinary to have studied psychosocial theory as part of social work training. This was exemplified in texts on casework and/or clinical social work by Hollis (1965) which had Freudian psychoanalytical thinking at their heart. Even though the nomenclature references 'social', the work had very little to do with 'social', in the sense of sociological or societal, and was criticised by much radical thinking from the mid 1970s for precisely this. Collective movements in social work such as 'CASE CON' in the 1970s sought to re-inject a socio-political dimension into such an individualistic approach (Lavalette 2011)

In clinical casework, as Hollis prescribed, and indeed also in some contemporary clinical psychology research and practice, the use the 'social' dimension of 'psychosocial' tends to mean the familial context of the individual, and occasionally other networks of relationships (e.g. Rutter 1987). Almost never does such work engage with structural sociology's concerns, of power, class and socio-political oppression. Issues, such as misogyny and racism, are rarely discussed. The intersection of structural and individual identity issues at the heart of 'new' psychosocial thinking, where the psychoanalytically theorised internal world tangles with the impact of e.g. class oppression, is missing.

Psychosocial theory is also not interchangeable with social psychology. The lack of a structural oppression dimension is one of the main distinguishing features between this and the psychosocial theory being discussed in this paper, even though social psychology often discusses the individual in context, and the impact of the external world on the psychic life of the individual. And indeed, there is a great deal of extremely useful work in the social psychology field. Goffman, for example, was hugely concerned with how the judgements and responses of people in the outside world impacted on individual identity, for good and bad. However, he does not theorise the internal world as such: no structure of the mind is offered in his work. Nor does he theorise social power relations, though his understanding of the 'top down' power of some societal institutions – e.g. as discussed in 'Asylums' – is a very helpful analysis (Goffman

1968). 'New' psychosocial theory, unlike most social psychology, tries to advance a psychoanalytical and social structural analysis.

Moving, now, from thinking about what psychosocial studies is not, to what it is, a little background may help. The development of what one might distinguish as 'new' psychosocial theory over the last two decades is building on the venerable tradition laid down by the mid-twentieth-century European critical theorists, to integrate psychoanalytical theory with forms of social theory, for example structural sociology and/or critical psychology, to better understand the human subject in context, and to apply this to research and practise.

The roots of this work are squarely European and mired in the concerns with social justice, liberation, truth, understanding of the nature of violence and persecution, the nature of human 'depth and surface' and repression: the modernist agenda of the twentieth-century Frankfurt School, which itself draws on the European Psychoanalytic Tradition of, e.g. Sigmund Freud and Melanie Klein and also, importantly, the political significance of Marxism. Contemporary psychosocial studies still has at its heart Adorno and Habermas's seminal attempts to elucidate human nature and social injustice with sociology and psychoanalysis. Insistence that such concerns as racism and other forms of social conflict can only be understood as the product of individual affect and social structure (e.g. Adorno's et al. [1951]) has continued to be a major driver in psychosocial thinking and research (Clarke 2005; Gadd and Dixon 2010).

'New' psychosocial theory has largely been developed in the last two decades initially driven from the disciplines of sociology and social policy, particularly by those theorists such as Hoggett who came to academia from backgrounds of political activism, and then added psychotherapy and/or psychoanalysis to their repertoires (Hoggett 2014). Similarly, some practitioners in areas such as mental health, whether qualified as social workers, psychologists or therapists bought this experiential sensibility into the world of theory when they moved into the academy (Frosh 2014).

Building psychosocial theory is an undertaking of those concerned with crossing or blurring boundaries and distinctions, and challenging some false dichotomies on the way: for example practice or theory, sociology or psychology, the internal or the external, the knower or the known.

Building psychosocial theory is also an ongoing project; unfinished and in the process of identity formation: hence definitions tend to be contingent and temporary. And, equally, because psychosocial theory is currently being written and developed, the boundaries of what is considered in the field and what its scope is, are still flexible. Psychosocial theory has mainly been driven in England and the USA, though other European nations have also developed the area. The Norwegian Psychoanalytic Society, for example, supports psychosocial initiatives, (e.g. The conference in Oslo in 2011, 'Nationalism and the Body Politic Conference'), and the psychosocial organisation 'Psychoanalysis and Politics' was co-founded by Norwegian scholar Dr Lene Auestad.

In the UK, there is now a psychosocial network, a psychosocial sub-group of the British Sociological Association, and a 'Learned [academic] Society' called The Association for Psychosocial Studies, whose launch at The British Library in 2014 confirmed academic legitimacy and disciplinary acceptance. Core academic journals have been founded with the USA, such as *Psychoanalysis, Culture and Society* (Palgrave Macmillan) and the online *Journal of Psycho-Social Studies*. Moreover, undergraduate, postgraduate and professional programmes have been developed to teach psychosocial approaches at a significant number of universities and institutes, for example: the

Department of Psychosocial Studies at Birkbeck College, London (e.g. M.Sc. Psychosocial Studies); The University of East London (BA Psychosocial Studies).

Perhaps as important as the teaching of psychosocial studies is the written contribution of psychosocial theory to understanding contemporary social life. In the UK, a substantial body of psychosocial literature and research has been generated from within the disciplines of sociology, criminology, psychology, social policy, psychoanalysis, social work and politics/social activism over the last decade or so (e.g. Hoggett 2001; Layton, Hollander, and Gutwill 2006; Gadd and Dixon 2010; Trevithick 2011; Hollway and Jefferson 2012; Froggett, Ramvi, and Davies 2014; Murray Parkes 2014).

The paper has now said a little about the history and growth of psychosocial studies: what it is not and what it is; where it is developing and for what purposes. Two further points may help with clarity before the discussion moves on. As much as anything definitive can be laid down about this fluid and developing set of ideas called 'psychosocial theory', it is its very specific notion of the subject – the person at the centre of the study – that psychosocial theory differently defines from other disciplines.

Psychosocial theory, then, theorises the human subject and their lived experience at the ontological centre of social theory, thus

> Subjects whose inner worlds cannot be understood without knowledge of their experiences in the world, and whose experiences of the world cannot be understood without knowledge of the way in which their inner worlds allow them to experience the outer world. (Hollway and Jefferson 2012, 4)

And the discipline overall, as the website of the Association of Psychosocial Studies captures, can, for now, be considered as follows:

> ... characterised by (a) its explicit inter or trans-disciplinarity, (b) its development of non-positivistic theory, method and praxis and (c) its orientation towards progressive social and personal change. (APS 2014)

What psychosocial theory offers overall is a 'rich' version of the subject in context: important for thinking sociologically, one might argue, as well as crucial for understanding the social work subject. The paper now goes on to consider a little of sociology and social work's far less compatible history.

Sociology and social work theory

Developing appropriate theory for social work is inevitably a complex process (Parton 2000). Part of the difficulty here lies in the relationship between social science subjects and social work and the drive within social work to claim a body of theory as its own. In reality it has had, since its rejection of psychoanalytically based theory four decades ago, mainly sociology, alongside positivist psychology, to draw on in the construction of this. It has also – though differentially in different countries – eschewed engagement with 'high' theory and attempted to substitute social policy and/or human rights discourse at its foundations. From anti-discriminatory practice to neoliberal managerialism, trends towards atheoreticism are in evidence over the last decades (Trevithick 2003). It is worth noting though that even given this, the influence on all social theory by 'the French turn' (Foucault, Lacan, Bourdieu) is also evident in social work (Bracher 1993; Parton 1994; Irving 1999; Powell 2001; Houston 2002; Garrett 2007).

Within social work courses exist academics who are formerly and currently sociologists, social policy writers and psychologists, who necessarily draw on their own disciplines for constructing, teaching and publishing theory for social work. The complex relationship between social science theory, social work theory and practice can bemuse or frustrate social work students. Disjunctures between lectures/lecturers and students can be the outcome.

Fook, for example, illustrates such a stance from her own background. Describing her experience of social work academia she comments

> What I found was … a world in which it seemed that male academic theorising sociologists tried to teach female practising social workers better social work by converting them to a world of theory (e.g. Althussar). (Pease and Fook 1999, 5)

And if social work struggled with structural sociology, structural sociology struggled with social work even more – especially psychodynamic or psychoanalytically informed casework, as noted above. Particularly from the 1960s, after sociology moved more firmly into the social work academy, and into social work practice, such work was heavily criticised for its perceived exclusion of any interest in power or inequality, and was seen to be too concerned with what is in people's heads to the exclusion of their material situation or concerns: the old but ongoing critique (Langan and Lee 1989).

Marxist sociologists' critique of social work – as essentially an instrument of state control: pathologising, labelling and further oppressing the already oppressed – dismissed its practices. Social workers more grounded in practice issues could see little chance of this Marxist critique realistically or usefully informing an alternative everyday practice, particularly in statutory contexts.

Fook's quote, above, also hints at a more structural struggle under the surface of the academic and disciplinary: that of gender. The surge in interest in sociology as a discipline in the 1960s and 1970s leads to far higher numbers of qualified male sociology graduates, some of whom had backgrounds in trade unionism and activist politics, and a proportion of whom became social workers and social work academics. Some came with no particular respect for or understanding of a feminised 'caring' profession that worked mostly with women and children.

That social work as a discipline has felt variously patronised by, and excluded by sociology and sociologists is not just a historical position but in many countries still very much the case. Italy for example has had an ongoing struggle, not over yet, to establish social work in the academy, and still appointments of senior academics for social work courses are far more likely to be male theoretical sociologists than women from social worker practice backgrounds (Campanini 2004).

And in the UK, sociology still seems to carry a certain ambivalence in relation to social work – certainly not making much of the connection. The current British Sociological Association website is keen to point out the links between sociology and more practice-based subject specialisms – but social work is not on the list.

> Now, as well as being an academic subject in its own right, sociology forms part of many other programmes such as business studies, medical training, geography and environmental science and the newer sports and health sciences http://www.britsoc.co.uk/WhatIsSociology/SocHist.aspx.

However, it also seems to be the case that problems and differences between sociology and social work theory tend to receive more attention than their, equally evident, congruence and mutual interests.

Part of the difficulty of connecting up sociology and social work certainly always was status hierarchies and political incompatibilities, and no doubt there were theoretical issues to. However, it seems clear that some of the theoretical incompatibilities may have related to *the kind* of sociological theory being utilised. In reality, there always were always alternatives to Althussar's particularly uncompromising form of structuralism (Elliott 1994). For example, it seems evident that theoretical strands from sociology such as labelling theory, deviance and connected concepts like 'moral panics' were more than helpful as aids to understanding the positioning and situation of service users as well as the potential role of the profession itself in exacerbating or minimising such forms of 'social damage' (Cohen 1973). Forms of social psychology such as symbolic interactionism, as typified in Goffman's work (discussed above), were also of considerable use. Such work can also usefully inform social work across a range of practice/theory dimensions. For example, 'Asylums' (1968) consideration of the erosion of identity within social and organisational structures is enduringly helpful for social work.

Although Fook, above, is critical of one aspect of one particular branch of Marxist theory, the ubiquitous social work language of 'emancipation', 'structural inequality' and 'critical social work' is inescapably elided to Marxist sociology in general, and Critical Theory in particular (Pease and Fook 1999).

Sociology, particularly when it was able to theorise both the subject and the society/social context in which they are located, as with the former example, could be of immense use in educating social workers, and educating them in ways that sociology was more comfortable to 'own'.

The social science curriculum for undergraduate social workers at the author's university draws on mainstream sociology, e.g. Giddens and Bourdieu, Foucault, Hochschild and Beck, to increase the students' understanding and how to apply it. It is not, staff here would argue, possible to understand the social work subject without understanding the sociological concepts of power, agency, identity, risk, emotional labour and cultural capital. In the curriculum though, it is sociology taken with the psychoanalytical ideas (e.g. from Bowlby, Winnicott and Lacan) – psychosocial studies, as this paper is arguing – that allows the social science curriculum to more closely address the needs of practitioners.

To the concepts listed above, attachment theory, object relations theory and ideas such as desire and identification are also crucial to even begin to make sense of the complexities and potential of not just the person but the relational social work encounter. To offer an example: a theory-into-practice student lecture and seminar session, on the subject of 'ill-being', focuses on three central issues: shame, loneliness and trauma. For the former, identity sociology, criminology and political theory contribute, psychology, sociology and critical psychology help with 'loneliness'; trauma is theorised from within psychotherapy and psychoanalysis, as well as the humanities and again political theory. In each case, work from psychosocial theory allows an integration of ideas, whilst putting the subject at the centre of the work (e.g. De Jong Gierveld, Van Tilburg, and Dykstra 2006; Walkerdine and Jimenez 2012; Eyerman 2013). Practice issues are under-pinned by these interwoven, psychosocial ideas. Shame, loneliness and trauma are core to many social work practice encounters.

From the end of 1980s to the present, sociology and social work have both developed more shared interests (e.g. identity, culture and anti-racism). However, in contradiction, they have also entered a new impasse. The attempt to integrate the post-structural 'turn' in sociology, or even the more vague tenets of 'postmodern' theory, has been highly problematic. How can social work (and indeed emancipatory sociology) maintain fundamentally modernist principles such as emancipation, structural inequality and (single) identity politics, in the face of such a sustained critique of humanism and an insistence on relativism and linguistic determinism, for example? The paper now considers the further rifts between sociological theory and social work theory inflicted by post-structuralism and postmodernism, and how psychosocial theory can provide an alternative.

Post-structural dilemmas and psychosocial resolutions

The conditions of academic production over the recent decades have ensured that sociological trends move quickly through to social work theory texts and teaching. This was the case with post-structural sociology (and the less disciplinary specific theories termed, loosely, postmodern). Careful critiques were also quick to emerge, and the multi-dimensional hybrid of 'critical social work', still containing elements of the other two strands, has been the most prevalent legacy (Adams 2001; Fook 2004). This section of the paper is concerned with the problems of merging post-structural sociological theory – particularly some of the anti-humanist work of the late twentieth-century French and American theorists, with social work thinking. A range of themes presenting dilemmas for social work theory and practice might illustrate this point, for example, conceptual dualism (particularly the 'agency vs. determinism' dichotomy). Here, though the example of psychosocial theory 'arbitrating' between sociological theory and social work theory in the realm of identity is now discussed. This seems to be an important area of confusion and practice paralysis that insistence on postmodern theory introduces. Strands of postmodernism theorise the subject (identity) as fluid, in process and organised within contingent narratives of personhood. By assuming this version of identity, then the answer to the question 'can people change?' for example, must be 'yes'; personal change, even self re-invention, is inevitable within this free play of multiple possible versions of selves. As well as postmodernism, recent social work theorising deriving from Giddens' structuration theory also suggests a rather voluntaristic version of welfare subjects who *choose* life-worlds and stances within flexible personal politics (Ferguson 2001).

On the one hand, this is helpful. Social work students are starting from an understanding of the welfare subject (any subject, including themselves) as having the ability to change. However, implicit in postmodern identity theory is also aspects which are incompatible with social work's theoretical, ethical and practical position.

Postmodern theory 'decentres the human subject', or in other words deletes the notion of human authenticity and individual worth as a fundamental feature and starting point in understanding identity, thereby abandoning humanism. This not only challenges the notion of an authentic self (in the sense put forward by modernist theorists on whom social work draws, such as Karl Rogers) but also argues the impossibility of coherent and clearly defined identities, including the politically expedient identities of 'black' or 'woman'. Practitioners are left to try and work out for themselves, for example, why, if identity is fluid and there is no essential self, the same kinds of problems often surface year after year in the same individuals and groups of people. And what is the point of, for example of instigating a women's consciousness raising group if there is no such reliable category as 'a woman'?

It seems that the body of sociology simply does not transfer well into social work theory and less still into practice situations. Psychosocial theory offers an alternative.

Psychosocial theorising offers a version of identity which can explain both the ability to *and* the reluctance to change, with some notion of possible movement also implicit. Hoggett, for example, suggests that

> ... our capacity to be a reflexive agent is often constrained by the difficulties we have in facing our own fears and anxieties. Some ideas and experiences are just too painful to think about, even with the support and solidarity of others ... (2001, 42)

Using psychosocial theory offers the opportunity to understand people as having multiple strands to their identities, some of which may be in conflict. Using this version, failure to change can be understood as the product of internal battles and ambiguities. This is not suggesting identities which are essential, unchanging or rational, which is a familiar critique of modernist identity theory. Nor is it arguing identity is primarily self-chosen or available for infinite revision, as strands of postmodern theory tend to suggest. Psychosocial theory suggests that identities might be messy and in process, but they do have authenticity, depth and value.

Importantly too, psychosocial theory understands people as existing within stratified social structures and complex but unequal power relations. Class, poverty, gender and other social structural determinisms are also part of identity and impact on agency. The version of personhood offered by psychosocial theory is of someone struggling, ambivalent, complex, passionate, having both internal and external forces and constraints. In other words, it offers a 'rich' version of the subject about whom knowledge, including self-knowledge, can only ever be partial and incomplete. For social workers, an issue such as 'why does this domestically abused woman still say she loves and wishes to return to that abusing man?' can be understood as demonstrating powerful ambivalence rather than wilful self-delusion or lack of self-esteem. The 'social' half of the psychosocial paradigm also connects this thinking to the social politics of gender oppression and the social construction of romantic love.

An engagement with psychosocial theory in sociology offers possibilities for informing new social work theory, which is coherent, comprehensible and useful. This goes beyond the notion of simply applying knowledge from the academic discipline to the practice of social work, in the problematic way identified by e.g. Parton (2000), but offers a complex, process-driven account of the fundamentals of identity, interpersonal relations and ways of knowing (an epistemology and ontology) with which students and social workers can make sense of the whole experience, including their location within it.

Sociology, including structural sociology, is of considerable importance to psychosocial theory. Sociologists concerned with the emotional/affective world of the human subject are invaluable. For example, Bourdieu's muscular social structuralism, concerned with power, oppression and practices in research and social justice, has also continued to be vital to inform the 'social' of psychosocial thinking. Bourdieu's concerned with the mechanisms through which society seeps into identity has a resonance with psychosocial concerns in itself, but also combined with, for example, Kleinian object relations theory, is particularly useful for thinking psychosocially about fundamental issues (such as 'social suffering'), which are also central to social work (Alford 1990; Bourdieu 1999; Walkerdine, Lucey, and Melody 2001; Grenfell 2008).

Understanding identity, and its social context, psychosocially is in itself of use to social work. What is of equal benefit, this paper now goes on the argue, is the reflexive nature of the discipline of psychosocial studies: that it questions the separation of the knower from the known – in other words situates the subject of knowledge production within their own theories and arguments and makes 'the expert' consider their own role in their expertise: as the paper now discusses.

Psychosocial theory and the theorist

Interestingly, the biographies of many of the key figures in the psychosocial movement in the UK and the USA at present include beginnings in social work, community work, clinical psychology and/or political activism. Currently, although these academics are to be found in departments of social sciences and/or social work, practice is still of paramount importance to the psychosocial: practices of activism around, e.g. climate change (Weintrobe 2013), community conflict (Hoggett, Mayo, and Miller 2009) and therapeutic practices within and outside the clinic (Scanlon and Adlam 2013). Socially engaged research might also be classed as a practice (see below, and also e.g. Mayo, Hoggett, and Miller 2007; Walkerdine and Jimenez 2012) as might some forms of art practices linked to social engagement Froggett et al. (2014). It is precisely the capacity of psychosocial thinking to dissolve boundaries between the 'academic' and the 'lived', the personal and the political, and also the knower and the known that extend the possibility of 'bridging' sociology and social work.

In the same ways as contemporary psychosocial research methods – as outlined by Hollway and Jefferson (2012) – insist on examining the inter-subjective relationship between interviewer and interviewee, the psychosocial approach overall highlights the relationship between the knower with the known. In other words how one studies a/the subject (what it means to be homeless or unemployed, a child in a working class family: a black older person in a traditional family, etc.) and perhaps even *why* we are looking at it, is also a product of what is in our heads, hearts and lives as people constructing knowledge. The researchers and theorists who are building the psychosocial knowledge base here are also implicated. They are not pretending to be objective or all-knowing, but accepting that personal experiences and leanings, class backgrounds and psychic worlds, impact on perceptions and discussions, the choices as to what counts and how it is written about it.

e.g. a text such as 'Growing up girl: psychosocial explorations of gender and class' discusses 'use of self' in research practice

> Our class background has remained a central issue in this part [data analysis] of the study … For example some of the middle class girls initially evoked our envy … Using our own subjectivity and experience of being envied by members of our families was part of the process of understanding envy in a more useful way and being able to use it as a tool with which to examine the psychic aspects of the lives of the middle class girls … (Walkerdine, Lucey, and Melody 2001, 84)

The academics, and the reader, are part of the process of trying to understand the 'lens' through which their findings are viewed – the commitments and loyalties and affiliations and damage they bring to this study of the class contexts of girls growing up.

Such reflexivity is an intellectual tool, for the social sciences, offering the capacity to identify and examine, rather than sweep under the carpet, the investments and perspectives bought to scholarly endeavour. In social work, it was ever thus, for students and practitioners, and never more so than now. As Froggett et al. succinctly comment

> It is because our students need critical contextual awareness and understanding of intersubjective relations at the practice interface that the classical social work concept use of self (Wosket 1999, Ward, 2010, Baldwin 2010) is useful. Froggett, Ramvi, and Davies (2014, 3)

But such thinking needs to be rigorous and analytical. Sociologically developed theories in relation to the self/identity, for example cultural capital (Bourdieu) or recognition (Honneth), 'pure' relationships (Elliott) and ontological insecurity (Giddens), autobiographic narratives or fateful moments (Giddens) offer conceptual frameworks for understanding self (and others). The sociology of identity, of the emotions, the family and so on, as well as the continued interlocking of sociology and psychoanalysis, facilitate both enhanced rigour and greatly extended breadth in examining who we are and what we bring to social encounters. The 'psych' element also offers frameworks and concepts for considering the 'beneath the surface' of the reflexive itself – e.g. object relations, splitting, anxiety (and envy). Psychosocial studies, then, legitimates reflexivity as a rigorous, theoretically coherent engagement with knowledge as a subjective and relational process.

Shared knowledge practices: psychosocial research

Following on from above, then, it is perhaps worth drawing this discussion towards a conclusion through the shared (between sociology, social work and psychosocial studies) concerns of research. Research methods and research practice have become core topics in psychosocial approaches; for example in terms of methodology, such as Hollway and Jefferson's (2012) revised *Doing qualitative research differently: a psychosocial approach* (alluded to above) and *Researching beneath the surface* edited by Clarke and Hoggett (2008). As we cited above, research-based studies drawing on such approaches have also contributed to how we are able to think psychosocially about the lived experiences of, e.g. (as above) class and gender, unemployment and 'shame', and these original studies have helped to develop the field: for example, Hollway's (forthcoming) study: 'Knowing Mothers/Mothers' Knowing' and 'Gender work and community after de-industrialisation: a psychosocial approach to affect' by Walkerdine and Jimenez (2012). Social problems and social practices have also become of core concern to psychosocial theorists, with racism providing a particularly rich focus, in for example, Clarke's (2003) *Social Theory, Psychoanalysis and Racism*, and Gadd and Dixon's (2010) *Loosing the Race: Thinking Psychosocially about Racially Motivated Crime*.

The final section of this paper will consider an extended example of a specific piece of social intervention that serves to highlight and epitomise the arguments advanced herein. It focuses on the psychosocial approach 'at work' as it was drawing from the dissolution of the boundaries between sociology and social work, practice and theory, structure and agency, research and reflection, and actions the power to address struggles and problems within the world. In other words, it is an example of 'the psychosocial' in practice ameliorating the perceived tensions in relation to sociology and social work.

The Centre for Psycho-Social Studies at UWE, Bristol, (2000–2012) was commissioned by the English funding body The Economic and Social Research Council to undertake a research project called 'Negotiating Ethical Dilemmas in Contested Communities'. This was part of the funders 'Identities' stream and allowed the researchers to focus on the identities of communities and workers within them.

Hoggett et al. (2007) undertook to use specifically psychosocial methodology to initially investigate the ethical commitment of community workers to their practice. They considered workers in the field of, loosely defined, community regeneration, and their, what they came to describe as, 'psychic roots of public commitment'. They found mixtures of class and gender positions, the internalisation of senses of 'outsiderness' and 'otherness', inextricably inter-twinned with political beliefs and social opportunities in developing and sustaining their work in and for the community. The psychosocial methodology employed, accessing the life stories and the 'under-the-surface' stories of their sample, leads the researchers to argue, essentially, that the profession is well-served by a strong commitment from its workers, and by workers who have been able to transform their family and/or individual identifications as sources of creative agency.

> So we come upon a final paradox. The identifications which fix and position us also provide us with the resources for their transformation. (Hoggett et al. 2007)

From this research, with its central concern of 'transforming identity', some of the team went on to look more closely at such 'regenerating' communities themselves: the deprived, mainly white working class communities on the fringe council estates of a medium sized provincial English city. Angry often, bitter and expressing high levels of grievance with the world, these communities had mainly cast themselves as victims of 'the system', whose needs and rights had been passed over, the argued bitterly, in favour of 'immigrants', black people, social security 'scroungers', 'thugs', single parents and other contemporary 'demons'. The team's psychosocial understanding of this community's grievances as grief, unmourned and 'nursed' and unrelinquished, was insightful in comprehending its static nature – how community work interventions had foundered on a resistance to change. Similarly to 'truth and reconciliation' initiatives in e.g. South Africa, the need for grieving, mourning, settling accounts and forgiving (a psychosocial bereavement model based on Freud's 'Mourning and Melancholia', 1917) was understood as a pre-requisite for repudiation of a passive victim position. With support for grieving the relinquishment of grievance was possible, and a capacity for moving on established (Hoggett et al. 2007).

Conclusion

The above example can perhaps stand in as a coherent definition of 'the psychosocial', in that it encapsulates the various dimensions and processes that one might wish to say about it: a useful beginning to a summing up. To continue, then: what this paper has argued, is that psychosocial theory is in the process of a re-emergence. It considers where it is being generated, and in what contexts. It looks at what it is not, as a discipline, and what, though still in process, it seems to be. It outlines its tradition in critical theory, and in social work. Having set out the context, the paper then focuses on some of the history of the relationship between sociology and social work theory, mentioning difficulties and areas of mutual support. The focus then shifts to specifically looking at some of the tensions in using post-structural and postmodern theory in social work, and why psychosocial theory offers more productive alternatives. Finally, the paper looks at two further areas where psychosocial thinking is useful to social work: reflexive identity, and in informing appropriate models of research. Through use of social work and sociological examples throughout, the paper has argued that social work and sociology need psychosocial studies for a productive and dynamic integration, offering renewed possibilities and injecting creative energy into the relationship. It has attempted to establish that psychosocial studies is a discipline that can offer social work a set of concepts and analytical tools that are genuinely useful.

Disclosure statement

No potential conflict of interest was reported by the author.

References

Adams, R. 2001. *Critical Practice in Social Work*. Basingstoke: Palgrave Macmillan.

Adorno, T., E. Frenkel-Brunswick, D. J. Levison, and R. N. Sanford. 1951. *The Authoritarian Personality*. New York: Harper Row.

Alford, C. F. 1990 *Melanie Klein and Critical Social Theory: An Account of Politics, Art, and Reason Based on Her Psychoanalytic Theory*. Vol. 1. Newhaven, CT: Yale University Press.

APS (Association for Psychosocial Studies). 2014. http://www.psychosocial-studies-association.org/

Bainbridge, C., S. Radstone, M. Rustin, and C. Yates, eds. 2007. *Culture and the Unconscious*. Basingstoke: Palgrave Macmillan.

Bourdieu, P. 1999. *The Weight of the World. Social Suffering in Contemporary Society*. Cambridge: Polity Press.

Bracher, M. 1993. *Lacan, Discourse and Social Change: A Psychoanalytical Cultural Criticism*. New York: Cornell University Press.

Briggs, S. 2008. "Working with the Risk of Suicide in Young People." *Journal of Social Work Practice: Psychotherapeutic Approaches in Health, Welfare and the Community* 16 (2): 135–148.

Campanini, A. 2004. "Italy." In *European Social Work: Commonalities and Differences*, edited by A. Campanini and E. Frost, 129–137. Rome: Carocci.

Clarke, S. 2003. *Social Theory, Psychoanalysis and Racism*. Basingstoke: Palgrave Macmillan.

Clarke, S. 2005. *From Enlightenment to Risk, Social Theory and Contemporary Society*. Basingstoke: Palgrave Macmillan.

Clarke, S., and H. Hoggett, eds. 2008. *Researching Beneath The Surface: Psycho-social Research Methods in Practice*. Basingstoke: Palgrave Macmillan.

Cohen, S. 1973. *Folk Devils and Moral Panics*. St Albans: Paladin.

Cooper, A., and J. Lousada. 2005. *Borderline Welfare: Feeling and Fear of Feeling in Modern Welfare*. London: Karnac.

De Jong Gierveld, J., T. Van Tilburg, and P. A. Dykstra. 2006. "Loneliness and Social Isolation." Chap. 26 in *Cambridge Handbook of Personal Relationships*, edited by A. Vangelisti and D. Perlman, 485–500. Cambridge: Cambridge University Press.

Elliott, G., ed. 1994. *Althusser: A Critical Reader*. Oxford: Blackwell.

Eyerman, R. 2013. "Social Theory and Trauma." *Acta Sociologica* 56 (1): 41–53.

Ferguson, H. 2001. "Social Work, Individualization and Life Politics." *British Journal of Social Work* 31 (1): 41–55.

Ferguson, H. 2005. "Working with Violence, Emotions and the Psychosocial Dynamics of Child Protection: Reflections on the Victoria Climbié Case." *Social Work Education* 24 (7): 784–795.

Fook, J. 2004. *Social Work, Critical Theory and Practice*. London: Sage.

Freud, S. 1917. "Mourning and Melancholia." In *The Standard Edition of the Complete Psychological Works of Sigmund Freud, Volume XIV (1914–1916)*, 237–358. London: The Hogarth Press.

Froggett, L., M. Conway, J. Manley, and A. Roy. 2014. Between Art and Social Science: Scenic Composition as a Methodological Device. *Forum Qualitative Sozialforschung* 15 (3).

Froggett, L., E. Ramvi, and L. Davies. 2014. "Thinking from Experience in Psychosocial Practice: Reclaiming and Teaching 'Use of Self'." *Journal of Social Work Practice, Psychotherapeutic Approaches in Health, Welfare and the Community* 29 (2): 133–150. doi:10.1080/02650533.2014.923389.

Frosh, S. 2014. "The Nature of the Psychosocial: Debates from Studies in the Psychosocial." *Journal of Psycho-Social Studies* 8 (1): 159–169.

Gadd, D., and B. Dixon. 2010. *Loosing the Race: Thinking Psychosocially about Racially Motivated Crime*. London: Karnac.

Garrett, P. M. 2007. "Making Social Work More Bourdieusian: Why the Social Professions Should Critically Engage with the Work of Pierre Bourdieu." *European Journal of Social Work* 10 (2): 225–243.

Goffman, I. 1968. *Asylums: Essays on the Social Situation of Mental Patients and Other Inmates*. Harmondsworth: Pelican.

Grenfell, M., ed. 2008. *Pierre Bourdieu: Key Concepts*. London: Acumen Press.

Hoggett, P. 2001. "Agency, Rationality and Social Policy." *Journal of Social Policy* 30 (1): 37–56.

Hoggett, P. 2014. "Learning from Three Practices." *Journal of Psycho-Social Studies* 8 (1): 179–196.
Hoggett, P., P. Beedell, L. Jimenez, M. Mayo, and C. Miller. 2007. "Identity, Life History and Commitment to Welfare." *Journal of Social Policy* 35 (4): 689–704.
Hoggett, P., M. Mayo, and C. Miller. 2009. *The Dilemmas of Development Work*. Bristol: Polity.
Hollis, F. 1965. *Casework: A Psychosocial Therapy*. London: Random House.
Hollway, W. 2014. *Knowing Mothers: Researching Maternal Identity Change* (Studies in the Psychosocial). London: Palgrave Macmillan.
Hollway, W., and T. Jefferson. 2012. *Doing Qualitative Research Differently: Free Association, Narrative and the Interview Method*. London: Sage.
Houston, S. 2002. "Beyond Social Constructionism: Critical Realism and Social Work." *British Journal of Social Work* 31 (6): 845–861.
Irving, A. 1999. *Reading Foucault for Social Work*. New York: Columbia University Press.
Langan, M., and P. Lee, eds. 1989. *Radical Social Work Today*. London: Unwin Hyman.
Lavalette, M., ed. 2011. *Radical Social Work Today: Social Work at the Crossroads*. Bristol: The Policy Press.
Layton, L., N. C. Hollander, and S. Gutwill. 2006. *Psychoanalysis, Class and Politics: Encounters in the Clinical Setting*. New York: Routledge.
Mayo, M., P. Hoggett, and C. Miller. 2007. "Ethics, Ethical Dilemmas, the Public Service Ethos and Caring." In *Care, Citizenship and Communities: Research and Practice in a Changing Policy Contex*, edited by S. Balloch and M. Hill, 75–88. Bristol: Policy Press.
Murray Parkes, C., ed. 2014. *Responses to Terrorism: Can Psychosocial Approaches Break the Cycle of Violence?* London: Routledge.
Parton, N. 1994. "The Problematics of Government, (Post) Modernity and Social Work." *British Journal of Social Work* 24 (1): 9–32.
Parton, N. 2000. "Some Thoughts on the Relationship between Theory and Practice in and for Social Work." *British Journal of Social Work* 30: 449–463.
Pease, B., and J. Fook. 1999. *Transforming Social Work Practice*. London: Routledge.
Powell, F. 2001. *The Politics of Social Work*. London: Sage.
Ruch, G. 2012. "Where have All the Feelings Gone? Developing Reflective and Relationship-based Management in Child-care Social Work." *British Journal of Social Work* 42 (7): 1315–1332.
Rutter, M. 1987. "Psychosocial Resilience and Protective Mechanisms." *American Journal of Orthopsychiatry* 57 (3): 316–331.
Scanlon, C., and J. Adlam. 2013. "Reflexive Violence." *Psychoanalysis, Culture & Society* 18: 223–241. Published online February 7, 2013.
Trevithick, P. 2003. "Effective Relationship-based Practice: A Theoretical Exploration." *Journal of Social Work Practice* 17 (2): 163–176.
Trevithick, P. 2011. "Understanding Defences and Defensiveness in Social Work." *Journal of Social Work Practice* 25 (4): 389–412.
Walkerdine, V., and L. Jimenez. 2012. *Gender, Work and Community After De-industrialisation: A Psychosocial Approach to Affect*. Basingstoke: Palgrave Macmillan.
Walkerdine, V., H. Lucey, and J. Melody. 2001. *Growing Up Girl: Psychosocial Explorations of Class and Gender*. Basingstoke: Palgrave Macmillan.
Weintrobe, S., ed. 2013. *Engaging with Climate Change: Psychoanalytic and Interdisciplinary Perspectives*. London: Routledge.

Complex issues, complex solutions: applying complexity theory in social work practice

Sheila Fish[a] and Mark Hardy[b]

[a]Social Care Institute for Excellence, London, UK; [b]Department of Social Policy and Social Work, University of York, York, UK

> High-profile service failures in social work have ensured that the demand that practitioner decision-making be both accurate and transparent has never been as vocal or persistent. Such expectations undermine both trust and legitimacy, and how best to respond represents perhaps the most challenging issue facing social work today. Of necessity, practitioners must make judgements in circumstances characterised by uncertainty and ambiguity, while the complexity of this undertaking is routinely cited as a confounding variable in efforts to generate and apply generalisable knowledge in a technical fashion. Here, we aim to utilise developments in complexity theory to elaborate on why this might be the case, but also what, practically, social work might do about it. In particular, we will respond to Eileen Munro suggestion that it is possible to differentiate areas of social work which can be proceduralised from those which should be judgement based. Utilising recent developments in complexity theory, we aim to explore whether this can be undertaken on the basis of a 'complexity continuum' which enables classification of roles and tasks on the basis of inherent certainty or uncertainty. In providing a reflexive account of the development and application of the continuum, however, the relationship between theory and practice is to some extent problematised. The findings demonstrate that although complexity theory can provide useful insights, it also has evident practical limitations. In turn, these limitations have implications for discussions regarding the real-world relevance of complexity theory, and for sociological theorising to social work more generally.

Introduction

The relationship between sociology and social work is longstanding and contested (Davies 1991). Sociology concerns itself with investigating and theorising the impact of social change on social life – people, groups, relationships, institutions and ideas. At least since the establishment of the Settlement movement, both theory and practice in social work have been informed by a broad sociological understanding of the role that social factors play in social problems and the individual circumstances and behaviours of which they are comprised. Social problems require – at least in part – social solutions and the social worker is invested with the power and authority to assess and intervene in ways which balance the needs and expectations of the individual with those of the wider collective. However, sociology is by no means the only, if even principal, influence on practice. In part, this is because it is itself characterised by disjuncture and cleavage – between, for example consensus and conflict models, empirical and postmodern and micro and macro. Nevertheless, without doubt, sociological theorising has enhanced practicing social workers' theoretical repertoires in helpful ways. In this paper, we continue this tradition, exploring the potential practical application of a relatively novel strand of sociological theorising – complexity theory – to one of the key issues that contemporary social work faces, namely the quality of the judgements and decisions made by its practitioners. The article provides a reflexive account of our efforts to think through the implications of a number of related issues: how social work should respond to a generalised problematic; how complexity theory can inform social work practice; our developing understanding of what we were seeking to achieve and how; and how our experience of 'thought in action' led us to reformulate some of our initial presumptions regarding the nature of the problem we were addressing, our approach to doing so and the relationship between sociological theory and social work, including social work research. Ultimately, this account raises important questions about the relevance of any generalised theory, sociological or otherwise, to actual practical professional activities, problematising some of the assumptions which underpin our understanding of the relevance of theory to practice.

Background

High-profile service failures across the domains of social work have ensured that the demand that professional judgements and decisions be both as accurate and accountable as possible has never been as vocal or persistent. Such 'failures' are of course hardly novel with certain iconic 'cases' known well beyond the distinct professional arenas in which they arose (Butler and Drakeford 2003). Nor are they necessarily limited to social work, as similarly high-profile and influential cases have occurred in health care and criminal justice. However, the challenges which they pose for the legitimacy of social work agencies, whose failings are seemingly perceived as qualitatively different from those of other agencies, are arguably distinct.

The case of 'Baby P' in the UK represents perhaps the most potent recent example of service failure and led to the Munro review of child protection (2011), as well as the establishment of the social work taskforce to reform social work training and practice. The review concluded that the ability of social workers to make accurate judgements is hampered by the burdensome degree of administration and scrutiny that they are subject to and their concordant impact on the time available to spend with children and families. Consequently, practitioners often have to make judgements in far from ideal situations, based on less than full knowledge, compounding rather than alleviating the uncertainty that characterises the complex work they must undertake. Subsequent, related reforms have sought to strengthen the status of social work by equipping it to deal with the related issues of the quality of day-to-day practice and the legitimacy of the profession.

Independently of her work for government, Munro has developed a body of work which seeks to combine the strengths of both analytic and intuitive, or formal and informal, approaches to judgement and decision-making so as to overcome their respective inherent limitations (Munro 2005, 2008, 2010, 2012). This broadly systemic model privileges notions of complexity and seeks to specify not how to eliminate uncertainty, but how to manage or engage with it. The assumption is that it is possible to improve and potentially standardise the quality of decision-making in practice under particular conditions where the appropriate style of reasoning informs particular judgements.

The challenge – and opportunity – faced in responding to the fallout from Baby P was how best to embed this approach within practice in children's services, and the recommendations contained in the final report – accepted in full by the government – represent a considered strategy to do exactly that. Munro (2010, 2011) distinguishes – in the abstract – between areas of practice which ought to be proceduralised and those which should be judgement based. However, she acknowledges that there is work to be done in establishing which areas of practice in which contexts and domains fit into each category. Although in health care and engineering, for example, there have been efforts to operationalise these distinctions (e.g. Braithwaite, Healy, and Dwan 2005; Woods et al. 2010), in social work, this is underdeveloped, both in terms of establishing criteria which might be used as the basis for such differentiation, as well as their utility in actual practice. Where suggestions have been made, these have been characterised by imprecision. Sheppard, for example, suggests that 'it is in the accuracy with which they are able to categorise a situation … that good social workers may be marked out' (2006, 210), but offers no criteria for distinguishing between what he calls 'straightforward' and 'non straightforward' scenarios. Pycroft (2014) provides a more theoretical but still inconclusive account of the distinctions between simple, complicated and complex scenarios. Munro (2011) herself, meanwhile, also utilises these distinctions, emphasising, on the one hand, the potential significance of proceduralisation, particularly in interagency and multi-professional contexts, especially for relatively inexperienced workers, and, on the other, the role of professional knowledge and skills in countering complexity. However, here too there is little in the way of specifics as to how these distinctions might actually be meaningfully applied in common social work scenarios by front line staff.

In this article, then, we explore whether the necessary differentiation can be undertaken on the basis of a classification framework which we provisionally refer to as 'the complexity continuum'. The model is informed by our understanding of complexity theory, and aims to enable the classification of judgements and decisions on the basis of relative certainty or uncertainty within routine social work scenarios. Were it to be viable, a model such as this might allow for relatively simple decisions to be addressed with a high degree of confidence that predicted outcomes would be achieved, as well as specifying those areas where such confidence is unwarranted and alternatives required. Complex judgements are not amenable to straightforward remedy. Rather, they challenge the efficacy of proceduralisation (Styhre 2013). Thus, in seeking to develop such a framework, we are not necessarily advocating its use. Rather, we are testing the extent to which it may or may not be practically useful as a means of enabling the differentiation which Munro regards as crucial to minimising inaccuracy in social work decision-making, and thus to enhancing the legitimacy of the profession. Our account of the development and application of the tool to some extent problematises formal efforts to proceduralise aspects of practice, including our own.

Uncertainty, ambiguity and complexity in social work

It has become commonplace to suggest that social work is characterised by uncertainty, ambiguity and complexity (Parton 1998). Indeed, Fook (2007) suggests that social work is *defined* by its relationship to uncertainty, while Webb (2001), in his influential critique of evidence-based practice, claims that empiricism disregards 'the complexity of actual decision-making processes in social work. A more complex relationship exists between social work interventions and decisions made by social work agencies which is governed by imperatives which fall outside the workings of a rational actor' (63). But what is at stake when such terms are utilised? What is 'complex' about social work?

The relationship between risk, uncertainty and complexity is not necessarily straightforward. Should it, for example, be conceived of as a positive relationship or a negative one? Is uncertainty indicative of the complex character of the subject of inquiry – an ontological issue? Or does it reflect our 'ways of knowing', an epistemological issue? Actually, it is both. The scenarios which social workers intervene in – their 'social' character – are characterised by intersections between multiple variables which are difficult to disentangle. Consequently, it is tricky to predict with any degree of certainty how a particular judgement or course of action will impact and so whether any intervention will 'work'. Social phenomena are distinct from those which concern the natural sciences, in that they do not emerge as a result of direct, unmediated stimuli which, when combined – in the manner of a chemical reaction – manifest in a predictable outcome. Social circumstances and relationships are inherently inter-subjective, reflecting the variable and (to some extent) individualised nature of the human beings they are comprised of. And because social phenomena are 'complex', we are quite rightly uncertain how to respond. Often, practitioners don't – and perhaps can't – know whether or not a decision will be the 'right' one, that a judgement will be accurate or that a particular intervention will be effective. In essence, the inability of social work to guarantee the accuracy and efficacy of its decisions and actions reflects the status of the knowledge upon which practice rests (uncertain) and the lack of consensus (ambiguity) regarding its aims, methods and achievements and how we might establish these. Uncertainty equates to lack of definitive knowledge regarding what will occur if particular approaches are adopted in specific situations (Koppenjan and Klijn 2004). Ambiguity about the purposes of practice – care, control, cure, safeguarding, protection or early intervention – is enduring. Clearly, the nature of the subject matter with which social work deals – human being under stress – is such that we are a long way from ever being able to accurately predict future outcomes. Considerable uncertainty and ambiguity are, then, 'the nature of the beast' (Sheppard 2006, 204).

So, does this mean that these 'complex' situations should therefore be responded to procedurally – to limit the potential for harm perceived to be associated with poor decisions or inaccurate judgements? Or conversely, does it suggest that the uncertainty inherent in complex situations is such that there is no option to deal with these other than on the basis of subjective, individualised judgements? Although particular authors have their preferred responses (compare, for example, Sheppard's (2006) emphasis on classification, schemas, verification and falsification as the basis for practical reasoning with the 'humane' judgements preferred by Featherstone, White and Morris (2014)), there are no clear-cut answers here. Consequently, of late, there has been increased attention paid to applying developments in complexity theory to make sense of contemporary mores within social work, and in particular, exploring how uncertainty and ambiguity might be managed, responded to and engaged with.

Complexity theory – key ideas and concepts

Complexity theory developed primarily within the natural sciences, though it has been utilised in many other disciplines, including health, epidemiology, computer science, politics, management and the social sciences, amongst others. It has a developed repertoire of concepts and terminology which can be off-putting, but is actually quite straightforward once the key ideas and principles underpinning complexity thinking are clarified. Some of these are familiar – systems, networks, dependence and bifurcation – and some less so – complex adaptive systems, emergence, dynamism, strange attractors, oscillation, power laws, fractals and the like. To add to the 'complexity', there is a diversity of perspectives within complexity thinking. There are various schools who use both concepts and terminology in slightly different ways, reflecting their different substantive and analytic foci. The original Santa Fe school, for example, is concerned with the implications of complexity for approaches to mathematical modelling in light of innovations in computing power, across the disciplines. According to Harvey, this represents 'an adjunct to standard science' (2001, 3) with ambitions to 'scientise' (via modelling) all disciplines, including the social sciences and humanities. The 'chaos' school associated with Prigogine, however, maps the boundaries of order and disorder in ways which reject the assumptions and principles of traditional truth-seeking. As Gleick puts it, 'Where chaos begins, classical science stops' (1987, 3).

Complexity theory explores the implications of recognition of the 'non-linear' nature of many phenomena. Non-linear thinking problematises the capacity of traditional linear approaches to knowledge development and application to produce generalisable knowledge, which incrementally can enable the development of law like statements regarding cause and effect. The potential for such laws to enable accurate predictions regarding (broadly defined) phenomena is therefore limited. Thus, in seeking to understand these, it is 'the system' rather than its individual component parts that ought to be the focus for analysis. Prediction is problematised within complex systems, which are adaptive (hence, 'complex adaptive systems') in light of positive and negative feedback loops with the environment, which dampen and accentuate the effect of action, such that very small factors can have a disproportionately large effect (Lorenz's 'butterfly effect' being the archetypal exemplar). Thus, central or top-down action may well be less dramatic in its impact than small-scale interactions, which contribute to largely unforeseen local emergence of phenomena/behaviour that analysis of individual elements would not have predicted. Such self-organising capacities within complex systems render control – the achievement of pre-set expectations via the manipulation of variables – more difficult than traditional, linear models assumed. Context matters equally as much as the variables and processes, which are occurring in the 'phase shifts' which emerge as systems, evolve.

Faith in linear models is undermined by recognition of the non-linear nature of the relationships between variables and thus also between cause and effect, and the environmental stimuli and multiple systems which characterise phenomena. Crucially, however, chaos scientists do not presume that disorder prohibits knowledge generation and application. Rather, as Mitchell (2009) makes clear, by contrast where others see disorder, they look for and find patterns. Thus, 'while systems appear random when they are initially studied, order and patterning are, in fact, observable' (Pycroft 2014, 18). Both 'systems' and 'chaos' approaches, then, are important to complexity thinking. Reed and Harvey (1992) explain that each is necessary as understanding their respective foci – internal sub-systems and external context – is a prerequisite for full comprehension of 'non-hierarchal inter-penetration' (Byrne 1998).

Complexity thinking, then, represents both 'solution' and 'problem'. It can simultaneously be regarded as helpful and problematic. On the one hand, it enables us to understand *why* it can be difficult to straightforwardly manipulate variables to achieve particular outcomes. On the other, by its nature, the understanding of the nature of phenomena embedded within this understanding renders the generation of useful, applicable knowledge very difficult.

Complexity thinking in the social and political sciences

The influence of such theoretical developments has impacted well beyond the natural sciences, including on particular strands of the social sciences, such as sociology and social work. Harvey is unsurprised by this: 'the goals of the policy sciences … are inherently nonlinear … research seeks to discover ameliorative solutions to social problems in which small changes in the initial conditions of the life course of a person, a community, or an institution will produce great changes in the final outcome' (2001, 7). Notable authors from sociology and related disciplines have argued that the lessons of complexity theory are equally as profound for the 'soft' disciplines as the 'hard'. Thus, Byrne (1998, 2001, 2011) has highlighted the positive role of the social sciences in generating data to illuminate causality and theory development, emphasising the interpretive nature of analysis of 'hard' statistical data. While Byrne's concerns are, in the main, methodological, the sociologist Sylvia Walby's work is more explicitly theoretical, applying complexity thinking to explore the implications of globalisation for our understanding of the nature and effects of social difference and inequality (Walby 2007, 2009, 2012). According to McDermott, 'Complexity theory is concerned with the intersection of systems … a concern that has been a prevailing analytical focus in sociology' (2014, 185). Walby focuses especially on reinvigorating aspects of systems thinking in light of, on the one hand, the rejection of deterministic Parsonian functionalism, and, on the other, recognition of the unbounded and thus reciprocally interacting nature of both institutions and their environment as complex adaptive systems. Robert Geyer, meanwhile, has used complexity theory to model political decision-making, both specifically, in international relations, and in public policy more generally (Geyer 2003; Geyer and Rihani 2010). There are many, significant, others (see Byrne and Callahan 2014; Hatt 2009; Urry 2002). Cumulatively, they demonstrate the utility and potential of complexity thinking in revisiting enduring issues in the social sciences and, in doing so, demonstrate its potential utility, particularly at a philosophical and conceptual level.

More practical work has occurred at the interface between 'theory' and 'practice'. Systems approaches have risen to prominence in attempts to understand human error, e.g. in areas such as air traffic control and nuclear engineering. Geyer, for example, demonstrates how 'fitness landscapes' and 'complexity cascades' – visual mappings of social and environmental variables – ensure that context or the 'surroundings in which living beings exist and behave' (Cairney 2012, 349) is privileged as a major contributory factor in social phenomena.

As well as the various 'schools' within complexity thinking itself, there are also different perspectives on complexity within disciplines which have adopted its thinking, each with distinct things to say about how best to engage, reduce, eliminate or manage it. These reflect the paradigmatic affiliations of particular authors. Byrne, for example, works within the realist tradition, while for example, Cilliers (1998) and Arrigo and Williams (1999, 2014) are more closely aligned with postmodernism. Thus, 'reductionist' complexity science aims to tame complexity in the traditional scientific manner, while 'soft' complexity science 'is closer to the postmodernist position where the metaphors of complexity can be used to modify current understanding and policy action' (Geyer 2012, 32). The latter is part of a wider form of 'complexity thinking' which rethinks in a more generalised sense the implications of the ubiquity of uncertainty for how we generate knowledge and apply it. Although long dominated by rationalist models, increasingly there is recognition that traditional reductionist methodologies are inadequate to the task of capturing complexity, an insight which is particularly apt with regard to practice-based disciplines.

The relationship between complexity and uncertainty, then, is recognised in diverse disciplinary contexts, with enduring debates regarding the nature of causal relationships and if and how perceived problems associated with operating in less than full knowledge might be responded to. This is as much the case in the 'hard' sciences as the soft, more social disciplines (Byers 2011), but of late, has become a source of much discussion in arenas where there are direct links between politics, policy and organisational practices (Kernick 2004; Nord and Connel 2011). The necessity of developing such thinking relates to the 'messiness' of the issues and problems which characterise these areas. In policy circles, Chapman's (2004) 'systems' approach has been influential. This suggests that linear approaches have inherent limitations when applied to 'social' phenomena which are characterised by ambiguity and uncertainty, regarding both the nature of the problem and how it should be addressed. The problems that contemporary public sector – including social work – organisations face cannot be resolved via tinkering – 'better' solutions, 'clearer' thinking. Instead, they require a radical reorientation of the ways in which issues, problems and dilemmas are formulated and responded to. Standard responses entailing clarification of objectives and means, rational planning, target setting and implementation are inappropriate in 'messy' situations – complex, unpredictable environments in which cause and effect relationships are unpredictable and there is often fundamental disagreement about the aims and objectives of particular organisations or agencies. This can be counter-posed with 'traditional' approaches which are regarded as reductionist and mechanistic. These include contemporary manifestations of modernist thinking such as 'evidence based' policy and practice, where a linear relationship between cause and effect, and thus the potential for control, is assumed without due regard being paid to the mediating impact of context. 'Traditional' thinking leads to unintended consequences, is often counter-productive, alienates ground level practitioners and undermines legitimacy.

The 'solution' to the problem of a lack of certain knowledge to enable predictability and control within 'complex adaptive systems' is an embedded commitment to ongoing learning, which is furthered via processes of reflection and modification. To enable this, individuals need to 'reflect on their way of thinking, the assumptions they are making and the real goals they are pursuing' (Chapman 2004, 14). At the same time, there is a commitment to evaluation and learning as a basis for ongoing modification. However, this is not to be achieved via privileged knowledge generation strategies – hierarchies of knowledge and the like – but via accommodating and integrating the varying perspectives of different stakeholders. This will not necessarily provide simple solutions to messy problems. But in *actual* learning organisations, responsiveness can facilitate effectiveness. The development of genuinely learning cultures, however, requires a shift within agency cultures which characterise public sector organisations of the contemporary neoliberal state, in particular the jettisoning of 'command and control' management models and counter-productive blaming systems (Hood 2011).

Such insights are not, of course, unique to complexity theory. Indeed, they are quite commonplace in the social sciences, particularly amongst those who are unconvinced of the virtues of broad brush reductionist linear approaches – positivism, experimental method, evidence-based policy and practice, etc. And so, to some extent, complexity theory had found a welcoming niche, and been integrated within the theoretical resources of critique as part of the resistance to 'conventional', top-down models. Cairney (2012) points to similarities of emphasis with established analytical frames in public policy analysis, particularly historical institutionalism and street-level bureaucracy. These tend to question the appropriateness of 'top down' approaches to social policy and social work practice (Haynes 2003). 'Soft' as opposed to 'hard' management approaches foster creativity and dynamism amongst front line staff, as well as tempering expectations of infallibility (Fook and Gardner 2007; Little 2012). There is also an associated critique of the value of risk factor research, attempts to predict behaviour based on actuarial knowledge and the large-scale modelling which characterises evidence-based practice (Fitzgibbon 2011; Webb 2006). McDermott, for example, suggests that 'complexity theory … is on a collision course with practices of risk management' (2014, 186). Case and Haines concur: 'the notion that human behaviour is amenable to mechanical (experimental) modelling and that cause and effect… can be understood in linear, consistent and predictable analyses necessitates a level of abstraction and generalisation as to render any conclusions so distant from the original social reality as to make them worthless artefacts' (2014, 126). Munro is more succinct: 'In a complex world, predictions are necessarily of limited value because even small changes in the value of one variable can lead to large differences in outcome' (2012, 230). As an alternative, we see a commitment to localism and, in the practice-based disciplines of health, social care and (as was) probation, holistic individualism (Kernick 2004; Sweeney and Griffiths 2002; Whitehead 2010).

Complexity thinking in social work

Much of this will resonate in contemporary social work, with its enduring emphasis on reflective, person-centred practice and recent highlighting of the merits of organisational learning. More generally, various authors have utilised complexity concepts to think through how social workers might respond to the diversity of situations which they are required to intervene in (Green and McDermott 2010; Halmi 2003; Sommerfeld and Hollenstein 2011; Stevens and Cox 2008; Stevens and Hassett 2007) and how social work agencies might understand the nature of the task they face in accommodating the ubiquity of uncertainty (Hudson 2010; McDermott 2014; Wolf-Branigin 2014). There is a degree of consensus amongst these writers, who generally suggest that 'quick fixes' are beyond the power of practitioners, but that in rejecting determinism, future possibilities are opened up which potentially can reflect the diversity of individual circumstances and needs, reaffirming that practice can make a difference. Byrne again: 'the great advantage of thinking about things in a complexity mode is that it opens up for us an exploration of what futures we might make to come to pass' (2001, 8). Pycroft emphasises 'the importance of understanding complex systems as … non-linear and uncertain precisely to help us analyse and intervene more effectively' (2014, 16), while Wolf-Branigin (2013) confidently asserts that complexity thinking enables the simple rules of the 'hidden order' of complexity to be revealed as patterns which can be usefully applied.

Within the literature, then, there are recurrent suggestions regarding how best to deal with complexity. In the main, this entails the rejection of simplistic theoretical frameworks based on deductive reasoning and rational analysis in favour of more holistic and individualised approaches based on inductive reasoning. The latter accommodate 'whole human beings in their social relationships and in their social environment' (Payne 2011, 125). It is clear that for many authors, complexity theory represents a useful framework for thinking about the challenges of practice. Although the very notion of complexity problematises the potential for practitioners to draw upon their professional knowledge base so as to effectively intervene, nevertheless, complexity theory offers some potentially useful conceptual tools to help make sense of social situations. For example, faced with uncertainty about how to respond in a particular case, in which there is no way of knowing what the outcome of a particular course of action will be, 'attractors' act a means of differentiation between potential alternative options, thus enabling their emergence and limiting positive alternatives, from which a choice can be made. Possible courses of action becomes limited and often boils down to a choice between as little as two competing alternatives 'oscillating' around 'bifurcation' points. Here, complexity thinking 'helps us to think through very complex, apparently intractable situations; it makes us feel less helpless. It reasserts our human capacity to deal with situations that have too many factors in them to understand' (Payne 2011, 125).

There have also been tentative efforts to think through what might be entailed in reducing the impact of 'the human factor' using systems analysis (e.g. Featherstone, White, and Morris 2014). In other sectors – high reliability organisations such as air traffic control and nuclear power, but also in human services, especially health care – the emphasis is less on eliminating risk and uncertainty and more about accepting the inevitability of error. Efforts to bring about 'safety cultures', whereby the culture within organisations helps to minimise error by learning from mistakes, exemplify this approach. Where effective, they are clearly beneficial. However, any efforts to transfer approaches derived from human factors research to social work face two challenges. First, the pervasiveness of blame cultures (Parton 1996) within the highly charged politics of risk makes vocal advocacy of fallibility politically difficult in social work. Secondly, as Taylor and White (2000) make clear, the nature of some of the decisions social workers make are qualitatively different than those of, for example, surgeons or airline pilots. These are less to do with technical proficiency under stress than moral judgements and are arguably less amenable to efforts to minimise 'inaccuracy' via proceduralisation.

In the main, then, the application of complexity thinking to social work has been either theoretical and, to some extent, utopian, or else impractical in its applications. Here, we aim to develop a potentially practically useful application of complexity thinking which addresses a particular problematic specific to social work, namely, a means to enable the differentiating of decisions and judgements which ought to be procedural from those which should be judgement based. The tool is underpinned by recognition of the relationship between uncertainty, ambiguity and complexity, which means that how practitioners intervene in genuinely complex situations cannot be specified, only enabled. In this sense, although procedural, it fits within the category of 'soft' rather than 'hard' complexity thinking. To some extent, then, we concur with Howe (2002) that the value of any theory – in this case, complexity theory – in practice-based disciplines ultimately rests in the extent to which it enables practitioners to understand and solve actual problems.

Developing the complexity continuum

Our efforts to think through and develop and apply the complexity continuum were informed by our awareness of other tools which have sought to 'model' complexity in other disciplines and our perception of the limitations of these already existing models for the practical task we were concerned to address. These include the Stacey diagram (Stacey 1996), the 'fitness landscape' and 'complexity cascade' (Geyer 2012; Geyer

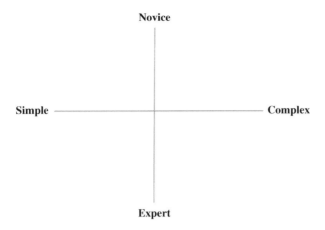

Diagram 1. The developing complexity continuum.

and Pickering 2011) and the 'complexity broom' (Lillrank and Liukko 2004). However, while Geyer's work provides a useful framework for understanding 'why things are as they are' in a particular policy domain (to do with the interplay between 'accidents' and 'regularities' that characterise 'punctuated equilibrium'), it is less applicable to the micro-level of practice. The complexity 'broom' is more useful here, but seems intended as a metaphor for the interaction between proceduralised and judgement-based approaches. It also has its roots in 'quality management' and so is geared towards the role that managers might play in decision-making. Nor were these models developed with social work in mind, and all seem to over complicate the process of simplifying complexity. Our preference was for a framework which might be straightforwardly helpful to either social work agencies or particularly to front line practitioners. The challenge, then, was to develop a model which suits social work and was applicable to the diverse domains of practice and the specific tasks and activities which define it.

Our intention was to respond to the recognition of complexity by providing a practical tool which might have utility in helping local actors to navigate complexity within their own specific practice context. To begin with, our original engagement with complexity theory as a theoretical resource to inform the practical task of differentiating areas of practice suggested that this would entail mapping judgements in practice according to how complex a particular type of decision appears to be. Where this was simple, practice might then be straightforwardly designated as procedural. Where it wasn't, it wouldn't be, as flexibility or adaptability would be required in light of the need for practice-based experimentation within 'discretionary spaces' (Woods et al. 2010).

The complexity continuum, then, potentially represents one means of differentiating those areas of practice which should be proceduralised from those which ought be judgement based, on the basis of the extent to which key decisions taken by practitioners are best characterised as defined by either relative certainty or uncertainty. It is informed by an understanding of the nature of the relationship between uncertainty and complexity that assumes it is possible to know some things with a greater degree of certainty than others, but that some situations are of a nature that preclude proscriptive responses and will remain elusive. Nevertheless, it is not the case that either human beings or their social relationships are so complex that we are not able to, in certain circumstances, generate useful knowledge and understanding which, with contextual caveats, will enable us to intervene with some expectation of success, whatever our objectives may be. In social work, this distinction – between areas of practice where we do have confidence regarding how to proceed, and those in which we do not – should form the basis upon which we selectively determine the extent to which in a particular situation we might draw upon formalised or informal knowledge sources.

In developing the framework, from the outset, we were aware of the need to acknowledge that the nature of practice is such that a dichotomous or static framework would probably not be useful. This is because there are gradations of complexity and thus uncertainty, in addition to which our knowledge and understanding is not fixed but changes constantly, both as individuals and as a collective. Any framework which seeks to differentiate therefore needs to be dynamic and adaptable. The continuum reflects these assumptions: it is premised on a belief that it may be possible to construct a continuum of areas of practice, against which judgements and decisions can be mapped. The assumption is that practice comprises a series of decisions and actions, and all of these entail processes via which judgements are made. The decisions which characterise social work are fairly generic and include both day-to-day choices that are part of a working routine as well as 'higher order' judgements which have direct implications for the welfare, security and liberty of service users and others. Examples of the latter include case formulation – what the nature of the issue is and how best to deal with it; which theoretical perspective best applies in understanding and intervening in particular scenarios; what resources to allocate to a specific case; which risk level to ascribe to a particular client; which interventions to utilise; whether or not to hospitalise someone; whether it is appropriate for a child to be removed from the family home or taken into care; and when to alter or end involvement. The distinction between lower and higher level decision-making was recognised as, to some extent, arbitrary. Nevertheless, distinguishing between them was necessary if we were to practically and meaningfully engage in what we were coming to recognise as a form of functional role analysis. This represented a type of process mapping, whereby practitioner responsibilities – the key judgements and decisions that they make, and the actions which follow from these – in a particular domain, agency and context are specified and categorised as a basis for allocation. The continuum was therefore aimed at these 'higher level' decisions.

Provisionally, we envisaged the categorisation and mapping of judgements between two poles of (as the name suggests) a continuum, according to a *subjective estimation* of their relative complexity, based on the extent to which multiple relationships between variables are in play in a particular scenario, and what we *perceive* the robustness of the existing knowledge to be at present (see Diagram 1). Some will be highly procedurally delineated, some will be mildly procedurally delineated, others will be mildly judgement based and some inherently judgement based, enabling allocation to one of the four quartiles between the poles.

Applying the complexity continuum

Our starting point for the continuum was to use the degree of complexity entailed in arriving at a judgement as a basis for categorising examples of decisions as either simple or complex. We sought to think through the issues that arise when applying it to the sorts of situations that practitioners confront during casework and the decisions and judgements which they need to make. As we thought this through, however, we quickly realised that our assumptions regarding the 'simplicity' of this task – as well as our own frustration at the lack of specificity amongst others who had undertaken this sort of designatory task in the past – were misplaced. For example, even the most straightforward model of professional competence assumes some progression from novice, through competence to qualified, experienced and expert status. We therefore needed to accommodate variability in levels of expertise in deciding how complex a particular scenario might be. Hence, it became apparent that of necessity, any such model must be individualised rather than generalised: a situation a novice finds inordinately complex might be perceived by an expert as very straightforward. While for the individual practitioner this might be helpful, it suggested that 'mapping complexity', according to generic classification of standardised judgements and decisions, might well be overly optimistic. Thus, two variables – complexity and expertise – would now intersect in determining how well equipped any particular individual practitioner was to undertake a particular task. We therefore amended our thoughts regarding how the continuum would function and adapted how it would be represented. The intersection between the axes would be represented on a grid comprising four quadrants, enabling the mapping and allocation of tasks according to the criteria already established, now to also include an estimation of the competence (for want of a better word) of the practitioner undertaking that particular task.

At that point, however, further 'complexities' emerged. Firstly, the assessment of competence raised questions regarding how this might be defined, according to which criteria it might be assessed and by who. The most straightforward models of competence are dichotomous, but recognised as limited because of their inability to accommodate degrees of expertise or accommodate specialisation. Even more expansive and responsive models depend on demonstration of accumulation and application of knowledge and understanding which the underpinning principles of complexity question. Secondly – and significantly, in terms of our thinking about the viability of the continuum – ongoing reflection on the strengths and limitations of complexity theory itself threatened the basis of the model we were developing. If we take complexity theory seriously, the distinction between 'lower order' routine, decisions and 'high order' judgements becomes problematic. Low-level decisions will have disproportionate effects elsewhere in the system such that aims and outcomes will be disturbed. But without the ability to disregard the significance of these 'happenings', the viability of assessing the actual complexity of a particular 'higher order' social work decision is compromised. Decisions regarding, for example, what day an appointment should be scheduled for, at what time, in which venue, using which room etc. become charged with possibility. Nor is it possible to disregard the significance of even more mundane eventualities – whether to drive to work or cycle, coffee or tea with lunch, the outfit that might be appropriate for a particular meeting, etc. Before we know it infinite alternative eventualities are apparent and the disorientation and doubt which Parton (1996) regards as characteristic of 'the vertigo of relativity' emerge, a relativism that Cilliers (2005) acknowledges has the potential to disable. Stewart (2001) refers to this as 'incondensible' complexity of a sort that complexity science, as developed in sociology, is as ill equipped to 'map' as any other social science perspective. Indeed, when thought of in these terms, it is difficult to envisage any judgement or decision in social work which is not infinitely complex. At which point, everything ... stopped.

Discussion

Although the literature on complexity theory has expanded rapidly, it remains a relatively recent and novel development. Coupled with the various differences of emphasis amongst the varying schools of complexity, this means that definitional and conceptual issues have yet to be resolved and continue to vex. In the social sciences, although there are many who believe its applicability and utility is now established, many of its social scientific applications are dependent on metaphor and analogy. This, of course, is not uncommon in the social sciences (Billig 2013) and has not hampered conceptual development. Indeed, Byrne, who arguably has done as much as anyone to demonstrate the real-world significance of complexity theory (e.g. 2011), nevertheless, acknowledges (in relation to social policy, but the argument holds for social work) that 'looking at topics in social policy and thinking them through with a complexity frame of reference … is the essence of complexity science as practice' (2001, 4). This was clearly the case in our efforts to develop and apply the complexity continuum. Although the logic of complexity thinking pointed in particular, developmental, directions, seeking to apply such ideas in the 'real world' of practice quickly threw up very significant obstacles. Indeed, once we got thinking again, with hindsight, this seemed inevitable. Despite the resonance of complexity thinking at many levels, common sense ought to lead us to question the relevance and utility of precepts and principles drawn from quantum mechanics to the day-to-day work of social workers. Thus, it is clear that the straightforward application of the principles and concepts associated with complexity theory, as developed in scientific disciplines, to social work is not as unproblematic as some suggest (Wolf-Branigin 2013). At best, the use of ideas from complexity theory in social work can be regarded as metaphorical, principally because the phenomena under consideration are of a wholly different nature and character to those which are typically the focus for complexity theory in science more generally. Payne suggests that 'it is important to realise that we are not applying a scientific theory here but using ideas … as an analogy to help us think through human complexities in a quite different context' (2011, 117).

The relationship between theory and practice, and between sociology and social work in particular, then, is best regarded as a contested one. Shaw (2014) points out that they are often conceived of as hierarchal, whereby (sociological) theory informs (social work) practice. Dominelli suggests that 'Sociological analyses provide theoretical perspectives that can subject policies and the work which practitioners do to systematic analysis'. Additionally, theory 'can be used to illuminate structures, processes and social relationships in social work and contribute to the development of more appropriate forms of practice' (1997, 5, italics added). Social work, it is assumed, can learn from sociology and improve its practice as a result. The psychiatric social worker turned sociologist Stan Cohen, however, expressed scepticism about the value of theorising more generally, suggesting that it produced 'remarkably few prescriptions that [can] actually be followed by social workers in any practical sense' (cited in Davies 1991). The lack of applicability of complexity thinking in the exercise recounted in this paper reflects a longstanding criticism of 'top down' conceptualisation, whereby sociological theory is useful for diagnosing problems, but limited in proscribing solutions.

Nevertheless, complexity theory does, however, explain why social work is so difficult to get right all of the time – because of the complexity, and thus unpredictability or difficulty of knowing whether a particular theoretical framework applies in 'this' case, if a judgement will be right or a specific intervention 'work'. Although this means complexity thinking is less useful as a practical remedy for the ills of social work, it does not, however, suggest that either sociological theory in general, or complexity theory in particular, are negated as potentially fruitful resources for thinking about practice. This is apparent, for example, when the similarities between the concept of 'emergence' and structure/agency are compared. Structure/agency, as operationalised by Giddens (1984), is one of the most useful sociological resources for social work, as it highlights the ways in which structures of society have both disempowering and empowering potential, and thus the *actual real* power that adheres within the role of the social worker. Complex systems clearly mirror the structure/agency distinction. Interactions within complex adaptive systems provoke the emergence of phenomena which are not reducible to agents' preferences. Equally, in the process of reacting to emergence, actors also develop perceptions of needs and wants and how to achieve these. Their interaction is reciprocal but weighted, in that agency is significant, but limited. For practitioners, however, awareness of 'the centrality of context and the patterning characterising that context' (McDermott 2014, 191) ensures that practitioners are not disabled by complexity.

As well as informing practice, there also remains potential for links between complexity thinking and social work research. As this exercise has demonstrated, the knowledge which research informed by complexity thinking might generate may not necessarily be straightforwardly applicable in practice, but can certainly enhance understanding of the importance of context to process and outcomes. As McDermott puts it, although 'the establishment of universal laws of causality may not be possible – with outcomes being the product of multiple causes in interaction and in context – research may enable us to discover what works in particular contexts and, thus, transfer the discovery to other similar contexts' (2014, 186). Recently, Nissen has usefully identified a key role for social work research in the development of a sociology of social problems for social work in which 'the complex relation between the societal context and the identification of and solution to social problems is addressed explicitly as a main research problem' (2014, 564). Central to this is the need to 'address the complexity of society as well as the complexity of welfare practices aiming to solve social problems collectively, and the relations between them' (p. 565). The aim is to 'discover a new and perhaps more practical sociological language about the complexities of social problems', which is 'adequate for social work' (p. 567). This is a pressing and laudable aim, and one which 'soft' complexity thinking (though perhaps not 'hard' complexity science) remains well placed to enhance.

Conclusion

The complexity continuum we attempted to develop and apply was useful as a means of thinking about how we might go about distinguishing between those situations and circumstances which lend themselves to procedural or judgement-based practice, but of little practical utility in achieving this end. Like all tools (e.g. risk assessment tools and critical appraisal tools), it is apparent that it replicates processes that agencies and practitioners already, to a greater or lesser extent, actually engage in, although mainly on an implicit or tacit basis. Despite its shortcomings, it usefully highlighted the difficulties in operationalising abstract theory – in this case, a combination of scientific method and sociological reflection – in practically helpful ways. It illustrated the inherent difficulties entailed in arriving at definitive statements regarding how best to make decisions in the social realm. Despite its 'failure', this was nevertheless an interesting exercise, and the continuum itself may well have merit in enabling practitioners to map and track the development of professional expertise in the various roles and tasks which characterise work across the domains of practice, particularly in social work education. Ultimately, however, it confirmed that there are many areas of social work practice which are not amenable to proceduralisation, and which thus of necessity must be addressed on the basis of professional wisdom, with all of its inherent strengths and limitations.

Disclosure statement

No potential conflict of interest was reported by the authors.

References

Arrigo, Bruce, and Christopher Williams. 1999. "Chaos Theory and the Social Control Theses: A Post Foucauldian Analysis of Mental Illness and Involuntary Civil Confinement." *Social Justice* 26 (1): 177–207.
Arrigo, Bruce, and Christopher Williams. 2014. "Complexity, Law and Ethics: On Drug Addiction, Natural Recovery and the Diagnostics of Psychological Jurisprudence", In *Applying Complexity Theory*, edited by Aaron Pycroft and Clemens Bartollas, 247–268. Bristol: Policy Press.
Billig, Michael. 2013. *Learn to Write Badly*. Cambridge: Cambridge University Press.
Braithwaite, John, Judith Healy, and Katherine Dwan. 2005. *The Governance of Health, Safety and Quality*. Commonwealth of Australia.
Butler, Ian, and Mark Drakeford. 2003. *Social Policy, Social Welfare and Scandal: How British Public Policy is Made*. Basingstoke: Palgrave Macmillan.
Byers, William. 2011. *The Blind Spot*. Princeton: Princeton University Press.
Byrne, David. 1998. *Complexity Theory and the Social Sciences: An Introduction*. Abingdon: Routledge.
Byrne, David. 2011. *Applying Social Science: The Role of Social Research in Politics, Policy and Practice*. Bristol: Policy Press.
Byrne, David. 2001. "Complexity Science and Transformations in Social Policy". *Social Issues*, 1, 2, Special issue, Complexity Science and Social Policy. http://www.whb.co.uk/socialissues/indexvol1two.htm.
Byrne, David, and Callahan Callahan. 2014. *Complexity Theory and the Social Sciences: The State of the Art*. Abingdon: Routledge.
Cairney, Paul. 2012. "Complexity theory in political science and public policy." *Political Studies Review* 10: 346–358.
Case, Steven, and Kevin Haines. 2014. "Youth Justice: From Linear Risk Paradigm to Complexity." In *Applying Complexity Theory*, edited by Aaron Pycroft and Clemens Bartollas, 113–140. Bristol: Policy Press.
Chapman, Jake. 2004. *System Failure: Why Governments Must Learn to Think Differently*. London: Demos.
Cilliers, P. 1998. *Complexity and Postmodernism: Understanding Complex Systems*. London: Routledge.
Cilliers, Paul. 2005. "Complexity, Deconstruction and Relativism." *Theory, Culture & Society* 22 (5): 255–267.
Davies, Martin. 1991. "Sociology and Social Work: A Misunderstood Relationship." In *The Sociology of Social Work*, edited by Martin Davies, 1–16. London: Routledge.
Dominelli, Lena. 1997. *Sociology for Social Work*. Basingstoke: Macmillan.
Featherstone, Brid, Sue White, and Kate Morris. 2014. *Re-imagining Child Protection – Towards Humane Social Work with Families*. Chap. 5. Bristol: Policy Press.
Fitzgibbon, Wendy. 2011. *Probation and Social Work on Trial*. Basingstoke: Palgrave Macmillan.
Fook, Jan. 2007. "Uncertainty – The Defining Characteristic of Social Work?" In *Social Work – A Companion to Learning*, edited by Mark Lymbery and Karen Postle, 30–39. London: Sage.
Fook, Jan, and Fiona Gardner. 2007. *Practising Critical Reflection – A Resource Handbook*. Maidenhead: Open University Press.
Geyer, Robert. 2003. "Beyond the Third Way: The Science of Complexity and the Politics of Choice." *The British Journal of Politics and International Relations* 5: 237–257.

Geyer, Robert. 2012. "Can Complexity Move UK Policy beyond 'Evidence-based Policy Making' and the 'Audit Culture'? Applying a 'Complexity Cascade' to Education and Health Policy." *Political Studies* 60: 20–43.

Geyer, Robert, and Steve Pickering. 2011. "Applying the Tools of Complexity to the International Realm: From Fitness Landscapes to Complexity Cascades." *Cambridge Review of International Affairs* 24 (1): 5–26.

Geyer, Robert, and Samir Rihani. 2010. *Complexity and Public Policy: A New Approach to 21st Century Politics, Policy and Society*. London: Routledge.

Giddens, Anthony. 1984. *The Constitution of Society: Outline of the Theory of Structuration*. Los Angeles, CA: University of California Press.

Gleick, James. 1987. *Chaos: Making a New Science*. London: Heinnemann.

Green, David, and Fiona McDermott. 2010. "Social Work from Inside and Between Complex Systems: Perspectives on Person-in-environment for Today's Social Work." *British Journal of Social Work* 40: 2414–2430.

Halmi, Aleksandar. 2003. "Chaos and Non-linear Dynamics: New Methodological Approaches in the Social Sciences and Social Work Practice." *International Social Work* 46 (1): 83–101.

Harvey, David. 2001. "Chaos and Complexity: Their Bearing on Social Policy Research" *Social Issues*, 1, 2. Complexity Science and Social Policy: Special Issue. http://www.whb.co.uk/socialissues/indexvol1two.htm

Hatt, Ken. 2009. "Considering Complexity: Towards a Strategy for Non-linear Analysis." *Canadian Journal of Sociology* 32 (2): 313–313.

Haynes, Philip. 2003. *Managing Complexity in the Public Services*. Maidenhead: Open University Press.

Hood, Christopher. 2011. *The Blame Game: Spin, Bureaucracy and Self-preservation in Government*. Princeton: Princeton University Press.

Howe, David. 2002. "Relating Theory to Practice." In *The Blackwell Companion to Social Work*, edited by Martin Davies, 81–87. Oxford: Blackwell.

Hudson, Christopher. 2010. *Complex Systems and Human Behaviour*. Chicago, IL: Lyceum.

Kernick, David, ed. 2004. *Complexity and Healthcare Organisation – A View from the Street*. Oxford: Radcliffe.

Koppenjan, Joop, and Eric Hans Klijn. 2004. *Managing Uncertainties in Networks: A Network Approach to Problem Solving and Decision Making*. Abingdon: Routledge.

Lillrank, Paul, and Matti Liukko. 2004. "Standard, Routine and Non-Routine Processes in Health Care." *International Journal of Health Care Quality Assurance* 17 (1): 39–46.

Little, Adrian. 2012. "Political Action, Error and Failure: The Epistemological Limits of Complexity." *Political Studies* 60 (1): 3–19.

McDermott, Fiona. 2014 "Complexity Theory, Trans-disciplinary Working and Reflective Practice", In *Applying Complexity Theory*, edited by Aaron Pycroft and Clemens Bartollas, 181–198. Bristol: Policy Press.

Mitchell, Melanie. 2009. *Complexity: A Guided Tour*. Oxford: Oxford University Press.

Munro, Eileen. 2005. "Improving Practice: Child Protection as a Systems Problem." *Child and Youth Services Review* 26 (9): 873–883.

Munro, Eileen. 2008. *Effective Child Protection*. 2nd ed. London: Sage.

Munro, Eileen. 2010. "Learning to Reduce Risk in Child Protection." *British Journal of Social Work* 40 (4): 1135–1151.

Munro, Eileen. 2011. *The Munro Review of Child Protection. Final Report, a Child Centred System*. London: Stationary Office.

Munro, Eileen. 2012. "Risk Assessment and Decision Making." In *The SAGE Handbook of Social Work*, edited by M. Gray, J. Midgley, and S. A. Webb, 224–235. London: Sage.

Nissen, Maria Appel. 2014. "In Search for a Sociology of Social Problems for Social Work." *Qualitative Social Work* 13 (4): 555–570.

Nord, Walter, and Ann Connel. 2011. *Rethinking the Knowledge Controversy in Organisation Studies*. Abingdon: Routledge.

Parton, Nigel. 1996. "Social Work, Risk and the Blaming System." In *Social theory, social change and social work*, edited by N. Parton, 98–114. London: Routledge.

Parton, Nigel. 1998. "Risk, Advanced Liberalism and Child Welfare: The Need to Rediscover Uncertainty and Ambiguity." *British Journal of Social Work* 28: 5–27.

Payne, Malcolm. 2011. *Humanistic Social Work: Core Principles in Practice*. Basingstoke: Palgrave Macmillan.

Pycroft, Aaron. 2014. "Complexity Theory: An Overview." In *Applying Complexity Theory*, edited by Aaron Pycroft and Clemens Bartollas, 15–38. Bristol: Policy Press.

Reed, Michael, and David Harvey. 1992. "The New Science and the Old: Complexity and Realism in the Social Sciences." *Journal for the Theory of Social Behaviour* 22 (4): 353–380.

Shaw, Ian 2014. "Sociology and Social Work: In Praise of Limestone?" In *The Palgrave Handbook of Sociology in Britain*, edited by John Holmwood and John Scott, 123–152. Basingstoke: Palgrave Macmillan.

Sheppard, Michael. 2006. *Social Exclusion and Social Work: The Idea of Practice*. Aldershot: Ashgate.

Sommerfeld, Peter, and Lea Hollenstein. 2011. "Searching for Appropriate Ways to Face the Challenges of Complexity and Dynamics." *British Journal of Social Work* 41: 668–688.

Stacey, Ralph 1996. *Complexity and Creativity in Organisations*. London: Berret-Koehler.

Stevens, Irene, and Pat Cox. 2008. "Complexity Theory: Developing New Understandings of Child Protection in Field Settings and in Residential Child Care." *British Journal of Social Work* 38: 1320–1336.

Stevens, Irene, and Peter Hassett. 2007. "Applying Complexity Theory to Risk in Child Protection Practice." *Childhood* 14: 128–144.

Stewart, Peter 2001. "Complexity Theories, Social Theory and the Question of Social Complexity." *Philosophy of the Social Sciences* 31 (3): 321–360.

Styhre, Alexander 2013. *Professionals Making Judgments*. Basingstoke: Palgrave Macmillan.

Sweeney, Kieran, and Paul Griffiths, eds. 2002. *Complexity and Healthcare: An Introduction*. Oxford: Radcliffe.

Taylor, Carolyn, and Sue White. 2000. *Practising Reflexivity in Health and Welfare: Making Knowledge*. Buckingham: Open University Press.

Urry, John. 2002. *Global Complexity*. Cambridge: Polity Press.

Walby, Sylvia. 2007. "Complexity Theory, Systems Theory, and Multiple Intersecting Social Inequalities." *Philosophy of the Social Sciences* 37 (4): 449–470.

Walby, Sylvia. 2009. *Globalization and Inequalities: Complexity and Contested Modernities*. London: Sage.

Walby, Sylvia. 2012. "Society and Social Change: Integrating the Analyses of Complex Social Inequalities and Globalization into the Heart of Social Theory Using Complexity Theory." In *The Shape of Sociology for the 21st Century: Tradition and Renewal*, edited by Devorah Kalekin-Fishman and Ann Denis, 61–79, London: Sage.

Webb, Stephen. 2001. "Some Considerations on the Validity of Evidence-based Practice in Social Work." *British Journal of Social Work* 31 (1): 57–79.

Webb, Stephen. 2006. *Social Work in a Risk Society*. Basingstoke: Palgrave Macmillan.

Whitehead, Philip. 2010. "Social Theory and Probation: Exploring Organisational Complexity within a Modernising Context." *Social and Public Policy Review* 4 (2): 15–33.

Wolf-Branigin, M. 2014. "Complexity and the emergence of social work and criminal justice programmes." In *Applying Complexity Theory*, edited by Aaron Pycroft and Clemens Bartollas, 79–96. Bristol: Policy Press.

Wolf-Branigin, Michael 2013. *Using Complexity Theory for Research and Program Evaluation*. Oxford: Oxford University.

Woods, David, Sidney Decker, Richard Cook, Leila Johannesen, and Nadine Sarter. 2010. *Behind Human Error*. 2nd ed. Aldershot: Ashgate.

What happens to the social in social work?

Jorid Krane Hanssen, Gunn Strand Hutchinson, Rolv Lyngstad and
Johans Tveit Sandvin

Faculty of Social Sciences, University of Nordland, Bodø, Norway

While international authoritative bodies of social work still keep the social tab high, with clear instructions to challenge the structures that create inequality, poverty and oppression, practitioners and researchers in social work increasingly report a practical reality that increasingly deviates from the professional policies. It is a widespread concern that the 'social' in social work is about to be diluted through processes such as individualisation, standardisation and demands for evidence-based practice. But what do we actually mean by the 'social'? The purpose of this article is to examine the idea of the disappearance of the 'social' in social work. Capitalising on theoretical resources derived from Bruno Latour and actor-network theory, we argue that the 'social' is not a property or dimension of its own that can expand or decrease. Instead, the 'social' comprises the relations and connections making up the sociomaterial practices in which people live and struggle with their lives. The article contend that it is not the 'social' as such that is about to fade, but rather the understanding of the complexities of human struggle, which in turn undermines forms of knowledge and practice central to social work.

Introduction

There is a growing international concern that the 'social' in social work is on the wane (Olson 2007; Ferguson 2008; Kam 2012). Some argue that the *social dimension* in social work and social welfare is about to be diluted through processes such as individualisation, standardisation and demands for evidence-based practice (EBP) (Dewe, Otto, and Schnurr 2006; Lavalette 2011). In our own country of Norway, 'social' is also about to disappear as a prefix in the naming of policies, schemes and institutions. There is no doubt that these changes are taking place and that they have profound implications for social work, but do they actually entail a decline of the social?

In professional social work discourses, there is a contemporary debate about what the 'social' in social work is. Programmatic statements from key organisations in the field like International Association of Schools of Social Work (IASSW), the International Council of Social Welfare (ICSW) and the International Federation of Social Workers (IFSW), point to the political aims and duties when emphasising the importance of the social, while others are more concerned with the relational aspects of social work practice. It is not only in social work but also in sociology that the meaning of the 'social' is under discussion, not least by adherents of so called actor-network theory

(ANT). One who has questioned the obvious understanding of the social is Bruno Latour, particularly in his book, *Reassembling the social* (2005). Here, Latour questions theoretical approaches that posit the existence of phenomenon such as 'society', 'social order', 'social practice' or 'social structure'. He argues that the meaning of the social has changed significantly since the founders of social science's early attempts to determine its content, and that the concept has become increasingly problematic. Today, he says: 'The social seems to be diluted everywhere and yet nowhere in particular' (2). Latour argues that the meaning of 'social' has become increasingly blurred, and calls for a sociology that moves the perspective from a 'science of the social' to 'the tracing of associations'. He insists that the word 'social' should not 'designate a thing among other things ... but *a type of connection* between things that are not themselves social' (5).

The aim of this article is to scrutinise the idea of the disappearance of the social in social work. We will argue that it is not the social as such that is about to fade, but rather the understanding of the complexities of human struggle, which in turn undermines forms of knowledge and practice central to social work. We believe that we may strengthen the knowledge base of social work by including perspectives on the 'social' derived from ANT.

The structure of the article is as follows. First, we show how the social and political are presented in the global definition of social work. Second, we present some of the research that shows how traditional social work is being put under pressure by both governments and other disciplines. Three trends are highlighted: (1) the ever-increasing demand for EBP, (2) standardisation of measures and procedures that undermines professional discretion and (3) the individualisation of social problems. Lastly, we present a theoretical perspective, taken from Latour and ANT, that we believe can help to shed light on both current trends in social work and on the question of what happens to the social.

What is social work?

Social work is a profession and discipline with a relatively clear self-understanding and perception of what elements (should) describe the profession. It is possible to trace these elements by looking into recent, authoritative documents adopted by the principal professional organisations. At the World Conference in Melbourne in July 2014, delegates from the IASSW, ICSW and IFSW approved a new definition of social work. Previous to the meeting in Melbourne, there were intense and comprehensive discussions and deliberations – both within and across national delegations – about the content of a definition that could unite social workers worldwide. The new definition reads as follows:

> Social work is a practice-based profession and an academic discipline that promotes social change and development, social cohesion and the empowerment and liberation of people. Principles of social justice, human rights, collective responsibility and respect for diversities are central to social work. Underpinned by theories of social work, social sciences, humanities and indigenous knowledge, social work engages people and structures to address life challenges and enhance well-being.

The definition is important in this context because it identifies and highlights some core elements in the profession's self-perception. The definition is clearly normative in that it emphasises core values and principles for social work. Building on these essentials, contemporary debates among social work professionals focus on the need for acting structurally and politically, as well as requiring more of a focus on what 'the social' in social work actually is. In professional discourses preceding and following the conference, the growing inequality in society is defined as the main problem, and there seems to be a unanimous understanding that there are primarily structural reasons for this unwanted development. Accordingly, social change and development is regarded a prime objective. It is therefore argued that social work strategies must confront and challenge oppressive power dynamics and structural sources of injustice in order to facilitate the empowerment and emancipation of people.

These perceptions of core social work challenges are recognisable in policy documents[1] in addition to the code of ethics, in which it is expressed that unfair distributions of resources are due to unjust policies and practices, and it is also necessary to challenge and change those structural conditions that contribute to marginalisation, social exclusion and oppression. Consequently, social workers have a duty to bring to the attention of their employers, policy-makers, politicians and the general public situations in which resources are inadequate or the distribution of resources, policies and practices are oppressive, unfair or harmful. Hence, it is argued that social workers have an obligation to challenge social conditions that contribute to social exclusion, stigmatisation or subjugation, and to work towards an inclusive society.[2]

Thus, there is an explicit professional attitude and conception that it is necessary to work politically to challenge and change the structural features producing these problems. However, these conceptions are not worth much if 'the facts on the ground' are very different. For this reason, it is important to take a closer look at professional discourses which focus on the relationship between social work practices and the normative foundations of the profession.

Social work under pressure

Discourses in social work are increasingly critical towards contemporary trends in which the 'social' in social work seems to diminish. Ferguson (2008, 12) is particularly critical of the neoliberal influence in society, including the social work profession, calling for 'a social work profession rooted in notions of social justice' that reclaims the social, the structural and the political in social work. Kam (2012, 2) asserts that, 'In the academic discourse, there is limited discussion and examination of the relationship between social workers' increasing neglect of the "social" in social work and the weakening of the practice of advancing social justice'. He also claims that, 'Social welfare has been changed from promoting the spirit of care and love to the advocacy of the value of individual responsibility and the achievement of the objective of "welfare to work"' (2012, 8). As a result of this, 'unfaithful angels' have forgotten to fight for social justice. Kam wonders what the term 'social' means for practitioners, and he presents a 6S framework to explain the 'social' in social work, which is comprised of social concern and consciousness, socially disadvantaged groups, social context, social construction, social change and social equality. Like Olson (2007), Kam questions a contemporary professionalisation strategy to reclaim the 'social' in social work practices, instead promoting social justice as a key professional purpose and arguing that professionalisation may undermine the social justice project. Olson argues that it is possible to change the professionalisation strategy 'so that professionalisation can be made to serve the ends of social justice' (2007, 45).

An increasing amount of research in Norway over the last decade documents a declining demand for the competences normally associated with social work, as well as a gradual disregard of the 'social' aspects of people's lives (Fjellstad 2007; Normann 2009; Røysum 2012; Ohnstad, Rugkåsa, and Ylvisaker 2014). These trends are also observable in other European countries (Dewe, Otto, and Schnurr 2006). We will highlight three trends in particular that we believe are contributing to the impression that the 'social' in social work is in vain: the ever-increasing demand for EBP, a standardisation that undermines professional discretion and the individualisation of social problems.

Evidence-based practice

Many scholars in social work are criticising the introduction of EBP in social work (Webb 2001; Simons 2004; Lorenz 2005; Olson 2007; Rubin 2007; Ferguson 2008; Solas 2008; Gray, Plath, and Webb 2009; Nothdurfter and Lorenz 2010; Petersén and Olsson 2014), and it can be argued that the professionalisation project and EBP are two sides of the same coin, in which an increasing professional status in competition with other disciplines is the real objective.

The interest for EBP must be viewed in the context of the New Public Management (NPM) that has increasingly influenced the public sector since the 1980s. Practice must document that it works because services must be effective. Services are expected to be more rights-based and should be more strongly standardised, following predefined guidelines. In such a way, practice can be reviewed and evaluated in order to determine what 'works' and at what cost.

The concept of an EBP seems to have its origin in medicine, which has now been firmly established in various welfare professions and in politics. It is appealing in that it is portrayed as an effort to improve the knowledge base for clinical work. Sackett et al. (1996) define EBP in medicine as follows:

> Evidence-based medicine is the conscientious, explicit, and judicious use of current best evidence in making decisions about the care of individual patients. The practice of evidence-based medicine means integrating individual clinical expertise with the best available external clinical evidence from systematic research. (1996, 71–72)

As we see from the above definition, they add an emphasis on creating a synthesis between personal experience and research in the field. Marthinsen (2004) points out that this subject seems to be prominent in several professional practices.

EBP also includes a criticism of practice-based knowledge and qualitative research as being too weak a knowledge base for practice. Some want a strict definition of what kind of research should be considered valid and will cast aside knowledge that seeks to provide insight into complex phenomena using types of studies other than the so-called randomised controlled trials (RCT). Hard data are set against tacit knowledge, reflection and in-depth studies. Sheldon and Macdonald (1999) have adapted the definition to social care, and have not included in their definition the idea of integrating experience and science in practice. They discuss their work in terms of conscientiousness, explicitness and judiciousness. The first term deals with the ethical obligations set out in the practice exercise, the need for the employee to keep up with developments, and to understand the social nature of the problem and the effects of various interventions. Explicitness is about being open to the user and being willing to discuss the different options, thereby offering varying chances of success. Judiciousness is about showing sober and good judgement, and Sheldon and Macdonald warn against fads, fashions and 'cause'.

Explicitness illustrates the democratic aspect that often accompanies discussions about best practice – that one should be user-oriented and that choice should be possible. Marthinsen (2004) questions whether these objectives are compatible with EBPs, in part because a discussion of options available to the user becomes illusory if the scientific evidence points in just one specific direction. Options are also complicated by lifestyle and personal taste because one cannot force solutions on people, even though the science might suggest other ways of living.

Perhaps the most profound criticism of EBP is put forward by Webb (2001), who asserts that EBP's inclination to separate processes into 'facts' and 'values' actually undermines professional discretion. Because of this, the epistemological assumption behind EBP is positivistic, and that makes it difficult for social work practices to be in accordance with a value-driven and change-oriented attitude difficult. Consequently, the 'EBP wave' (Vedung 2010) in the social work profession is not very appropriate if the main features laid down in the definition and policy documents of the profession are to be realised. It could even be counterproductive if the goal for professional social work is to reclaim 'the social, the structural and the political' in social work.

However, there are different opinions on the various conceptions of EBP and on how useful they will be in moving professional social work forward. Avby, Nilsen, and Dahlgren's (2013) opinion is that a moderate version of EBP can be useful, as they call for a reflective debate about EBP in social work in order to:

> compose a supportive atmosphere for EBP to thrive and to realize a social work practice that utilizes various knowledge sources, both research-based knowledge and practice-based knowledge, to the benefit of clients. (2013, 16)

Others criticise EBP for having a too narrow view of evidence at the cost of relevance in social work (Petersén and Olsson 2014), and they want to bring Aristoteles' concept of phronesis, the wisdom and virtue of practical thought, back onto the agenda. They argue that a praxis-based knowledge strategy is better to help identify 'what works' than the instrumental rationality underlying NPM or EBP.

Standardisation

The ideas from EBP and NPM have increasingly come to dominate the ways in which social work is practiced in the Nordic welfare states today. Focusing on predefined guidelines and a cluster of ideas retrieved from the private sector, the ultimate goal for the public sector seems to be 'more value for money'. Both EBP and NPM have a top-down rationalistic perspective that tends to promote evidence and rules independently of context. Professionals and public officials are supposed to successfully implement these ideas and functions in practical situations through standardised treatments and general techniques (Petersén and Olsson 2014). Reisch (2013, 718) claims that this widespread acceptance of neoliberal assumptions has shifted the focus of social work practice away from structural transformation and change, to adaption, resilience and compliance within this 'disciplinary regime'.

The ideas challenge traditional government models in favour of market and business-like principles, and imply a standardisation of services that puts into question the possibility for social workers to exercise professional discretion. If we focus on the definition of social work and the code of ethics (see Introduction), social workers have a responsibility to promote social justice, which also implies the opportunity to put this into practice. One can certainly ask if neoliberal assumptions give the social workers this opportunity. Røysum (2012) finds that social workers are often demanded to stay loyal to predefined guidelines and working methods. In a study done by Lundberg (2013), the clients express the view that the services they get from NAV are merely top-down and standardised solutions. Standardisation may be a reasonable way of organising social work if clients need only minor help, but standardisation may prevent the opportunity of helping clients with complex problems who are in need of extensive help.

As a consequence, there is a tension between organising the social services in the welfare state and the opportunity for social workers to practice social work according to their code of ethics and professional discretion. The social worker and the client may negotiate solutions for what is the best for the client, though within standardised frames and on the system's premises.

Individualisation

Current developments in the Nordic welfare states tend to favour individual explanations to people's problems at the expense of structural factors, including those relating to welfare institutions themselves. This increasing individualisation primarily implies that clients must be prepared to go through a personal process in order to change their position from being clients to becoming full members of and contributors to society. These individual processes correspond with changing demands on how social work should be practiced in welfare state institutions. In other words, it is not just any process that clients are supposed to go through; rather, it is the process that welfare institutions regard as necessary in order for the individual to benefit from self-help (Mik-Meyer and Järvinen 2003).

In the Nordic countries today, social work mostly means helping clients who are categorised as 'drug addicts', 'criminals', 'homeless', etc. The categorised client is offered the opportunity to escape such categorical positions through an active participation in the change process, which means willingly following the prescribed path laid down by the institution in question. This reflects a neoliberal perspective, in which social problems are perceived to be purely individual and not in any way inflicted by structural power relations within politics, law and economy (Villadsen 2004). Perspectives derived from evidence-based knowledge and neoliberalistic ideas frame social justice in individual rather than structural terms, emphasising personal transformation and discipline rather than solidarity and social change (Schram 2006; Hasenfeld 2010).

However, the workings of welfare institutions depend on clients complying with institutions' strategies and demands. Therefore, if clients have needs and expectations that are in conflict with institutional solutions, they are perceived and portrayed as 'difficult', 'weak', 'lacking self-awareness' and 'wishing to remain in a client position'. Still, the fact that some clients cease to comply with institutional requirements contributes to the questioning of institutional policies, thus presenting a challenge to their legitimacy.

The above indicates that in order to understand, prevent and resolve social problems, it is necessary to focus on the relation between the individual social worker and the individual client – though of course within the rational framework defined by welfare institutions regarding what it takes for clients to take part in self-help measures. From this perspective, social work becomes a rather restricted field of practice. Villadsen (2003, 223) claims that 'the discourse on "the social" is on the wane (…), and that the subjects of social work are increasingly described in cultural and economic terms', indicating that social work is about to 'give up the perception of the welfare state as a social community that binds all citizens together'.

What do we mean by the social?

We have seen that, while key organisations in social work flag the social and political dimension at least as high as before, this dimension is under immense pressure in day-to-day social work practice. This includes both the discipline's grounding in the *social* sciences, as well as the social worker's traditional orientation towards *social* aspects of people's lives. The grounding in social sciences is being challenged by growing demands for *evidence*, which is increasingly understood as a claim for RCT and evidence grading schemes (Boruch and Rui 2008). The emphasis on the social aspects of people's lives is challenged by increasing both the individualisation of the understanding of people's problems and a standardisation of responses. But what is actually this social dimension being under pressure? What does it social consist of?

Today, it seems almost odd to ask such questions. The social is something we simply take for granted, which was not the case for the early founders of social sciences. For them, the social was a matter of discovery and definition. In order to form a separate subject area for the new science, it was important to clearly delineate its object, particularly in relation to biology. According to Durkheim ([1895] 1966), the *social* should refer to ways of acting, thinking and feeling that were 'external to the individual', that is, actions and expressions that were learned or otherwise imposed on the individual from outside, from society or from the institutional sphere. To Durkheim, these phenomena constituted a set of *social facts* that were clearly separated from biology, 'and it is to them exclusively that the term "social" ought to be applied' ([1895] 1966, 3).

Max Weber, who was less concerned about facts and more about the *intentionality* of people's actions, defined the social as being the 'relationships among persons' ([1904] 1949, 71). What makes an action a *social* action is that it is directed towards or coordinated with other people's actions. The point to make here is that the social is defined as something concrete, something that can be observed and accounted for. Since then, Latour contends, the social has inflated and diluted into something increasingly vague.

According to Latour (2005), the orthodox position in social sciences today is that 'social' points to a specific property, or a specific domain of reality, that differs from other reality domains such as the biological, mental, economic, etc. When talking about 'social' *order*, 'social' *practice* or 'social' *problems*, it points at an order, practice or problem that belongs to this specific reality domain, and to which one can designate a 'social' *explanation*. According to Latour (2005, 3), the problem with this is that this property or reality domain becomes both the explanation and the phenomenon to be explained: 'Once the domain had been defined, no matter how vaguely, it could then be used to shed some light on specifically social phenomena – the social could explain the social'.

Contrary to this, and more in line with Weber's conception, Latour offers a different answer, in which the 'social' is neither a property nor a separate domain of reality, but *relations*, or rather *associations*, between elements that are not themselves social. As for Weber, people are not social in themselves; instead, the social is what connects people together. What Latour and other representatives of ANT add to this is to claim that the social should also comprise associations between human and non-human actors.

Reading a manual could be equally decisive for a person's action as the power exercised by another human being. It means that people's associations with things such as written material, drugs, money, weapon, prisons, etc. are part of the social as well, which should make sense to any social worker. The point is that the social is all about associations between elements that are not in themselves social.

This may seem confusing at first glance, but is actually the opposite. What Latour aims at is clarity in something he finds extremely vague, insofar as any science must be able to construct its object so that it can be accounted for. Nevertheless, the orthodox conception of the social as a separate domain of reality is not easy to account for. What is the stuff that the social domain is made of? We tend to think and talk as if it was self-evident, while it is in fact rather blurred. We talk about social relations, but what is it that makes relations social? Latour insists that relations are themselves social. Social workers claim to promote social justice, but what is social justice? Justice is all about relations, and is therefore social. Fighting for justice involves analysing and remedying relations between elements that are not in themselves social.

Similarly, Latour insists that there is no such thing as a 'social' *order* or a 'social' *structure*, apart from those associations constantly ordering or structuring people's lives. Social workers sometimes defend their jurisdiction by insisting on the social forces affecting people's lives, in addition to psychological and biological factors. Latour insists that 'no "social force" is available to "explain" the residual features other domains cannot account for' (2005, 4). The forces affecting people's lives, sometimes in a coercive manner, is all about relations and connections, between people, and between people and material artefacts, but may also involve psychological and biological elements, such as is the case with substance abuse.

The argument given by Latour has some ontological implications. To say that the social is not a property or a reality domain does not mean that it does not exist. What it means is that the social does not have a substance of its own, but that it consists of associations which exist in concrete practices. Because practices are contingent, constantly shifting and never stable, so is the social. Mol (2002, 6) contends, 'That ontology is not given in the order of things, but that, instead, ontologies are brought into being, sustained, or allowed to wither away in common, day-to-day, sociomaterial practice'. Care and cohesion, as well as neglect and oppression, all exist and have real consequences in people's lives, but they do not exist outside the relations and practices in which they are created and maintained. And their shape and strength varies constantly, both between and within practices; they are brought into different things. The same goes for a diagnosis, for instance a clinical depression, which exists, but the depression brought into being in a diagnostic practice is not the same as the one experienced by the person diagnosed in his/her everyday practice.

The epistemological implication of this is that 'social reality' is only accessible through practice. Knowledge can only be derived from practice, from what people do and what is done to people in concrete settings. Tracing the social, then, means tracing the associations making up the sociomaterial practices within which people are living and struggling with their lives. We cannot know an object or a phenomenon from general aggregates produced about them; aggregates, or rather abstractions, can only be made or produced on the basis of local practices. A family problem, a drug addiction or a crime do not exist as 'social facts' independent of the practices that produce them. A drug addiction is produced by people and artefacts connected in the practices of drug dealing and drug use (Ursin 2014), but it is also produced by social workers through professional practices and by scientists through scientific practices. And, importantly, through these various practices drug addiction is made into different things (Mol 2002).

Our aim is not to provide an exhaustive introduction to Latour's conception of the social, which would require significantly more space than we have at our disposal. Rather, our aim is to show that the alternative understanding of the social offered by Latour and ANT may prove useful in attempting to understand what happens to the social in social work, and thus also to form a better armour in the defence of the discipline and practice of social work.

The trends reconsidered

Let us first consider the trends described earlier in the article. Talking about EBP indicates that evidence is something independent from practice, although the production of evidence is a practice of its own. The idea that scientific practices conducted in one location should produce evidence for how to act in practices in multiple sites is not only naïve, but also potentially harmful. First, the practices in which the evidence is supposed to be applied are quite different from the practices in which the evidence is produced. Scientific practices require a type and amount of control that would be unthinkable in most practices within which social work is performed. Even so, any sensible and necessary adjustment will be inconsistent with the idea of evidence. Secondly, since we then must assume there is only one 'evidence' for each conceivable problem, then EBP would imply that all (seemingly) similar problems are treated exactly the same, irrespective of their site and circumstances. Apart from the unreasonable in this practice, it will unavoidably produce one of the other trends described above, namely that of standardisation.

As indicated above, randomised controlled trails require that the conditions under which it is performed can be controlled; meaning that all associations (or 'influences') other than the one under investigation are kept constant, or at least accounted for. This is probably impossible under any circumstances involving human agents, and particularly with regard to those practices producing or dealing with problems perceived to be 'social'. Consequently, in order to produce outcomes passing as evidence (i.e. meeting the scientific requirements), it is likely that problems will increasingly be perceived to be individual, rather than 'social,' which helps to make scientific conditions more controllable.

This means that the evidence-making practices will produce not only standardisation, but also individualisation. It also means that the practices in which problems are produced and maintained become ever more invisible. This is probably one of the reasons why the social seems to wane in social work. But the social, understood as the connections making up the practices in which human problems are produced, maintained and dealt with, has certainly not disappeared, or even diminished. What is diminishing is the recognition of the complexity of relations producing and upholding social problems, and it is precisely this relation that makes them social.

A better theoretical and practical armour

In order to recapture some of the territory lost to other fields, such as health care and behavioural sciences, and thus to provide more adequate assistance to people struggling with complex problems, we believe that social work must be better armed to justify their distinctive contributions, both as a field of knowledge and as a professional practice. In particular, we believe that social work must be better able to account for the social component so vital to this knowledge and practice. We believe that Latour and others complying with a similar ontology have something to offer in this respect.

First, the conception of the social presented above could provide social work with an ontological and theoretical framework to contest the evidence-based regime locking social work stuck in individualised and standardised procedures. Using Latour's approach, the idea that remotely produced 'scientific knowledge' can form the bases for standardised 'packages' that can easily be transported out to the frontline to solve problems in very diverse settings is utterly incommensurable.

Secondly, it may help to explain that the understanding of people's problems must be derived from the practices within which these problems are located. Accounts of the social are then the associations making up these practices that may produce or maintain problematic situations; practices that obstruct, exclude, suppress, exploit or keep people trapped in poverty and deprivation. It is by tracing the associations producing such problems that provide social workers with the understanding to intervene in such practices and to support people in gaining more authority over their lives.

This conception of the social is more practical and easier to apply than the rigorous talk about a social domain of reality. It is far easier to defend that a social problem is located in a person's association with other people, and with things like drugs or money, or even with institutions, labels or service schemes, than to claim that the problem is due to social structures or social forces. Structural problems are also social in the sense that they are comprised of unfortunate associations. Inequalities, be they economic or related to ethnicity, gender, sexuality or disability, are all caught up in relations between people and between people and public institutions, physical environments, wage systems, cultural perceptions, texts, etc, of which the most also represent power relations. Understanding power relations requires a precise tracing and understanding of relationships between people and other things that serve as means and mediators of power (Foucault 1982; Mik-Meyer and Villadsen 2007; Law and Singleton 2013). In practice, power always operates through the relations it manages to produce, including those between social workers and their clients. Social workers can rightly claim to possess special qualifications to track such associations and to understand their complex problem-generating capacities, which may create a far better base for the communication of social work both as a discipline and as a profession.

Conclusion

We have seen in this article that the international authoritative bodies of social work still keep the social tab high, perhaps even higher than before, by their clear instructions to act politically in order to challenge the structures that create inequality, poverty and oppression. We have also seen that practitioners and researchers in social work report a practical reality that increasingly deviates from the professional policies. Many social workers feel that they are fighting in vain for perspectives and values that are central to social work, while others resign and give in to prevailing discourses.

This means that social work is subject to disciplinary power, exerted by an alliance of politics and 'science,' through which social workers are made to submit to prevailing forms of knowledge and practice. This exercise of power, which is also parallel to the current activation policy, has developed slowly, but seems to have been exacerbated by the most recent financial crises.

What we have attempted to do in this article is to point at theoretical resources that could contribute to social work's understanding of a theoretical consistent conception of the social. This conception is not only easier to justify, but it also points directly at what are the objects of social work, the multiple associations forming the practices in which people are living and struggling with their lives. As seen through the lenses of Latour and ANT, the social is not in vain. Instead, it is the productive and destructive connections constantly shaping the conditions of people's lives, just waiting to be traced.

Notes

1. http://www.iassw-aiets.org/uploads/file/20121025_GA_E_8Mar.pdf.
2. http://www.iassw-aiets.org/uploads/file/20130506_Ethics%20in%20Social%20Work,%20Statement,%20IFSW,%20IASSW,%202004.pdf.

References

Avby, G., P. Nilsen, and M. A. Dahlgren. 2013. "Ways of Understanding Evidence-based Practice in Social Work: A Qualitative Study." *British Journal of Social Work*. Accessed January 8, 2013. http://bjsw.oxfordjournals.org/content/early/2013/01/07/bjsw.bcs198.full.pdf+html

Boruch, R., and N. Rui. 2008. "From Randomized Controlled Trials to Evidence Grading Schemes: Current State of Evidence-based Practice in Social Sciences." *Journal of Evidence-Based Medicine* 1 (1): 41–49.

Dewe, B., H.-U. Otto, and S. Schnurr. 2006. "New Professionalism in Social Work – A Social Work and Society Series. Introduction." *Social Work & Society* 4 (1): 1–3.

Durkheim, E. (1895) 1966. *The Rules of Sociological Method*. Chicago, IL: Free Press.

Ferguson, I. 2008. *Reclaiming Social Work: Challenging Neo-liberalism and Promoting Social Justice*. Los Angeles, CA: Sage.

Fjellstad, R. 2007. *Både sosialarbeider og terapeut? Sosionomers profesjonelle rolle i psykisk helsevern for barn og unge* [Both a Social Worker and a Therapist? Social Worker's Professional Role in Child and Youth Psychiatry.] Oslo: Høgskolen i Oslo, Masteroppgave sosialt arbeid.

Foucault, M. 1982. "The Subject and Power." *Critical Inquiry* 8 (4): 777–795.

Gray, M., D. Plath, and S. A. Webb. 2009. *Evidence-based Social Work: A Critical Stance*. New York: Routledge.

Hasenfeld, Y. 2010. "Worker–Client Relations: Social Policy in Practice." In *Human Service as Complex Organizations*. 2nd ed., edited by Y. Hasenfeld, 405–426. Los Angeles, CA: Sage.

Kam, P. K. 2012. "Back to the 'Social' of Social Work. Reviving the Social Work Profession's Contribution to the Promotion of Social Justice." *International Social Work*. Accessed October 5, 2012. http://isw.sagepub.com/content/early/2012/10/05/0020872812447118

Latour, B. 2005. *Reassembling the Social. An Introduction to Actor-network-theory*. Oxford: Oxford University press.

Lavalette, M., ed. 2011. *Radical Social Work Today – Social Work at the Crossroads*. Bristol: Policy Press.

Law, J., and V. Singleton. 2013. "ANT and Politics: Working in and on the World." *Qualitative Sociology* 36: 485–502.

Lorenz, W. 2005. "Social Work and a New Social Order – Challenging Neo-liberalism's Erosion of Solidarity." *Social Work and Society. International Online Journal* 3 (1). http://www.socwork.net/sws/article/view/205/475.

Lundberg, K. G. 2013. "Individualiserte mål, standardiserte løsninger, lokalt skjønn og brukernes kompetanse." [Individual Goals, Standard Solutions, Local Discretion and the Clients' Competence.] In *Nav – med brukeren i sentrum?* [Nav – A Focus on the Client?], edited by H.-T. Hansen, K. G. Lundberg, and L. J. Syltevik, 91–110. Oslo: Universitetsforlaget

Marthinsen, E. 2004. "'Evidensbasert' – praksis og ideologi." ['Evidence Based' – Practice and Ideology.] *Nordisk Sosialt Arbeid* 4. http://www.idunn.no/ts/nsa/2004/04/evidensbasert_-_praksis_og_ideologi.

Mik-Meyer, N., and M. Järvinen. 2003. "Indledning: At skabe en klient." [Introduction: To Create a Client.] In *At skabe en klient. Institutionelle identiteter i socialt arbejde* [To Create a Client. Institutional Identities in Social Work], edited by N. Mik-Meyer and M. Järvinen, 9–29. København: Hans Reitzels Forlag.

Mik-Meyer, N., and K. Villadsen. 2007. *Magtens former. Sociologiske perspektiver på statens møde med borgeren* [The Shapes of Power. Sociological Perspectives on the Relations between the State and Citizens.] København: Hans Reitzels Forlag

Mol, A. 2002. *The Body Multiple*. Durham: Duke University Press.

Normann, S. 2009. "Er det rom for sosialt arbeid i BUP?" [Is there a Room for Social Work in Child and Youth Psychiatry?] In *Jubileumsskrift Norsk Sosionomforbund 50 år* [The 50th Anniversary Celebration for the Norwegian Social Worker Federation], edited by A. Grønningsæter, 125–135. Oslo: The Norwegian Social Worker Federation.

Nothdurfter, U., and W. Lorenz. 2010. "Beyond the Pro and Contra of Evidence-based Practice: Reflections on a Recurring Dilemma at the Core of Social Work." *Social Work and Society. International Online Journal* 8 (1). http://www.socwork.net/sws/article/view/22/62.

Ohnstad, A., M. Rugkåsa, and S. Ylvisaker. 2014. *Ubehaget i sosialt arbeid* [The Discomfort in Social Work.] Oslo: Gyldendal Akademisk.

Olson, J. J. 2007. "Social Work's Professional and Social Justice Projects." *Journal of Progressive Human Services* 18 (1): 45–69.

Petersén, A. C., and J. I. Olsson. 2014. "Calling Evidence-based Practice into Question: Acknowledging Phronetic Knowledge in Social Work." *British Journal of Social Work* 1–17. http://bjsw.oxfordjournals.org/content/early/2014/03/30/bjsw.bcu020.full.pdf+html.

Reisch, M. 2013. "Social Work Education and the Neo-liberal Challenge: The US Response to Increasing Global Inequality." *Social Work Education* 32 (6): 715–733.

Røysum, A. 2012. "Sosialt arbeid i nye kontekster. En studie om sosialarbeideres erfaringer med Nav reformen." [Social Work in New Contexts. A Study of Social Workers' Experiences within the Nav Reform.] PhD diss., Høgskolen i Oslo og Akershus: HIOA.

Rubin, A. 2007. "Improving the Teaching of Evidence-based Practice: Introduction to the Special Issue." *Research on Social Work Practice* 17 (5): 541–547.

Sackett, D., W. Rosenberg, J. Gray, R. Haynes, and W. Richardson. 1996. "Evidence Based Medicine: What It is and What it isn't." *BMJ* 312: 71–72. http://cebm.jr2.ox.ac.uk/ebmisisnt.html.

Schram, S. F. 2006. *Welfare Discipline: Discourse, Governance, and Globalization*. Philadelphia, PA: Temple University Press.

Sheldon, B., and G. M. Macdonald. 1999. *Research and Practice in Social Care: Mind the Gap*. Exeter: Centre for Evidence-Based Social Service, University of Exeter.

Simons, H. 2004. "Utilizing Evaluation Evidence to Enhance Professional Practice." *Evaluation* 10 (4): 410–429.

Solas, J. 2008. "What Kind of Social Justice Does Social Work Seek?" *International Social Work* 51 (6): 813–822.

Ursin, M. 2014. "'Crack Ends It All?' A Study of the Interrelations between Crack Cocaine, Social Environments, Social Relations, Crime, and Homicide among Poor, Young Men in Urban Brazil." *Contemporary Drug Problems* 41 (2): 171–199.

Vedung, E. 2010. "Four Waves of Evaluation Diffusion." *Evaluation* 16 (3): 263–277.

Villadsen, K. 2003. "Det sociale arbejde som befrielse." [Social Work as a Relief.] In *At skabe en klient. Institutionelle identiteter i socialt arbejde* [To Create a Client. Institutional Identities in Social Work], edited by N. Mik-Meyer and M. Järvinen, 192–228. København: Hans Reitzels Forlag.

Villadsen, K. 2004. *Det sociale arbejdes genealogi* [Social Work's Genealogy.] København: Hans Reitzels Forlag.

Webb, S. A. 2001. "Some Considerations on the Validity of Evidence-based Practice in Social Work." *British Journal of Social Work* 31: 57–79.

Weber, M. (1904) 1949. *The Methodology of Social Science*. Translated and edited by E. Shils and H. Finch. Glencoe, IL: Free Press.

Index

Note: Page numbers followed by 'n' refer to notes

academic journals 87
academization 80
Addams, J. 8, 21n, 33
added value 79–82
agency: impacts on 92; society 25; structure 111; theory of 32
ambiguity 100–1
American culture 33
Americanization 33
Applied Social Theory 67–8
article structure 72
autism: randomised controlled trials (RCTs) 58, 59
autonomy: relative 81

Baby P (UK) 99–100
Baldwin, J.M. 47
Bartlett, H. 12, 16, 20; biographical sketch 11; idea of the case 13
Berelman, W.C. 47
Bernard, L.L. 12
biculturation 34
bio-politics: quantitative surveys 63
biographical sketches 9–11
blame cultures 106
blanket terms: language 16
borrowing field 43–5
bottom-up development: society 61
boy life: common language 15
Brante, T.: scientific position of social work 43–4
Burgess, E. 12, 13, 15; interviewing 13; letter 19
Byrne, D. 103, 105, 110

Campbell, D. 62
Campbell Institute: systematic reviews (SR) 57
capitalism: market 79
Case Study of Possibilities (Burgess) 12
case work: centrality of 12; theoretical foundation 42–55

case worker 11–12, 47–8; selection of facts 15–16
Catholicism 33–5
certainty: judgment 101
Chalmers, I.: systematic reviews (SR) 57
Chambon, A. 8
change: personality 48
Chicago: immigrants 27; men and women 26; population 27
Chicago School 5, 62; legacy 37–8; the other 24–41
child protection: Munro review 99–100
children: immigrant families 27
choice: individual agency 27
citizens: conflicts 64
City (Park): individual agency 29
civil rights movement 63
class: and gender 93
classical theorists: functional differentiation 72
cleavage: disjuncture 98–9
clients 12, 75
clinical sociology 62–4
Cochrane Collaboration: systematic reviews (SR) 57
Cohen, S. 110
collective consciousness 3
common language: boy life 15
communication 78; systems 73, 74
Condition of the Working Class in England, The (Engels) 30
conduct: social situation 16
conflict: citizens 64
connection 116
constructionism: proto-social 15–16
contemporary social theory 3
control: individual agency 31–3
criminology 31
curriculum: undergraduate study 90

Dahle, R.: borrowing field 44
decision-making: rational 63, 64
Deegan, M.J.: Park, R. 32

INDEX

deviance 90
direct social work 52
discipline 80–1
discourse 117; Foucault 10; power structures 79
disjuncture: cleavage 98–9
diversity 59
Dominelli, L. 110
drug addiction 122
Durkheim, E. 3

economic theory 76
effects: history of 46
Ekeland, T.-J.: randomised controlled trials (RCTs) 58
emancipation 90
empirical pragmatism: randomised controlled trials (RCTs) 58
empiricism: pragmatic 59–60
Engebretsen, E.: *t al.* 42–55
engineering: healthcare 100
England 87
entire social settings 12
environment 11–12, 50, 51, 53; personality 47
Europe 7
evaluation: realistic and institutional ethnography 66–7
evidence: New Public Management 64–5; research designs 56–70
evidence-based knowledge 56
exclusion 73; management 75

facts 15
family problems: intervention 62
Ferguson, I. 117
Fish, S.: and Hardy, M. 5, 98–114
Fjeldheim, S.: *et al.* 42–55
Fook, J. 90
Foucault, M. 4, 8, 63; discourse 10
four wishes theory (Thomas) 32
Frankfurt School: modernist agenda 87
Frost, E. 5, 85–97
function systems 72, 77, 78; self-descriptions 76
functional differentiation 71, 72–3; classical theorists 72; modern society 72; observations 73

Gadamer, H.-G.: hermeneutic circle 46; hermeneutic readings 46; hermeneutic tradition 66; hermeneutical key principles 46
Gang: A Study of 1313 Gangs in Chicago, The (Thrasher) 31
gender 89; and class 93
Geyer, R. 103, 107
Giddens, A. 111; structuration theory 91
Goffman, E. 63
Gordon, L.: Hull House 30

Gothenburg: World Congress of Sociology (2010) 1
Graduate School of Social Service Administration 16

Haldar, M.: and Seltzer, M. 25–41
Hall, T. 26
Hanssen, J.K.: *et al.* 115–26
Hardy, M.: and Fish, S. 5, 98–114
healthcare: engineering 100
hermeneutic circle (Gadamer) 46
hermeneutic readings: Gadamer, H-G. 46
hermeneutic tradition (Gadamer) 66
hermeneutical key principles (Gadamer) 46
high reliability organizations 107
historical research 26
historical separation 1–2
history: applied social research 67–8; review of 67–8
Hoggett, G. 91–2
Høgsbro, K. 5, 56–70
Holter, H. 44
homelessness 75
Hull House 26, 30, 33–4, 36; quantitative work 30; space 29; urban life 29–31; women 29, 29–31, 33–5, 36
Hull House Maps and Papers report (Kelley *et al.*) 30, 35
human conflict 62
human interdependence: process 46–8, 52, 53
human nature 64
human subject: lived experience 88
Hutchinson, G.S.: *et al.* 115–26

identity 80; fundamentals of 92; self 93–4; uncertain 80
immigrants: Chicago 27; children 27, 33–4
inclusion 73
indirect work 49–50, 52; mass betterment 50; social reform 50
individual agency 27; choice 27; *City* (Park) 29; control 31–3; notion of temperament 28
individualistic approach 49
individually orientated methods 2
inequality: structural 90; welfare system 3
institutional ethnography: realistic evaluation 66–7
international journals: systematic reviews (SR) 57
intervention 13–15, 49; family problems 62; interviewing 15; micro-sociological approach 63; randomized controlled trials (RCTs) 58; and Sheffield 13; and Young 13
interview 14; Burgess on 13; early development of practice 14; informal 15; intervention 15; Karpf on 18

INDEX

Introduction to the Science of Sociology (Park and Burgess) 28
Italy 89

judgement 100; certainty 101; decision-making 107–8, 109

Kam, P.K. 117
Karpf, F. 18
Kelley, F. 30; and Starr 30
key organizations 115
Kieserling, A. 76
knowledge 14, 122

labelling theory 90
language 15–16; blanket terms 16; difficulties of 16
Latour, B. 116, 121, 122
Lee, R. 14
Lengermann, P.: and Niebrugge-Brantley, G. 34, 35
Levin, I.: *et al.* 5, 42–55
liberalism: market 79
life-history method 13
lived experience: human subject 88
Lyngstad, R.: *et al.* 115–26

McDermott, F. 103, 105, 111
man and his environment 49–51; personality 53
management: hard 105; quality 107; soft 105
market: capitalism 79; liberalism 79
Marxist sociologists: critique of social work 89
mass betterment 50; indirect work 50
mass movements 79
Mead, G.H. 32, 47; symbolic interaction 17; thinking of 15–16
medicine 44
men 31–3; Chicago 26; group of 25; temperament 29; University of Chicago (1892) 2
mental experiences 13
metropolises 62
Michailakis, D.: and Schirmer, W. 71–84
micro-sociological approach: intervention 63
minority groups: mobilization 61
modern society: functional differentiation 72
modernist agenda: Frankfurt School 87
Mol, A. 122
moral panics 90
Munro, E.: child protection 99–100; proceduralization 100; serious case review 99–100
Musolf, G.: personal agency/in everyday life 32
mutual expectation: structure 74

natural disposition: temperament 29
Negro: temperament of 38

New Public Management (NPM) 80; evidence movement 64–5
Niebrugge-Brantley, G.: and Lengermann, P. 34, 35
North America 7; randomized controlled trials (RCTs) 59
Norway 117
Norwegian Psychoanalytic Society 87

obscurity: relative 19–20
observations: functional differentiation 73
organizations: high reliability 107; key 115; private social care 80

Park, R. 28, 29, 31–2, 33, 35; Negro temperament 28; spiritual instability 34
Pearson, M.: systematic reviews (SR) 57
pedagogy 76, 79
personal agency 32
personality 12, 48–9; change 48; development of 49; environment 47; man and his environment 53; situation 11
policy: goals of 103; systems approach 104
policy-making 61
political theory 76
Popkewitz, T.: situation 32
population: Chicago 27
positivistic illusion 60
post-structural dilemmas 91–3
post-war Europe 61
postmodern theory 91
poverty 62, 64; USA 64
power: reproduction of 4
power relations: social structures 92
power structures: discourses 79
practical profession: science 43
practice 62–4; and theory 81, 103, 110
pragmatic empiricism 59–60
private social care organizations 80
proceduralization 100
process: human interdependence 46–8, 52, 53
professions: randomized controlled trials (RCTs) 59
programmes: psychosocial approaches 87–8
prosperity 36
prostitution 78
proto-social constructionism 15–16
psychology of sentiment 19–20
public administration: randomized controlled trials (RCTs) 58
public interventions 56
public sector 104
Pycroft, A. 100, 105

quality management 107
quantitative surveys: bio-politics 63
quantitative work: Hull House 30

129

INDEX

Queen, S. 12, 17; unpublished autobiography 17
questionnaires 16

randomized controlled trials (RCTs) 58–9; autism 58, 59; Ekeland 58; empirical pragmatism 58; intervention 58; North America 59; professions 59; public administration 58; reflection 58; sample of people 58; systematic reviews (SR) 57
rational decision-making 63, 64
rational ideal form 61
Reagan administration (USA) 64
Reassembling the Social (Latour) 116
Reckless, W. 17
reflection: randomized controlled trials (RCTs) 58
reflexivity 93
relations 121–2
relative autonomy 81
relative obscurity 19–20
representation 15–16
research: historical 26; interview 14; psychosocial 94–5; resource 13–14
researchers: theorists 93
Richmond, M. 4, 5, 8, 19, 22n
risk: trust 59–60; uncertainty 101
Ritzer, G.: Hull House 36
Robinson, V. 22n; on Sheffield 19

Sandvin, J.T.: *et al.* 115–26
Schirmer, W.: and Michailakis, D. 71–84
Schwendinger, H.: and Schwendinger, J. 31
science: practical profession 43
scientific disciplines 76
scientific position 43–4
selection of facts: case worker 15–16
self: identity 93–4
self-descriptions: function systems 76
Seltzer, M.: and Haldar, M. 25–41
sentiment: psychology of 19–20
separation: historical 1–2
serious case review 99–100
service failure: high profile 99
Settlement movement 98
shared knowledge practices: psychosocial research 94–5
Shaw, I. 7–24, 110
Sheffield, A. 11, 12, 20; biographical sketch 9–10; intervention 13; Robinson on 19
Sheppard, M. 100
Simmel, G. 62
situation: definition of 32–3; personality 11; Popkewitz 32
Small, A. 26
Smith, D. 66
social action 121
Social Diagnosis (Richmond) 43, 45, 49, 50, 53
social dimension 115

social engineering 53, 61, 62
social order: social structure 122
social reform: indirect work 50
social situation: conduct 16
social structure: power relations 92; social order 122; solving problem of 33–5
social systems 73
social work: defined 44, 100
Social Work in the Light of History (Queen) 17
society: agency 25; individual 49; structural understandings 31; structure 73
sociologists: early 28–9
sociology: definition of 19
sociotechnics 62–4
Soydan, H. 44
space: Hull House 29
speech-habits 16
spiritual instability 34
Starr, E.G. 30
structural inequality 90
structural problems 124
structural understandings: society 31
structuralism 3
structuration theory (Giddens) 91
structure: agency 111; article 72; factors 65–6; mutual expectation 74; society 73
suppression 63
symbolic interaction 17
symbolic interactionism 90
systematic reviews (SR) 56–8, 61, 66; Campbell Institute 57; Chalmers 57; Cochrane Collaboration 57; international journals 57; Pearson 57; randomized controlled trials (RCT) 5, 57
systems approach: policy 104

Taylor, C.: and White, S. 106
temperament: individual agency 28; men 29; natural disposition 29; Negro 38
textbooks 79
theology 76
theoretical intersections 3–4
theorists: researchers 93
theory: and practice 81, 103, 110
Thomas, W. 33, 35; theory of four wishes 32
though-in-action 99
Thrasher, F. 31
trained skill 52
trends 123; association 123
trust: risk 59–60

undergraduate study: curriculum 90
United Kingdom (UK) 9, 89, 93; Baby P 99–100; literature and research 85; psychosocial literature 88
United States of America (USA) 8, 9, 14, 25, 34, 87, 93; poverty 64; Reagan administration 64

INDEX

University of Chicago 62; (1892) men/women 2
urban disorganization 32
urban life: women at Hull House 29–31
use of self 93

values: problems 66

Walby, S. 103
Weber, M. 60–2, 121; rational decision-making 63, 64; rational ideal form 61
welfare system 3
welfareaholics 64–5
What is Social Case Work? (Richmond) 42, 43, 45, 46, 52, 53
White, S.: and Taylor, C. 106

Wolf-Branigin, M. 105
women: at Hull House 29, 29–31, 33–5, 36; Chicago 26; University of Chicago (1892) 2; urban life 29–31
World Conference (Melbourne, 2014) 116
World Congress of Sociology (Gothenburg, 2010) 1
World War, Second (1939–45) 63

Young, E.F.: biographical sketch 10
Young, P. 14, 16, 18, 20; biographical sketch 10–11; facts 115; intervention 13; knowledge 14; letter to Bernard (1928) 13, 21n; research interview 14
Young, V. 22n